THE SEARCH FOR BEULAH LAND

THE SEARCH FOR BEULAH LAND

THE WELSH AND THE ATLANTIC REVOLUTION

GWYN A. WILLIAMS

HOLMES & MEIER PUBLISHERS, INC.
NEW YORK

First published in the United States of America 1980 by
Holmes & Meier Publishers, Inc.
30 Irving Place
New York, N.Y. 10003

Library of Congress Cataloging in Publication Data

Williams, Gwyn A.
  The search for Beulah Land.

  Includes bibliographical references and index.
    1. Wales – Politics and government.   2. Nationalism –
Wales.   3. Wales Civilization – American influences.
4. United States – History – Revolution, 1775-1783 –
Influence.   I. Title.
DA720.W496   942.9'07'3   79-24193
ISBN 0-8419-0589-4

Printed in Great Britain

CONTENTS

For all the Children of Madoc in the Americas,
with a particular filial homage to
the Morgans of Alberta and the Pritchards of Ohio

When night has fallen on your loneliness
And the deep wood beyond the ruined wall
Seems to step forward swiftly with the dusk
You shall remember them. You shall not see
Water or wheat or axe-mark on the tree
And not remember them.
You shall not win without remembering them,
For they won every shadow of the moon,
All the vast shadows, and you shall not lose
Without a dark remembrance of their loss
For they lost all and none remembered them.

Stephen Vincent Benét

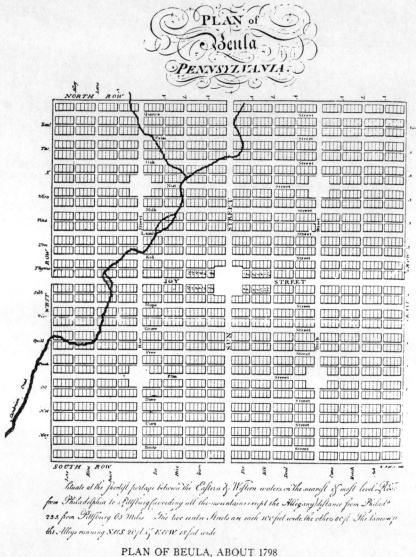

PLAN OF BEULA, ABOUT 1798
Courtesy Erie Book Store

Original Town Plan of Beula, filed with Recorder of Deeds, Somerset
County, Pennsylvania, 18 September 1798

PREFACE

The late eighteenth century was a hinge of fate for the people of Wales. The first modern Welsh 'nation' was born with the American and French revolutions; so was the first Welsh democracy. It was a time of beginnings. The population graph jerks upwards into a century and more of unremitting and accelerating growth; industrial capitalism plants itself in the south and east, dislocates north and west, propels the Welsh into industrialisation and urbanisation, highly distinctive in character, turning the south-east into an export metropolis of the imperial economy of Britain, geared to the Atlantic. In the same period, the Welsh, by the thousand and the thousand score, begin their long march out of Establishment and into the spiritual world of Dissent even as south and east begin theirs into West Britain.

It is in the 1790s that this decisive change registers on the historical consciousness, in a crisis of modernisation which cracked a society and a crisis of identity which created a 'nation' and generated a millenarian migration to the USA. One young Welshman rode the entire length of the American Republic, fought for a black church in Georgia and for Indian identity in Ohio, to launch a new Wales on the frontier. An even younger Welshman, entering the service of Spain, went further up the unknown Missouri than any white man before him, turning himself into a pioneer of American exploration and Spain's last conquistador in the New World, on a search for Welsh Indians. For all of them carried in their heads some vision of Prince Madoc who, they believed, had discovered America three hundred years before Columbus and had left a tribe behind him, those Lost Brothers out there somewhere across that wide Missouri. In common with that of several other peoples, the experience of the Welsh during the 1790s cannot be understood outside that Atlantic dimension which for a generation of Europeans and Americans, north and south, became a lived historical reality.

Those of us who want to compose a history of modern Wales with something of the stature and the power of Pierre Vilar's magisterial study of Catalonia within the history of Spain face an exacting programme of work, quantitative and conceptual. The enterprise is in train, but it will take team-work and time. I felt, however, that it was possible now to write an essay on this particular moment in the history of the Welsh, to locate the Wales of the 1790s in its multiple contexts.

1

In consequence, I have written two books. One is this volume, which attempts such an essay; the other is a study of the Madoc myth, which tries to trace its history over a 400-year span but which, inevitably, finds its focus in the decade of revolution. The books are, of course, radically different in character, but on the 1790s share a common patrimony of evidence. I am therefore grateful to the respective publishers for permitting me, on a few occasions, to reproduce passages which are virtually identical, thus absolving me from the sin of plagiarising myself, a concept I find as theologically difficult as it is ideologically intriguing.

This book, I think, speaks for itself, except in one particular: it makes repeated and serious use of Antonio Gramsci's concept of 'organic intellectuals'. Gramsci considerably extended the notion of 'intellectuals'. 'All men are intellectuals,' he said, 'but not all men have in society the function of intellectuals.' He used the word, in effect, to describe 'mental labour'; he applied it to all who exercised analytical, organising, directive capacities, creative power in any craft, the agents of initiative. Organic, as opposed to traditional, intellectuals were those produced more or less directly by social groups or classes coming into historical existence as modes of production and social formations shifted and changed and who, whatever else they did, defined, articulated and expressed the consciousness of those groups and classes.

I find this idea particularly apposite to the history of Wales. No less apposite is the notion which must, at some time or other, afflict any Welshman who tries to write the history of his own country: how comfortable it must be to belong to a people which does not have to shout at the top of its voice to convince itself that it exists.

Gwyn A. Williams

University College of South Wales,
Cardiff

ACKNOWLEDGEMENTS

To Eyre Methuen for permission to use material from my *Madoc: the Making of a Myth* (1980) and to the editors of the *Welsh History Review* and the *Bulletin of the Board of Celtic Studies* for permission to reproduce material which first appeared in articles.

To the American Council of Learned Societies and the John Carter Brown Library for Fellowships at the University of Pennsylvania and Brown University, Rhode Island, which enabled me to work in American archives; to the staffs of the John Carter Brown Library and the University Library, Brown University, of the Historical Society of Pennsylvania, the Veterans' Building, the City Hall and the University of Pennsylvania Library, all in Philadelphia; of the National Library of Wales, Aberystwyth, the National Museum of Wales, the University Library, Salisbury Library, City Library in Cardiff; to Edna Lehman of the Cambria Historical Society and Fred McCann of the Courthouse, Ebensburg, and the staff of the Courthouse, Somerset, both in Pennsylvania, and to my kinsfolk in Youngstown, Ohio and Newcastle, Pennsylvania, for enabling me to do field-work.

To Mrs Mary Murray Brown, Mount Kisco, New York, for a copy of the Rhys journal and to the Cartographical Section, Department of Maritime Studies, University of Wales Institute of Science and Technology, Cardiff for invaluable help with the maps. For challenge and companionship, to my friend, colleague and co-worker Dr David B. Smith and the students of the History of Wales at Cardiff.

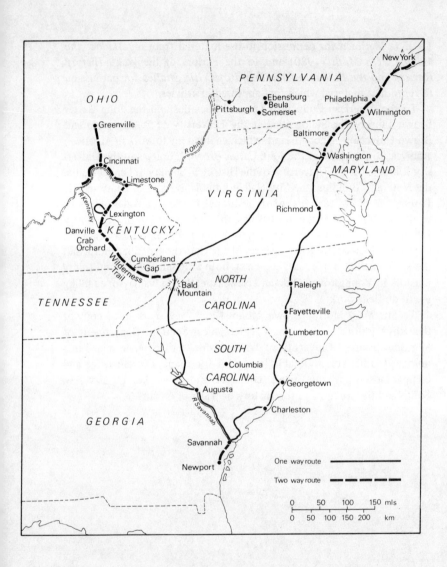

Morgan John Rhys's Journey, 1794-1795

PROLOGUE

It was in the autumn of 1796, or the fall as they called it now, that the first party of settlers came across the Allegheny Mountains into the wilderness of western Pennsylvania.

They came up from Philadelphia and the Great Valley of the Appalachians by boat and on foot, since only Esquire Jones the surveyor had a horse as yet. They found their way to the place by compass, cutting through a rolling sea of endless, blazing forest, down on to Blacklick Creek and the Connemaugh, under the Laurel Hills, where they could see the lower ground sweeping on west towards the Ohio and that far Missouri where even now their compatriot John Evans might at last have found their Lost Brothers, the Welsh Indians of Prince Madoc who had reached this hard and empty continent three hundred years before Columbus.

Captain of the first party at grips with the forest was Thomas Watkin Jones the surveyor, a man of property from Glasbury in Breconshire, south Wales, an able and passionate young free thinker, barely 24 years of age, who was to give himself with a cold and total fury to this knuckle-hard edge of wilderness and to leave his still-young bones there. There were other men of spirit. Rees Lloyd had been minister to the Independents at Ebenezer in Pontypool, Monmouthshire, and was now painfully teaching himself the English language. His deacon, George Roberts, came from Llanbrynmair in Montgomeryshire, north-central Wales, and from a family which was to become celebrated in Welsh-American annals. Theophilus Rees, a man of small property who had led over the Baptists from Salem at St Clears in Carmarthenshire in the south-west, was a friend of one of the liberal luminaries of his cause, William Richards, Welsh Baptist minister of Lynn in Norfolk, a dedicated defender of the American and French revolutions who was to bequeath his library to Brown University in Rhode Island, 'the sacred island of Roger Williams'. Twelve families and four bachelors, they ringed trees, planted their axe-crop and huddled before the winter.

'My first habitation here', wrote Rees Lloyd years later, 'was a little cabin covered with spruce limbs or rather spruce brush and Providence covered that with snow two feet deep, where now the town of Ebensburg is. In this place my child Rachel was born.' In that place he lost her to the wilderness which was to break the spirit of half of them.

5

But though they had to go 26 miles for seed-corn and iron, their hearts were high, for in the spring the second party came — John J. Evans and William Rees, John Roberts (Penbryn) and William Williams (South) — twelve more families and six bachelors, with Simon James the Baptist elder from St Dogmael's, Pembrokeshire, south-west Wales, who had ministered to them back in the Great Valley and among the old Welsh churches of eastern Pennsylvania. With them also came their leader who held, under mortgage, the land they laboured at.

Morgan John Rhys, or Rhees as he spelled his name now, came to lay out a town and to give names to the land. He brought with him *The Heroic Elegies of Llywarch Hen Prince of the Cambro-Britons*, which was to be the first book in the town library. But he had also been reading his Isaiah:

> Surely I will no more give thy corn to be meat for thine enemies; and the sons of the stranger shall not drink thy wine ... but they that have gathered it shall eat it and praise the Lord. Thou shalt no more be termed Forsaken neither shall thy land any more be termed Desolate, but thou shalt be called Hephzibah (that is, my delight is in thee) and thy land Beulah (that is, married) for the Lord delighteth in thee and thy land shall be married.

So Morgan John Rhys planted his town and gave it the name of Beula. The creek and the country he called Cambria.

Morgan John Rhys was fulfilling a pledge. For five years and more he had been on a Mission for his Nation, a mission which had taken him to revolutionary Paris to battle for Protestant liberty, to Savannah in Georgia to battle for a black church, to Greenville in Ohio to battle for the Iroquois coming in to surrender. He who had stood on the ruins of the Bastille and, in his own words, felt the earth shake to the principles which were breaking an old and making a new order of things, had fifteen months earlier stood on 'the unbroken grass' of the newly-liberated Ohio and, on Bastille Day 1795, claimed the American frontier as a National Home for the Welsh People.

1 INDENTURED SERVANTS TO FREEDOM

Politics in Wales begin with the American Revolution. Among a people still substantially monoglot Welsh, the first political publication in its own language was a translation of a pamphlet on the British dispute with the American colonies, which appeared at the same time as Adam Smith's *Wealth of Nations* and Major Cartwright's *Take Your Choice!*, the first effective democratic text in the English of England. For a few years even the homespun ballad-mongers were disturbed; non-political Tories most of them, they were temporarily unhinged by the 'conflict between Old England and New'. Some even showed a transient sympathy for errant brethren across the water before lapsing with relief into their customary John Bull jingoism on the entry of France and Spain into the war.

From that point, *politics* thrust its enquiring snout into the meagre but influential book production of the Welsh-speaking Welsh. In the 1760s, there were some 230 publications in Welsh; by the 1790s the total had climbed to nearly 500 and, among them, the number of political texts multiplied sixfold. Over a hundred appeared, mostly in the 1790s, and their message echoed through the larger number of historical studies, antiquities, biographies, verse, left its impress even on the serried ranks of volumes (600 and more out of a total of 1,300 printed between 1760 and 1799) devoted to theology, sermons and hymns.[1]

For this response to the American challenge was peculiarly that of an alternative society slowly forming in Wales under the crust of squirearchy. Its public philosophy that alternative society was acquiring from Dissent, in particular from the minority liberal Dissent of the Enlightenment and its spiritual derivatives, however heterodox. An embattled but initially self-confident minority was beginning to shape a dissident *pays réel* beneath the *pays légal* of the gentry.

In the eighteenth century those gentry had Wales sewn up.[2] They had entered formally into their political hegemony under the Tudors, a dynasty part-Welsh in origin and widely regarded as Welsh, who had liberated the principality from colonialism, incorporated old British traditions of the Welsh into a new national mythology and integrated Wales into the English shire and gentry system. That critical century had witnessed one of the recurrent explosions of the marginal Welsh into English society (which left the Cecils, for example, as formidable offspring of carpet-baggers from the Welsh-speaking districts of Hereford-

shire), an enriching of economic and cultural life and a characteristic
contradiction: a Protestant Welsh Bible to shape and direct the survival
of the language on the one hand, official discrimination against and
social scorn for that language on the other. As the revolutionary seventeenth century decimated the multitudinous lesser gentry of Wales, a
product of its kindred social structure and critical to its separate identity,
and left some three score strongholds of Puritan Dissent inching into
infidel parts from the borderlands and the south-west, official Wales
slithered into an ambiguous 'Anglicisation'. In the eighteenth century,
Welsh landowners were painlessly integrated into the broad, acquisitive,
astute, ruthless and flexible oligarchy of England and subjected to a
handful of magnates, often Anglo-Scottish in origin.

Some thirty to forty parliamentary families, worth perhaps £3,000-
5,000 a year, monopolised Commons seats and the vital local patronage
which went with them, in a small and marginal country notorious for
poverty before its mineral wealth had been seriously expropriated (a
process which was just beginning). Beneath them, the local gentry, the
£500 men of long pedigree and short purse, perhaps 25 to 50 families a
county, served as JPs with their parsons and ran the place through their
country club of a Quarter Sessions and an independent Welsh judicial
circuit. In some counties, the forty-shilling freehold voters could be a
force, though in the tiny parliamentary boroughs, forty glorified villages
in the squirearchy's pocket, grouped from poverty and for convenience
in a uniquely Welsh contributory system, voters could be created
virtually at will to ward off local malcontents or some new-rich 'nabob'
horning in. In large and comparatively affluent shires like Glamorgan in
the south or Denbigh in the north, as many as 1,500 men could vote
and, during the constitutional arguments of the late eighteenth century,
the novelty of ideas and commitments which were genuinely political
occasionally intruded. Rarely, however, did such deplorable lapses from
good practice disturb the tenor of public life among the 20,000-25,000
Welshmen who possessed the franchise, unless there were vendettas or
intruders, when elections became a matter of Eatanswill orgies and
bankruptcies.

Encrusted with its dependent interest groups, buttressed by its
myriad hungry servitors and lubricated by deferential but robust
Church-and-King ideologies which could find room for Welsh sentiment
or sentimentality if safely antiquarian or anodyne in cultural content,
the system worked well enough for its purposes. It proved durable. Even
after Wales had experienced an economic and social transformation
dramatic in speed and revolutionary in its impact on community, the
country's parliamentary representation remained firmly in the grip of

the gentry. In the early nineteenth century, the system was occasionally dislocated by the intrusion of iron-masters and a new bourgeoisie or by the episodic break-in of an unaccustomed radical; it was buffeted by great gales from outside. But not until the advent of manhood suffrage and the county councils from the 1880s did it go under.

The abrupt totality of its collapse at that point, however, its brutal expulsion from the political community of the new Welsh, its even more brutal exile from the historiography of that new Welsh 'nation' (which threatened to eliminate the gentry almost entirely from the 'history' of 'the Welsh') exemplify the *unreality* which had come to characterise the whole outwardly imposing but inwardly vacuous structure. To the new society struggling to life within its apparently undisturbed carapace, its parliamentary and political conventions had been for generations *irrelevant*.

A lost corner of the Atlantic basin, that eighteenth-century Wales of theirs, edging into its 'modernisation': two peninsulas of Britain with half a million people scattered over a bony mountain heartland, clustering in the thin coastal and interstitial plains of north and west, spilling out more abundantly in the relatively more open lands of the south. Merchant capitalism had concentrated some of them around the quays, counting-houses and copper plants of Swansea and its hinterland, linked to the mines of Anglesey, in and about the markets of Wrexham and its dependencies on the north-eastern coalfield. Through Cardiganshire, Pembrokeshire, Caernarvonshire and elsewhere, there was a scatter of lead mines, coal levels, slate scrapings and the handful of fertile stretches nurtured in Carmarthen, Neath, Haverfordwest, Brecon, Denbigh, Caernarvon, lively little towns of hucksters, artisans, underemployed professionals, over-employed printers and preachers and a brisk but forgotten fraternity of seamen. But most of the Welsh on their upland farms and at their treadmill of loom and spinning-wheel were trapped in a bleak and back-breaking poverty and an economy of unremitting colonial dependence, its most vivid symptoms the great droves of skinny cattle and skinny people seasonally tramping into England to be fattened.

It was in the late eighteenth century that the novel economy of that buoyant England thrust its hungry tentacles into this relatively un-exploited corner. As the population spurted up and through the 600,000 of the first census of 1801, industrial capitalism raised its cloth factories along the Severn, commandeered the minds of magnates and improving gentlemen, to disrupt traditional rural community to west and north; it planted its vertically integrated and technologically advanced iron industry in the empty hill country of Monmouth and Glamorgan, sent pulses of change radiating through slow-moving parishes and, with the export-oriented south as fulcrum, levered Wales out of the margin and into a new world. In particular, and a matter of central intellectual and spiritual significance, it directed the Welsh towards that Atlantic which was being increasingly shaped, as a living historical experience for a generation, by the new commercial and maritime power of Britain and by those two decades of disturbing political impulse radiating from the new imperial democracy of the USA and the populist, terrorist democracy of France. It was as part of this very process that the Welsh experienced the phenomenon which in their historiography goes under the name of *Revival*.

The successful establishment in Welsh historiography of the concept of Revival implies the parallel establishment of the concept of a *Decadence*. The Welsh, an old people with long but fractured memories, had, since their brief moment of Tudor prestige, lived through two centuries on the margin, often in contempt and self-contempt. It was their new and self-appointed spokesmen in the late eighteenth century who told them that these had been centuries of Decadence. Apart from its stubborn but equally marginal language, this was a people which lacked almost every attribute of a nation; but a *nation* is what its new spokesmen told it it was.

That 'nation' and the Revival which created it represented in fact a complex of contradictory movements and aspirations, themselves the product of the accelerating growth, with all its attendant ambitions, frustrations, achievements and conflicts which characterised the European and American littorals of the Atlantic from the early years of the eighteenth century. Wales experienced a major evangelical campaign for literacy, intimately associated with the charity schools and mission drives of an essentially Anglo-American world. In its climax, the finely tuned circulating schools of Griffith Jones, effectively geared to the rhythms of life and work of hill communities, this must have turned a majority of the adult population technically literate in Welsh, at least for a stretch of the late eighteenth century; in those years, certainly, a literate public emerged in Wales, a wider reading public than has been assumed and one, moreover, more versed in English than has been believed. This was one source, though by no means the only or perhaps the major one, of a Calvinistic Methodist movement whose origins in the 1730s were independent of those of English Methodism and whose victory during the social transformation which becomes visible from the 1790s was to prove so stunning that it posthumously distorted the entire historiography of the new Welsh 'nation' of the nineteenth century. Literacy was certainly one root of the renaissance of Old Dissent which swiftly followed Methodism into its trajectory of irresistible growth from the 1790s onwards, particularly in west and north. Within this new and populist Dissent, clusters of intellectuals and missionaries emerged who rapidly distanced themselves from Calvinism; from the 1780s, the Old Cause generated rationalist and radical movements and societies whose minority but trenchant spokesmen were to be remembered a century later as 'precursors' of Welsh democracy. Parallel to these drives, sometimes in harmony with, sometimes in contradiction to them, ran a surge of renewed interest in Welsh antiquities, literature and language. At first respectable and traditional, it gripped in particular the vivacious societies of the London-Welsh, for long the virtual 'capital' of the principality. In the last twenty years of the century, the decades of Atlantic revolution (and all these movements had strong American affiliations), those London-Welsh societies were themselves transformed, largely as the result of the modernisation of the economy of north Wales which provided most of their recruits. With revolution coming hard on the heels of revolution, and a Tom Paine in every parish asserting that men could start the world all over again, they were swept by the multiple millenarianisms of the age of revolution, a more scholarly and measured version of which equally convulsed Dissent. They committed themselves to the regeneration of their people. With their allies and dependents in the parishes of Wales, they resurrected Welsh history and literature, inventing them where they could not be found; they 'revived' the eisteddfod as an embryonic national academy, they created a *Gorsedd* (Order) of Bards of the Island of Britain as people's remembrancers and the directive elite of a new nation conceived in liberty. In their practice and their propaganda, they began briefly to shape a half-formed national ideology. Their enemies called them *Jacobins*.[3] The accusation was just, for these new intellectuals of the Welsh were operating in precisely the same manner and to precisely the same rhythm as their counterparts in Europe during the age of revolution, those minority peoples emerging, in the eyes of their spokesmen, from a 'non-historic' existence, the Czechs, the Catalans, Serbs, Croats, indeed some Venezuelans, some Argentines and some Americans. This was, after all, the time when people discovered 'the people' and when antiquarians, philologists, dictionary-makers and historians stamped nations out of the ground and wove new tricolours out of old legends.[4]

The direct and immediate consequence in late-eighteenth-century Wales was the formation of an organic intelligentsia, contradictory and incoherent in composition and divorced from Establishment. Its

formation coincided with, was in truth an integral element of, the first
trauma of innovation among a largely traditional people who had hitherto
made room for living in a quasi-colonial dependency. The population
explosion precipitated slow, dragging crisis in rural Wales. This was
abruptly sharpened and accelerated by the wars against revolutionary
and Napoleonic France, the war that lasted a generation. The partial
but remorseless transformation of even this marginal agriculture into a
capitalist industry, in circumstances of wartime inflation and emergency
economy, was accompanied by the massive penetration of the iron and
coal industries into the south-east and the appearance of the first large
towns in the Welsh landscape. In little more than two generations after
1790, there was a spectacular shift of population to the south-east and
a wholesale secession of the people from Establishment, many of them
into the Nonconformist sects which by then included the Methodists,
driven into Dissent by official repression in 1811.

The whole country, but south and east in particular, was more closely
absorbed into British society and British nationalism. In response, a
new and semi-political Welsh 'nation' clawed its way into half-existence,
rapidly displacing and dismissing into limbo the nascent *Jacobin* 'nation'
of the 1790s. Although increasingly a numerical minority among a
population being sucked into the modernising and English-speaking
south-east, this new 'nation', forming along a language line and a religious
line which was also a class line, assumed moral hegemony over many of
the Welsh by the middle of the nineteenth century. After the advent of
democracy in the 1880s, it equipped itself with institutions and began
to claim a monopoly of 'Welshness' even as there was, simultaneously,
another explosion of the aspirant Welsh into English society and a
massive, buoyant and innovatory immigration into south Wales second
in intensity only to immigration into the USA itself. The catastrophic
Depression of the 1920s, which brought a century of accelerating expansion to a brutal stop, unhinged this polity, devastated its communities,
dispersed a quarter of its people and thrust the Welsh into those multiple
crises of identity which have plagued their contemporary experience.

Not until the 1790s does this remorseless old mole of a revolutionary
process begin to register visibly in Welsh annals: in riot, rebellion, the
marching and counter-marching of redcoats in rural west and north, in
the Jacobinism, to use the jeer of its enemies, of the industrialising
south-east, most vividly of all in a nationalist and millenarian migration
to the USA.

Before that disconcerting decade, the gentry had been more alarmed
by Methodism which, however quietist its adepts, offered a challenge to

a local authority unquestioned for centuries. The gentry and Anglican clergymen of eighteenth-century Wales have been mercilessly pilloried by the triumphantly populist and Nonconformist historiography of the new nation. In fact, they seem to have been more paternalist and even, instrumentally, more Welsh than tradition (like many such British 'traditions', manufactured in the nineteenth century) has allowed. Possibly even the much maligned 'Anglicisation' of the gentry was as much a consequence as a cause of the new order. Popular loyalty and deference were for a long time strong, at least in those regions of social experience where they were necessary. As iron furnaces reared in the hill country of Monmouth and Glamorgan, there was a symptomatic transfer of such loyalties to ironmasters, until a spasmodic working class and a more continuous Dissenter consciousness eroded them and much of the old folk-culture with them. But over whole reaches of social experience, from the late eighteenth century, such manners and modes were beginning to shrink into a particular, ritual, sometimes insulated area of living.

The turmoil in rural and Welsh-speaking Merioneth, Denbighshire and Cardiganshire in the 1790s shows how thin their Welsh life-blood really was. The gentry panics over Methodism and Jacobinism, the quasi-permanent revolt against the magistracy in the south-west, the highly self-conscious American migrations and even more, that widespread *hunger for migration* which could not find the means to satisfy itself, which characterised that decade, are symptomatic. During those 1790s and into the 1800s, in some parts of Cardiganshire, Carmarthenshire and Pembrokeshire, in the smallholder south-west which was to breed the guerrilla war of the Rebecca Riots, in whole districts of the cloth country of Montgomeryshire and Merioneth in north and north-centre which lapsed into some years of quasi-permanent disorder, which fed people into the newly opened Ohio territory of the USA and supplied the father of its first native-born Governor, in the isolated farmer-fisherman Llŷn peninsula of the north-west, on the edge of the slate-quarry country, which broke into revolt over enclosures and pumped out a significant proportion of its small population into upstate New York, there was something of an Irish atmosphere.[5]

In more general terms, among organic intellectuals and populist leaders generated in this conjuncture, in both rural west and north (where they did not emigrate, that is) and in the more open, more socially civilised and more rapidly modernising south and east, a new Wales began to take shape and for two generations continued to grow, *outside* the political nation. It bears the stigmata of its birth to this day.

Its political ideology this new nation, a pugnacious little minority in
the 1790s, learned from Dissenters of a liberal and often unorthodox
temper who were so *American* in spirit that they joined men from far
less Biblical traditions in that 'true Whiggism' of the minority, radical
Britain of the age of revolution, which self-consciously adopted the blue
and the buff of George Washington as its colours. The Americans, so often
cousin by creed if not by birth to that British minority, won through to
independence and broke the first British empire in 1783. Barely six
years later the Bastille fell in France, in the very year Washington assumed the Presidency of a new US republic which, on its official seal,
proclaimed itself a New Order of the Ages. It was in these years of contagious revolution, during Britain's first post-colonial crisis, which was
also a time of unprecedented economic growth, that the old libertarian
tradition of England gave birth, to the mingled pride and apprehension
of its progenitors, to its obstreperous offspring: militant democracy.[6]

Welshmen from Glamorgan presided at the birth. This was the richest
and most literate of Wales's counties, one of the nurseries of the democratic ideology in a time of Atlantic revolution.[7] Swansea, the largest
town in Wales with 6,000 inhabitants, was already a fully articulated
little social and intellectual capital, with its merchant class, its artisans,
its brisk and wide-ranging commerce, the copper and metal industries of
its anthracite hinterland. In the hill country, novel communities were
clustering around the ironworks; before the century was out, Merthyr
Tydfil with its 7,000 people crowding into a single parish could boast
a bookseller taking weekly consignments from London. Here were
launched the Unitarian Association of South Wales and the Cyfarthfa
Philosophical Society, Wales's version of Priestley's Lunar Society in
Birmingham. To the south, in Glamorgan's broad and beautiful Vale, one
of the rare regions of Wales where a cereal culture nurtured nucleated
villages, not scattered hill hamlets, Cowbridge Book Society served a
lively and inquisitive world of artisans, small merchants, cultivated
parsons and ministers, aspiring farmers; Bristol, a jewel in England's
eighteenth-century necklace of cultivated provincial cities, was the
region's capital and London itself was within reach. The villages of the
Vale of Glamorgan were peopled by clubs and friendly societies, itinerant craftsmen, booksellers, schoolmasters, poets and antiquarians. A
Dissenting network dating from Cromwell's time, with its own academy
and its access to Bristol colleges and local grammar schools, linked
comfortable congregations in the Vale (*Bro*), wide open to the trade
winds and to the liberal and scientific currents which coursed through
eighteenth-century Dissent from its often heretical academies, to the

tough-minded chapels of the hill-country (the *Blaenau*) which, with their congregations of smallholders, auctioneers, artisans, opening up to the master colliers, engineers, skilled puddlers and ironstone miners of the new iron complex, went over to liberal Presbyterianism on their route into Unitarianism.

The county was strong in a bilingual artisanry and an aspiring lower-middle class, precisely those groups which, in England, Scotland, America North and South, France, the Low Countries and the Rhineland, generated the radical thrust. A whole coterie of craftsmen, poets, antiquarians and patriots Welsh and universal clustered, for example, around Lewis Hopkin, joiner, carpenter, glazier, wire-worker, stone-cutter, farmer, shopkeeper and surveyor in constant demand. Hopkin's house was full of books, Welsh, English, Latin, French, the grammars of Welsh poetry and the latest numbers of the *Spectator*. William Edward, who built the lovely single-span bridge at Pontypridd, was one of this bilingual circle, as was John Bradford of Betws near Bridgend, traditional nursery of Glamorgan's Welsh poets. A fuller and dyer, often in Bristol and London, classical scholar and at ease in the literatures of France and England, Bradford was a bold Deist and no less passionate in the cause of Welsh revival, as was the more gentle Edward Ifan of Aberdare, apprenticed in wood and verse to Hopkin and on tramp, like most of them, before he settled as the first Unitarian minister of the district.

Out of this lively, open but frustrated society living in the interstices of gentry politics and so similar in intellectual and social tone to that Philadelphia which was the spiritual capital of most of them, came the maimed and towering genius *Iolo Morganwg*, Edward Williams the stone-mason Bard of Liberty, who invented the *Gorsedd* of Bards and the no less *Jacobin* and Unitarian Druids of a 'revived' tradition and offered the Welsh a revivification of that 'tradition' which was in truth the driving ideology of a new and radical 'nation' built on the principles of the American and French revolutions. Not far away from the birthplace of this demiurge of the new Wales, Morgan John Rhys himself, founding father of an even newer Wales in the Land of Liberty, was born, in Llanfabon on the scarp edge of *Bro* and *Blaenau* and into the Baptist community of celebrated Hengoed, just across the line in Monmouthshire which cherished a very similar society, with an even tougher tradition of Dissent transmuting into an equally tough liberalism.

It is no accident that it was this region of Wales which produced two of the most famous British radicals of European and American reputation of the entire epoch. Ty'n Ton, near Bridgend, lay in what was the traditional heartland of Welsh poetry and Welsh poets in Glamorgan.

Here Rees Price, one of the craggier Independents of a craggy denomination, ran a school which was the direct successor of the first Dissenter
school in the area and was later to merge into the Carmarthen Academy
of the Independents. The eldest son of his second marriage was cousin
to a girl who served as model for the tragic heroine of *The Maid of Cefn
Ydfa*, an enormously popular Welsh romance of love frustrated by class.
The boy was brilliant. Educated at Neath grammar school and a Dissenter
seminary, Richard Price was sent to the Independent Academy after its
flight from the Arminian heresy into Breconshire. To no avail: Richard
broke with his father's Calvinism, moved from Arminianism through
Arianism into Presbyterianism, moved physically to Hoxton academy
and later to Hackney and became the minister of a Presbyterian chapel
at Stoke Newington near London. Statistician, actuary, social scientist
by temper (his friends and William Pitt's were to dispute the authorship
of the latter's Sinking Fund), he became one of the best known of the
political Dissenters, a friend of the celebrated American Benjamin Franklin, and a member of that remarkable circle which Franklin gathered
around him like some eighteenth-century Fabian Society.

When the American War broke out, Richard Price published his
Observations on the Nature of Civil Liberty, which raised the whole
issue to the high plane of popular sovereignty and the natural rights of
man. Sixty thousand copies were printed within a year and it scored a
decisive success in America. Price followed up with more pamphlets,
including one in 1784 on the means of making the American revolution
'useful to the world'. He commented trenchantly on the new American
constitutions. Franklin, Arthur Lee and John Adams were deputed by
Congress formally to invite him to serve as financial adviser to the new
Republic.

At home, he strongly supported the renewed struggle for civil equality
for Dissenters which grew directly out of the American crisis during the
1780s and he was on one of his annual visits to south Wales when news
of the French Revolution reached him. He preached a sermon to one
of the many societies formed to commemorate the centenary of the
Glorious Revolution of 1688: the light of liberty, set ablaze by America,
was penetrating France and would soon illumine benighted Britain. It
was this sermon which jarred Edmund Burke into writing his classic of
conservatism, the *Reflections on the Revolution in France*, but when
Price died in 1791, the French National Assembly went into mourning
for him.

David Williams, a younger man, was born in Caerphilly, not far from
Morgan Rhys's Llanfabon, into the family of a man who ran a small

colliery which went broke. David was propelled by his father into the Presbyterian chapel of the Watford nearby and then to the Academy which had returned to Carmarthen and to heresy. He took up charges in Frome and Exeter but settled at Highgate, London, where John Wilkes's father was a member of his congregation. By this time, he had moved right off the Christian spectrum into Deism. His congregation would not follow him, though he was active in the campaign for civil rights and freedom of expression, publishing outspoken pamphlets. He opened an academy himself in Chelsea, read widely in Rousseau and the *philosophes* and became a friend of Benjamin Franklin. He and Franklin formed a club to reform religion. With the American's approval, David Williams created the liturgy of a Natural Religion (his own religious credo is said to have been the shortest on record: 'I believe in God. Amen.') This he submitted to Frederick the Great of Prussia and to Voltaire; a copy was passed to Rousseau. All of them approved. It may have influenced Robespierre's cult of the Supreme Being. It certainly touched Iolo Morganwg's Druid-Bard Directory of a new Welsh nation conceived in Liberty. David Williams tried to organise churches around this creed, translated Voltaire and brought out a pamphlet on intellectual freedom.[8]

It was at the crisis of the American War that he broke into political print with his *Letters on Political Liberty* in 1782 which argued the full democratic programme and was in fact a tract in support of the newly formed and seminal Society for Constitutional Information which was to be the matrix for the unprecedented popular societies of the 1790s. This captured the mind of the future leader of the French Girondins, Brissot, author of a classic study of America. It was translated into French and when the Revolution broke out five years later, read by Mirabeau and Siéyès. From 1789 indeed, David Williams was busy criticising the new French constitution, to such effect that, on the overthrow of the French monarchy in August 1792, he was invited over to advise Condorcet and the Girondins. He lived through the mortal crisis of the winter of 1792-3 in Paris and, a shattered man, came home on the outbreak of war between France and Britain, carrying remarkable last-minute peace proposals from the French government. Suspect and shunned, he retired to Soho to direct the Literary Fund and write a history of Monmouthshire.

Despite this experience, David Williams had no hesitation in locating the birth of Jacobinism, not in France but in England. He dated that birth precisely in 1782: 'The year 1782 should be distinguished in History as having in England given birth to an organization, the spirit of

Jacobinism, which afterwards displayed itself in the French Revolution.'[9] This was an *American* birth for democracy in Britain; its midwife was the Society for Constitutional Information. It was even more visibly an *American* birth for Jacobinism in Wales.

In that year of 1782, William Owen, a leading figure of the Welsh Revival, joined the premier London-Welsh society, the Gwyneddigion; he was accompanied by most of the London-Welsh intellectuals. The Gwyneddigion, veritable powerhouse of the new Welsh nation, lived and had its being in the heart of the London of John Wilkes and Horne Tooke and John Thelwall, of the SCI and the London Corresponding Society. Its members moved on the fringes of the circle of William Blake and the radical poets, William Owen himself was a follower of the millenarian Joanna Southcott. In that same year of 1782, Sir William Jones, a celebrated Orientalist and a Welshman, published an attack on the American War. His brother-in-law, the Dean of St Asaph in north Wales, printed it, was tried for seditious libel, defended by the renowned lawyer Erskine and acquitted. The Wrexham-Ruabon area was disturbed, as it was to be later by the propaganda of the *Jacobin* entrepreneurs Wilkinson and Wedgwood. It was certainly during the disastrous last years and the aftermath of the American War that serious and sustained reform campaigns got under way in Britain.

The main thrust among the respectable came from Christopher Wyvill's county association movement (which touched parts of Wales), the movement for pragmatic reform which carried Burke and Pitt to popular leadership.[10] Its Westminster committee, however, was much more tough and doctrinaire, published a full democratic programme in 1780 (the programme the Chartists were to fight for sixty years later) and budded out the SCI. The latter came to life again after the catastrophic Gordon Riots in 1780 in London and one of its main preoccupations was the mass dissemination of radical literature. Thomas Hardy the shoemaker, future leader of the major popular society, the London Corresponding Society, got his basic political education from it. The debating clubs of working men owed a lot to it. Its members were steeped in American experience, men associated with them corresponded with and sent libraries to the USA.

Their first sortie was ineffective. After some measures of 'economical' reform in the immediate aftermath of war, the campaign for parliamentary reform was defeated by 1785. These men came to regard Pitt and Burke less as enemies than as renegades, but during the 1780s the parallel campaigns against the slave trade and against the anti-Dissenter Test and Corporation Acts could channel their energies. In 1787 and

1789 Bills for the political emancipation of Dissent were presented to the House: the latter scored a near-success. In 1788-9, to celebrate the centenary of the Glorious Revolution, societies were organised and the reform drive acquired new impetus, at the very moment when news came of the fall of the Bastille.

In this, the first honeymoon period of the French Revolution, its universal message was in fact received into a strictly Anglo-American universe. Thomas Paine is a classic expression of the conjuncture. The conservative response to the Revolution was unnaturally 'early' (Burke's *Reflections* came out in 1790) precisely because Church and King had already mobilised against threats to the Glorious Constitution (revered with an almost American zeal!) before the events in France had made any real impact. Church and King clubs had mobilised in physical reality, in particular against the Dissenters' campaign in several localities, such as Manchester and Birmingham, where social change, clusters of Dissenters and radical intellectuals seemed to pose a threat to local authority. The first spasm of violence against *Jacobins* broke out precisely in Birmingham, home of the Lunar Society, when a crowd, manipulated by shadowy Anglican-Tory magistrates, attacked Joseph Priestley and destroyed his laboratory. The Unitarian celebrated the anniversary of the 14 July; he was a French traitor.

It was America which had first exposed such men as 'traitors'. Thomas Paine's *Rights of Man* is much more American than French in its tone. Before August 1792, when the overthrow of the monarchy and the eruption of the populist, democratic and terrorist *sans-culottes* added a whole dimension to Revolution, France was to the British a glorious or terrifying myth, a dramatic example of the overthrow of Catholic tyranny; it gave the British a new vocabulary, a new style, a new universalism. But that universalism simply added resonance to an essentially Anglo-American tradition. In many respects, after all, America was a minority British radical sensibility made flesh. The James Burgh whose *Political Disquisitions* was so widely read in America was a political mentor to the British *Jacobins* of the 1790s. In those 1790s, the British civil war which the American Revolution ought to have been broke out, in book and pamphlet and sermon and song. After 1792, when what looked like a populist *sans-culotte* movement began to grow in Britain, even as the respectable shied away from France at the bloody advent of militant democracy, it became a matter of treason trials, witch-hunts, Botany Bay — and emigration to the spiritual homeland.

Wales was even more directly affected by the American thrust of this British Jacobinism. For while Welsh liberal Dissenters might be a thin

and scattered minority at home, in America they were over-represented
and in the critical transatlantic perspective of British radicalism they
were much more visible. From the beginning, Welsh migrations, notable
in quality if not in quantity, had been Dissenter, missionary and quasi-
millenarian in tone.[11] John Miles, founder of the Welsh Baptists, had
taken his people over to New England early in the Restoration and the
Quakers, who had gone later, had intended to found a *Gwladfa*, a
National Home for the Welsh, in their promised Welsh Barony in Penn's
commonwealth. It never materialised, but Welshmen were very prominent in the early history of Pennsylvania, Thomas Lloyd of Dolobran in
north-central Wales serving as Penn's deputy. Compatriots overflowed
into the Welsh Tract in neighbouring Delaware, and in eastern Pennsylvania and the Great Valley there were clusters of Welsh place-names
in a great arc round from Meirion to Pencader.

Welsh adventurers were everywhere in the New World, from the West
Indies to Spanish Louisiana and western Canada, but generally speaking,
people moved in denominational groups with a strong missionary motiva-
tion. Arminian Baptists had gone with the Quakers to Pennsylvania;
they were followed in 1700-1 by an important inflow of Calvinistic
Baptists from the critical zone of the Carmarthenshire-Pembrokeshire
border where the mother church of Rhydwilym had its roots. These
quit the Arminians to people the Welsh Tract and Pencader. From these
nuclei, the Welsh grew in considerable strength, planting significant
offshoots in the Carolinas, particularly at the Welsh Neck on the Peedee
river, South Carolina. Missionary waves reinforced the southern settlements, but Pennsylvania remained the Welsh heartland. The St David's
Society was launched in Philadelphia in 1729; Welsh books were published there, including the first Welsh Biblical concordance.

It was the Baptist network in particular which maintained contact
with the homeland and sprang into renewed life in the crisis of the
1780s.[12] The oldest of their churches in Pennsylvania was Pennepek,
Lower Dublin township, north-east of Philadelphia. It was served by a
succession of Welshmen. Philadelphia First Baptist was a daughter church,
opened by Jenkin Jones. Ministers from Cardiganshire served the
equally Welsh churches in the Great Valley and Pencader. Abel Morgan
ran their celebrated academy and from the middle of the eighteenth
century the Baptists entered another cycle of rapid growth. By 1770
there were said to be 300 Baptist churches in America and sixteen years
later the denomination claimed that numbers had tripled, with the new
settlements in the south and Kentucky, where a new Baptist college
was projected, particular conquests. Welshmen and Welsh-Americans

remained prominent in the leadership.[13] A prime mover was Morgan Edwards, a Monmouthshire man who settled in Philadelphia in 1761, rode 3,000 miles on circuit and collected material towards a twelve-volume history of the American Baptists. He was one of the founders of Rhode Island College (later Brown University) from 1762.

His colleague in this enterprise was a remarkable Welsh-American, Samuel Jones. Dr Jones had been born in Betws, Bridgend, in Glamorgan's 'Welsh Parnassus', into a family with strong roots in south Cardiganshire and nearby Pembrokeshire. He had been taken to Philadelphia as a boy, graduated from its college and served Pennepek from 1762 to 1814. He was the real author of Rhode Island College charter and the patron of its first student, the Dr William Rogers who became a celebrated Principal of Philadelphia. Samuel Jones, a man of fine physique and lively liberal mind, became 'a sort of bishop among the Baptists', and proved to be a key figure in the transatlantic world of the new Welsh radicalism.

It was, characteristically, in the late 1780s that the Baptist international was revivified. The connection had been renewed when Morgan Edwards began to exchange material with the historian of the Welsh Baptists at home, Joshua Thomas of Leominster; Edwards returned to Wales to solicit funds for Rhode Island College. The American demand for preachers was one factor; it was to be a motor force in the Welsh migrations. By 1793, the famous American geographer Jedidiah Morse was writing from Charleston to George Lewis, Independent minister at Caernarvon, listing the areas of the USA where ministers were badly needed and naming members of immigrant societies in the eastern states.[14] More significant, however, was the crisis of American Independence. Several Welsh-Americans were prominent in the rebel leadership; David Jones, minister of Great Valley Baptist, had a price put on his head by the British. So well represented were they, in fact, that the people at home firmly believed that a majority of the signatures to the Declaration of Independence were Welsh![15]

The American struggle, the American example of civic equality and freedom, added a whole dimension to the world of Welsh Dissent during the reform campaigns of the 1780s in Britain. In the process it adds a historical dimension to the Jacobinism of Wales. It is a curious assumption of several Welsh historians that writers of international repute like Richard Price had no effect on their homeland because they wrote in English and in London. Welsh historiography on the *Jacobins* is mechanical and unreal. Taking as basic assumptions the minority character of this Jacobinism and the impermeability of gentry-controlled political society, which are without doubt accurate assessments, it makes a further distinction between radicalism, conceived essentially as an intellectual force, and the social tension and turmoil which ravaged north and west Wales in the 1790s, which is somehow regarded as 'non-political' (where this upheaval is noticed at all, since it has signally failed to register in the Welsh historical consciousness). It then differentiates three *levels* in Welsh Jacobinism, all of them intellectual: writers in English like Richard Price, the publishers of short-lived journals often linked with the London-Welsh, and the handful who wrote in Wales and in Welsh. Treated in this manner, such a Jacobinism becomes a brief, transient phenomenon without significance.[16]

This analysis misses the reality. That this Jacobinism — and the *nationalism* it expressed (which also tends to escape the historical net) — was short-lived cannot be denied, but to divorce it from the ongoing process of which it was one expression is to distort. What is missing above all is the transatlantic dimension. One central feature of the social crisis in rural Wales was a migration movement, strongly political in tone and Dissenter in character, which sent Welsh families by the hundred to the America boats. To find the Welsh *Jacobins* of north and west Wales, you need to look to the Ohio, Pennsylvania and New York. In the south-east, on the other hand, in the more open and varied society being created by industry, *Jacobins* could find a home at home. The Unitarian cousinhoods of the south colonised the new town of Merthyr Tydfil and neighbouring communities in Monmouthshire to such effect that they created an unbroken political tradition stretching from the 'sturdy old Republicans' of Merthyr in the 1790s to the first generation of the Chartist leadership.[17]

More directly, the Baptist international linking Wales and America became perhaps the most lively of all the transatlantic connections during the age of revolution. From the late 1780s Dr Samuel Jones, Pennepek, began to act as corresponding secretary and clearing-house for a flow of letters from Wales on migration, denominational affairs and politics. By 1789, William Richards of Lynn was opening a sustained correspondence with him, followed by Morgan Jones who ran an academy in Hammersmith. The circle of Samuel Jones's correspondents rapidly widened. By the mid-1790s this 'bishop' of the American Baptists was acting as an unofficial Welsh consul in the USA.

His correspondence brings to light a fascinating and extraordinarily lively transatlantic world. There was a constant two-way traffic in ideas, books, letters, pamphlets, information. This Baptist international had its own ships, three or four favoured vessels, notably the *Pigou* of Captain Benjamin Loxley of Philadelphia, who had married a kinswoman of

Morgan Jones and belonged to a celebrated revolutionary family which was a pillar of Philadelphia First Baptist. The letters from Wales were overpoweringly *Jacobin* in tone, full of the prices, the rents, the poverty, the iniquities of landlords and the Church, full of irritation at the endless anti-American propaganda in British pulpits and newspapers. Of the dozens of people who wrote to Samuel Jones, Dissenters almost to a man, *every single one* at one stage or other called himself 'a sans-culotte Republican'. Hardly surprising, when over whole tracts of Merioneth, Montgomeryshire and Denbighshire public order virtually broke down, great crowds assembled in defiance of the magistrates and soldiers, and ordinary farmers drank *Jacobin* toasts in the pubs of Bala, the Mecca of Calvinistic Methodism, and when an excited curate in Anglesey could shout (in a message passed directly to the King) that 'hordes' of Methodists were 'overrunning' north Wales and 'descanting on the Rights of Man'. Hardly surprising too, at a time when inhabitants of Newcastle Emlyn in the south-west petitioned William Richards Lynn to arrange for their township's transportation *en bloc* to the USA, when George Lewis of Caernarvon would seriously discuss the whole-sale transfer of the Independents of north Wales to the Ohio, when in Carmarthen 3,000 people could offer to fight a way through the press gangs and the militia for a handful of migrants from Montgomeryshire to escape to the New World.[18]

During the 1790s, as the celebrated emigrants' handbooks poured out in 'the rage to go to America' as Mrs Lindsay called it, Samuel Jones had to deal with a flow of letters of dismission, appeals for help or information, warnings of the arrival of 'another seven score' from Pontypool or Newcastle Emlyn or Llanbrynmair. It was the Philadelphia Baptist Association which initiated the revival of the Welsh society in the city and the formation of an immigrants' aid committee precisely to deal with the sudden inflow of people from Wales. There was a recognised Baptist network in the States for the reception of immigrants, with Rhode Island College and the Great Valley as foci. It was this alert, living, constantly renewed connection which was the prime channel of entry at that critical moment in the 1790s when it looked for a while as if half the Welsh nation was ready to transplant itself.

Welsh Dissent and the Jacobinism which at least in part derived from it were a sector of an international movement. To assume that the latter's internationally renowned spokesmen made no contact with monoglot Welsh at home is grotesquely to exaggerate the insulation of those Welsh. William Jones, a vinegary Voltairean who was a prime mover of the migration, never left his remote parish of Llangadfan in north-central Wales for more than a fortnight, but he was one of the best-informed men on America (and on millenarian speculation) in Britain.[19] Joseph Priestley could bring pious Welsh divines in deepest Cardiganshire to the point of fist-fights. The Unitarian hub in Wales was in that county, 'buried' in the heart of Welsh Wales. Richard Price went home every year; his kinsfolk, the Morgans, Williamses, Coffins of Llandaff and the Vale of Glamorgan were radical colonisers of the upland Valleys and Merthyr Tydfil.[20] Some men's words can become so much the common speech that they are never quoted except unconsciously and the language of Richard Price was the common discourse of radical Dissenters, whatever tongue they used. Priestley's impact was more visible. David Jones, the *Welsh Freeholder*, made Priestley preaching a life's work. The Unitarian's political writing charged that of many a Dissenter who disagreed with his theology. By 1807, a miner in Merthyr could be teaching his chemistry to apprentices, as a matter of course.

Deism, certainly, could shut a man out, even if David Williams did write a history of Gwent (in the review of it in the new *Cambrian Register*, the gritting of teeth is almost audible!). But Williams certainly influenced Iolo, and William Jones Llangadfan was by no means the only Voltairean in Wales. Thomas Watkin Jones of Breconshire, who was to serve as land-agent to the New Wales in the West, named his son after the *philosophe*; Morgan John Rhys would have published him in Welsh translation had not his printer taken fright; in Merthyr, at the height of the wartime repression, people were reading him in clandestine groups on Aberdare Mountain. Freethinkers lurked under the half-respectable umbrella of Arminianism and Unitarianism. Iolo's Druidic Religion of Patriarchal times which was to inspire the Welsh in their resurrection had been forced to disguise itself as Freemasonry, he admitted, the *'forbidden* GOD' of his poems. The resemblances between his *Gorsedd* and the radical *Illuminati*, the *Jacobin* Religion of Nature and the Masonic conspiracies of the Continent were clear enough to authority, which took some pains to suppress it. Many of the leading figures of the Welsh revival seem to have been Freemasons. One of the first public buildings to be erected in the Welsh liberty settlement in America was a Masons' Lodge.

In short, a developing intelligentsia emerging from the Welsh people in the first travail of modernisation, however varied its provenance — London-Welsh bohemians, isolated and bookish individuals in the parishes, the multiplying ranks of Dissenting and Methodist ministers, began to cohere and to acquire form in a strictly transatlantic context.

Its emergence coincided with the first serious crisis of that modernisation in Welsh society which registered painfully and inescapably in rural Wales to west and north, where Methodism, closely followed by Dissent, was entering a phase of explosive growth. This crisis, too, and its interaction with the enterprise of the intellectuals operated in a transatlantic context. It is this dimension which makes the 1790s a conjuncture of some significance in the emergence of modern Wales.

Notes

1. J.J. Evans, *Morgan John Rhys a'i Amserau* (University of Wales Press, Cardiff, 1935), pp. 121-2, tabulates book production, but gives no source; the best approach to this period is through the works of David Williams: bibliography in the special number of *Welsh History Review* (1967) in his honour.

2. There is a useful survey of the political structure of eighteenth-century Wales, based on his own comprehensive work, in Peter D.G. Thomas, 'Society, Government and Politics' in Donald Moore (ed.), *Wales in the Eighteenth Century* (Christopher Davies, Swansea, 1976). The general context I derive from my own reading, teaching and writing about the history of Wales over 25 years.

3. For convenience, I refer henceforth to people of this temper as *Jacobins*, following the current cant parlance.

4. Stimulating on this theme is the opening chapter of Peter Burke, *Popular Culture in Early Modern Europe* (Temple Smith, London, 1978).

5. The vital text here, whose material has to be correlated with other types of evidence, is the admirable study by my colleague David Jones: D.J.V. Jones, *Before Rebecca: Popular Protest in Wales 1793-1835* (Allen Lane, London, 1973); there is a wealth of retrospective reference in David Williams's classic *The Rebecca Riots* (University of Wales Press, Cardiff, 1955); still outstanding despite its age, and a book that cries out for translation into English, is R.T. Jenkins, *Hanes Cymru yn y Ddeunawfed Ganrif* (University of Wales paperback reprint, Cardiff, 1972: a short social and intellectual essay on eighteenth-century Wales).

6. Central to the understanding of British radicalism in these years, with its strong American affiliations, are Bernard Bailyn's brilliant *Ideological Origins of the American Revolution* (Harvard University Press, Cambridge, Mass., 1967) and Caroline Robbins's comprehensive *The Eighteenth Century Commonwealthman* (Harvard University Press, Cambridge, Mass., 1959); the most recent British study to focus on some of these problems is Albert Goodwin, *The Friends of Liberty* (Hutchinson, London, 1979) which is particularly strong on Dissent and the radicalism of the 1780s.

7. I derive my picture of Glamorgan and its organic intellectuals from the fascinating G.J. Williams, *Traddodiad Llenyddol Morgannwg* (University of Wales Press, Cardiff, 1948: on Glamorgan's literary tradition), Ceri W. Lewis, 'The Literary History of Glamorgan from 1550 to 1770' in Glanmor Williams (ed.), *Glamorgan County History*, Vol. IV (Cardiff, 1974) and from my own work, some of which is reported in my *The Merthyr Rising* (Croom Helm, London, 1978).

8. From the voluminous literature on Richard Price and David Williams, Goodwin, *Friends of Liberty*, and the work of David Williams listed in *Welsh History Review* (1967) would serve as good introductions.

9. From a manuscript autobiography in Cardiff Public Library, quoted in J.J. Evans, *Dylanwad y Chwyldro Ffrengig ar Lenyddiaeth Cymru* (Hugh Evans, Liverpool, 1928: an essay on the influence of the French Revolution on Welsh literature), p. 30.

10. In addition to Goodwin, *Friends of Liberty*, E.C. Black, *The Association: British Extra-parliamentary Organisation, 1769-1793* (Harvard University Press, Cambridge, Mass., 1963) and C. Bonwick, *English Radicals and the American Revolution* (University of North Carolina Press, Chapel Hill, North Carolina, 1977) are very useful; the seminal works by Caroline Robbins and Bernard Bailyn are essential. I touch briefly on some themes in my *Artisans and Sans-culottes; Popular Movements in Britain and France during the French Revolution* (E. Arnold, London, 1968, reprinted 1973).

11. The best general survey of Welsh migration to the USA is E.G. Hartmann, *Americans from Wales* (Christopher, Boston, 1967).

12. My thinking on this theme has been transformed by the discovery of a mass of Welsh-American correspondence among the papers of Dr Samuel Jones, Pennepek, in Mrs Irving H. McKesson Collection: Jones section, Historical Society of Pennsylvania (Philadelphia) (henceforth Pennepek).

13. There is a great deal of information in the letter which the Welsh Baptist historian Joshua Thomas wrote to a colleague, reporting on his correspondence with Morgan Edwards and Samuel Jones: J. Thomas—J. Sutcliff, 26 September 1788, National Library of Wales (henceforth NLW) 1207.

14. J.Morse—G. Lewis, 15 January 1793, NLW 13713.

15. The basis for this whole section is the papers of Samuel Jones, Pennepek.

16. The work of David Williams (see *Welsh History Review*, 1967) first established this perspective; specific studies are the works of J.J. Evans cited and an older, ill-ordered but still useful text, David Davies, *The Influence of the French Revolution on Welsh Life and Literature* (W.M. Evans, Carmarthen, 1926).

17. *The Merthyr Rising* and 'South Wales Radicalism: the First Phase' in S. Williams (ed.), *Glamorgan Historian*, vol. ii (1965).

18. Samuel Jones papers, Pennepek; Jones, *Before Rebecca*; see below, Chapter 6.

19. Many letters by him in the voluminous papers of William Owen, NLW, mainly NLW 13221: see below.

20. Some intriguing information in Caroline E. Williams, *A Welsh Family* (London, 1885).

2 RESURRECTION OF THE WITNESSES

That conjuncture found its focus in London.[1] In a country with poor internal communications and no natural centre, the north looking to Liverpool, the south to Bristol, the communities of London-Welsh had acquired the character of a surrogate capital. The early Tudor migrations made the London-Welsh a decisive factor in both the economic and the cultural life of Wales. They were followed by waves of seasonal migrants, the drove herds of cattle, Wales's 'Spanish silver fleet', bringing back currency and breeding banks, the tramping hosiers, the even poorer weeders and migrant labourers, accompanied by more permanent residents. Out of this movement had grown the premier London-Welsh society dedicated to a revival and purification of Welsh letters and life, the Cymmrodorion. At its head, the Morris brothers of Anglesey had recaptured traditions and established a Welsh classicism. Snobbish, sectarian, cluttered with useless aristocratic ornaments and a crowd of piously Welsh and philistine climbers, this society yielded in the late eighteenth century to the more active and populist Gwyneddigion.

In some significant senses this change parallels a shift visible in all the developed nations of the Atlantic basin at this time: the move from academies to *sociétés de pensée* in the French-speaking world, the *amigos del pais* in the Spanish, the philosophical societies and debating clubs of the Anglo-American polity. The Gwyneddigion reflected changes in social composition no less than in practice and style. The new men, markedly more active and committed, were also more popular. The printing trade attracted a surprising number of Welshmen; they peopled middle-class and lower-middle-class professions, teaching jobs, intellectual taverns, overflowed from literary societies into Grub Street. And a striking number of them came from Denbighshire.

For Denbighshire was the Glamorgan of north Wales, a fulcrum of the new economy there.[2] Varied, populous, relatively affluent and modernising, Denbighshire embraced not only a rough cloth district producing 'webs' in characteristic northern style, but the fertile vales of Conway and Clwyd and a covey of 'spirited proprietors'. Wrexham, capital of the north-eastern coalfield, was in 1801 the strongest single concentration of people in Wales, with 8,000 people in its parishes and its fair the biggest in the principality. The eastern coalfield, which ran through neighbouring Flintshire, was the theatre of a strong, if ultimately abortive, thrust of industrialisation, powered in part from the adjacent iron industry of Shropshire with its *Jacobin* entrepreneur John Wilkinson. Ironworks and collieries around Holywell and Wrexham turned the district into a centre of mixed if small-scale production whose impact sent ripples of change through north Wales. Communities began to emerge, bristling with men of small property and big aspiration; newly articulate groups among them, often influenced by Liverpool and Shrewsbury, led protest meetings, the mushrooming conventicles of Dissent and Methodism and the characteristic migration to London.

During the 1790s, soldiers were constantly crossing and recrossing Denbighshire. In 1795, it was reported that the 'lower orders' of the county had totally lost faith in the magistracy and that artisans in Wrexham were denouncing the King. In the great Denbigh riot of 1795, crowds imprisoned magistrates, rejected all taxes which had not been voted by the people and demanded the abolition of the militia and the emasculation of the Navy Act. John Jones, a small farmer of Aerdden, could thunder out speeches bubbling with America, France and a native Jacobinism. By 1801, there was a panic over pikes and rumours of systematic plans for insurrection; troops were once more in the streets of Denbigh and Holywell.

Straight out of this Denbighshire, from Cerrig-y-Drudion, came John Jones, celebrated keeper of the King's Head Ludgate and very voice of a populist radicalism which would ultimately become a Welsh national style.[3] Coiner of the by now hallowed expression 'Dic Sion Dafydd' to describe that familiar kind of Welshman who on crossing Severn suffers a sea-change into something poor and strange, John, as 'Jac Glan-y-Gors', brought out two pamphlets in 1795 and 1797 which convulsed literate Wales and were virtually Thomas Paine in Welsh. When the Gwyneddigion created a new political club during the revolutionary decade, the Cymreigyddion, Jac wrote its initiation song.

More central to the London-Welsh in a material sense was Owen Jones, nicknamed 'Owain Myfyr', 'The Scholar'. Born in Denbighshire in 1741, Owen Jones went up to London a radical and stuck to his guns, come hell or high water. Labouring for years as a currier in the fur trade, he ended owning a business and a wealthy man. That wealth he devoted to the service of Welsh history and literature. He spent £180 on the society's edition of the poems of Dafydd ap Gwilym, over £1,000 on its great collection the *Myvyrian Archaiology*, named after him despite his protests. He helped to send the brilliant Walter Davies, 'Gwallter Mechain', up to Oxford, subsidised Iolo Morganwg and a host of others, and paid for scores of volumes of transcriptions.

Around him gathered a cluster of antiquarians, intellectuals, poets, meeting constantly in pubs, often riotous, sometimes raucous, always felicitous. About their discourse at its best, there was something of the flavour of the correspondence of John Adams and Thomas Jefferson. They were the last, warm, free-thinking, sometimes pagan glow from an old but awakening Wales before the Calvinist curtain came down.

The hardest worker was William Owen, 'Gwilym Dawel', Will Friendly. Born in Merioneth in 1759, educated at Altrincham, Will went up to London in 1776, worked at a number of jobs and became a free-lance writer, copying reams for Owen Jones. Something of an eighteenth-century polymath, skilled with pen and brush, widely read, he became a Fellow of the Society of Antiquaries with an Oxford degree. He edited a version of the early poems, *Llywarch Hen*, in 1792, produced a Welsh dictionary between 1793 and 1803, published a *Cambrian Register* and a *Cambrian Biography*, translated *Paradise Lost* and was a pillar of the *Myvyrian Archaiology*. No mean poet himself, his occasional writings were numberless and he above all was the contact between the London-Welsh and the parish-pump intellectuals back home.

There were many others: John Edwards, 'Sion Ceiriog', another Denbighshire man, wit, musician, astronomer and professional gadfly; David Samwell, 'Dafydd Ddu Meddyg', Black David the Doctor, who had served as surgeon to Captain James Cook on the *Resolution* and the *Discovery* and, an accomplished botanist and amateur anthropologist, had made the first written record of the Maori language at Queen Charlotte Sound.[4] He was Iolo Morganwg's great crony, went with him on pilgrimage to Sterne's grave and joined him in scurrilous verse on the vagaries of treacherous patrons. Fond of their glass, he and Iolo were equally fond of challenging people (especially eisteddfod adjudicators) to duels, though they were once kicked downstairs for their pains by Ned Môn, an Anglesey poet. Duelling, after all, was an aristocratic indulgence!

Not all of them were radicals: Iolo suspected that Edward Jones, a brilliant harpist and musician who collected and published Welsh scores and served as harper to the Prince of Wales, had shopped him to the Privy Council during the anti-*Jacobin* witch-hunt of 1794. But most of them were and the tone of the society was certainly *Jacobin*. The medals for the would-be national eisteddfods they launched in 1789 were struck by M. Dupré, engraver to the French National Assembly, and the competition titles were radical. The Gwyneddigion had taken characteristic form at a climax of the reform campaigns of the 1780s; during the 1790s they organised clubs for political debate, the Caradogion, open to non-Welshmen and the equally uproarious, Welsh and democratic Cymreigyddion. They were hit by the repression of 1794, their publications were denounced as subversive and many of them peeled away during the years of iron. In 1797 a majority of the Caradogion were to support Pitt's Two Acts which suspended English liberties for the duration; Iolo Morganwg and Jac Glan-y-Gors were to write in praise of Nelson and the Volunteers. This all too familiar trajectory of apostasy, however, has been exaggerated by a historiography with a vested interest in the deprecation of Jacobinism. Iolo greeted the panic and the anti-Dissenter witch-hunt which followed the French landing in Fishguard in 1797 with scatological and subversive comment which could certainly have landed him in the Tower.[5] Many of the men associated with the London-Welsh were as hard as nails in their Jacobinism, Owen Jones at their head. One of their men, Thomas Roberts, Llwynrhudol, brought out the most specifically and concretely Welsh of all the *Jacobin* texts, *Cwyn yn erbyn Gorthrymder* (*Protest against Oppression*) as late as 1798, while a friend, Thomas Evans, 'Tomos Glyn Cothi', a Unitarian who ran a short-lived journal, was jailed for singing Welsh versions of *Jacobin* songs in 1801. Iolo himself, after running a 'subversive' shop in Cowbridge, shifted towards Merthyr, with its 'sturdy old Republicans', its Philosophical Society and its Cymreigyddion, while Tomos Glyn Cothi took up the Unitarian cause in nearby Aberdare.

The Jacobinism of the Gwyneddigion and their kin did not in fact wither; it tended to lose purchase on reality when the French Republic was displaced by Napoleon (though many switched their loyalties to the Soldier of the Revolution),[6] but in effect it was *driven* out of public sight. It surfaces again, not only in private correspondence, but in a new political tradition in south-east Wales and, no less characteristically, in the new Wales in America, with its singing of the Ça Ira, its toasts to Jefferson and 'the brave sans-culottes', in the Masons' lodges of trans-atlantic Cambria.[7]

Central to their vision of a new Wales, however, was the misty perception of an old. The translation of their historical-literary enterprise into nation-building took the form of a journal and a 'revived' national eisteddfod. The latter, launched from 1789 in alliance with obsessive individuals in the localities, particularly of north Wales, was intended to initiate the re-engagement of an interrupted tradition. Their heroic efforts in locating, editing and publishing forgotten Welsh texts were directed to the same end. That they were credulous, pre-scientific and unscholarly by twentieth-century standards is a truism; they could hardly have been anything else. More important to the historian is the fact that, in common with men like them in the Europe of that French Revolution which tried to create a revolutionary new nation on the model of classical democracy, they tried to root a Wales which was to be a radical and total breach with the immediate past in a remote past re-lived in romantic, Utopian and increasingly millenarian spirit. The Orientalism of the great scholar Sir William Jones, himself a Welshman, drove them into a search for a possible connection between Sanskrit and the languages of a once great Celtic world. Was Welsh the degener-ate descendant of Earth's Mother Tongue? William Owen became obsessed with the need to 'purify' the Welsh language, to purge it of the encrusted corruptions of centuries of servitude. Addicted to bizarre linguistic theories in his quest for a basic human language, he advocated a 'reformed' orthography for Welsh which merely stupefied the stay-at-homes. In this, however, he did not differ much from millenarian Americans, like Noah Webster, who wanted to turn old Gothic English into the Esperanto of Liberty, or Dr Benjamin Rush who wanted New World medicine to be a new world medicine. Their futurism was in fact a Return — to the original principles of human community in their purity. This millenarianism — Owen became a dedicated follower of Joanna Southcott, one of the populist prophets whose dramatic pro-clamations punctuated the revolutionary decade — could evoke an echo among Dissenters of liberal temper who also called for a purge and a return to the purity of the original gathered church of believers. Central to the kind of millenarianism which was possessing Dissenters and bohemians (both radical innovators, and both confronted by an ap-parently Atlantic-wide revolution), was the concept of the Resurrection of the Witnesses in the Last Days.[8]

It was precisely here that Iolo Morganwg could work his magic; it was precisely this which made his collaboration with the Londoners in the 1790s so seminal.[9] Born Edward Williams in 1747, in a village in the Vale of Glamorgan, Iolo by his death in 1826 had established him-self as one of the most remarkable, if maimed, geniuses Wales has ever produced. His father, intelligent and literate, was a working stonemason, his mother, frail, aloof, a dreamer, was the poor kinswoman of a dis-tinguished gentry family and a descendant of one of Glamorgan's dynasties of Welsh poets. She instilled in her son a passion for the twin traditions of his native county and country. Iolo became a stonemason, but on his tremendous walking feats as he went on tramp through Wales and southern England, he plundered libraries, collections, poets' homes of documents. Taught lexicographical and antiquarian skills by local literary gentlemen, steeped in the beery eisteddfods and vivid folk-culture of Glamorgan, he locked into the active world of poets and hymn-writers, north and south, and, completely bilingual, was free of English writing. Failed shopkeeper, shipper, farmer, jailed for debt in 1786, he emerged from Cardiff prison to establish contact with the London-Welsh and found his life's mission. He spent several years in London, returned to set up a *Jacobin* shop in Cowbridge and towards the end of his life shifted his interest to the new town of Merthyr where his son Taliesin was running a celebrated school.

In his own day, he was acknowledged to be the most learned man in Wales on Welsh literature, history and antiquities. He was much cherished by Southey and the first generation of English Romantics who saw in him an Original Bard out of the Celtic Twilight, an image he unscrupulously cultivated. His imagination was no less unscrupulous; in a time of great and high-minded forgers, he invented poets, chroniclers, bardic guilds and ancient traditions by the dozen. It has taken the heroic labours of a dedicated Welsh scholar of the twentieth century to cut Iolo clear of his fabrications. Yet in that very process, Iolo himself is not seriously diminished. His forgeries have a certain logic, embody a perception in depth which no one else could have achieved. After a while, buried in his little cottage at Flemingston, awash in manuscripts and laudanum, Iolo himself could no longer distinguish between fact and his own inspired fiction. What he had was an intuitive grasp of the *historical* function of Welsh traditions and of their functional utility to the starved, neglected and often self-despising Welsh of his own day.

To balance his forgeries, there were his genuine achievements as a scholar and an antiquarian. He projected a Welsh national library, a national museum, a national eisteddfod; he was one of the first serious folklorists in Wales. His central perception was of Druidism, Bardism and the *Gorsedd*. He broke through to it in 1791, his happy London summer in the springtime of the French Revolution. Versions of it appeared piecemeal in William Owen's edition of the *Llywarch Hen* in 1792, in his own *Poems, Lyrical and Pastoral* of 1794 and in a host of occasional writings.

Welsh poets, Iolo perceived, had not been poets as the English used the word; they were the directive spiritual elite of a society, people's remembrancers. The London-Welsh were trying to create a national eisteddfod which would be strict and professional, a kind of national academy. Iolo went much further. Arthur and his knights, he argued, had regulated Welsh poetry in a *gorsedd*, a term which had come to mean an open-air tribunal. Iolo at first used the word in this sense. But Druids were coming into fashion, along with the Gothic, the remote, the Noble Savage, the cult of Nature, Rousseau and Wordsworth. It was the time of revolution, natural religion, William Blake and no less that of forgers in a good cause, Macpherson, Ireland, the Chatterton whom Iolo frequently invoked. Henry Rowland's essay on Anglesey had identified the island as the heartland of Druidism; learned and apparently learned works traced the Druids of the vast and ancient Celtic lands to the Patriarchs, noted similarities to the Jewish Cabbala and Brahminism, yoked the Celtic tongues to Sanskrit.

Iolo's *gorsedd* grew into an Order of Bards who were the last European representatives of the ancient Druids. Druidism itself took on the lineaments of Rousseau's natural religion, a unitarian creed uncorrupted by priestcraft; the traditions of this universal and original truth, liberty, equality and natural religion had been transmitted to the Welsh Bards, remembrancers of the people and sole survivors of the ancient and uncorrupted race. The instrument for the recreation of their libertarian world was the *gorsedd*, which was to supervise every aspect of Welsh life, to engender pure theology, genuine morality, the art of the poets, law-givers to mankind in the search for 'rational principles of government . . . truth and universal peace'.

To this end, Iolo devised ('discovered' in his own words, and in Glamorgan naturally!) a *gorsedd*, with its ranks, ceremonies, robes and ritual, to be the directive intelligentsia of the Welsh people. The London-Welsh had launched their eisteddfods in north Wales over 1789-91. They held the first *gorsedd* on Primrose Hill in 1792. By 1819, a pale shadow of it was incorporated in the eisteddfod, where it has remained to this day. This is hardly the *gorsedd* that Iolo had in mind: the responsible elite of a Welsh nation, itself to be an exemplar of universal liberty. When Iolo devised a plan for a Welsh liberty settlement in the USA, it was to be run by just such a *gorsedd*. And though Iolo denied it because he had to, his Bards were inevitably *Jacobins*, Unitarians, Freemasons. He read his famous poem *The Rights of Man* within the *gorsedd*'s stone circle. When the Cowbridge Volunteers dispersed a *gorsedd* on Garth Mountain as 'democratic' and threatened to wreck the Flemingston cottage for its subversive documents, they knew quite well what they were doing.

Not many people embraced Iolo's bubbling theories in their entirety, but around a half-acceptance of him, so much dedicated work could crystallise.[10] Freemasonry and Unitarianism run as underground currents throughout this first phase in the recreation of the Welsh. Iolo offered a unifying thematic to the scattered and disparate clusters of intellectuals, each busy in its own way about the rescuscitation of a people:

antiquarians, revivers of the eisteddfod, speculators in language and anthropology, Dissenters anxious to restore religion to purity. They were no longer mere antiquarians, lexicographers, poets, they were moral legislators to a nation, they were 'bards', people's remembrancers.

So Iolo's half-formed national ideology found its way into William Owen's *Llywarch Hen*, to cause a minor sensation in France, into his own poems, into the voluminous texts and correspondence of the London-Welsh and into their great compilation the *Myvyrian Archaiology*, which started to come out in 1801. All the other subsidiary enterprises of these new organic intellectuals of the Welsh could fit into this problematic, this half-formed, half-accepted but very real world-view, the Welsh vision of the Restorative Revolution.

It was therefore among the London-Welsh in alliance with Iolo Morganwg that the 'restored' but revolutionary 'nation' of the Welsh began to take shape and to act as a co-ordinating force. From London, in turn, through its eisteddfod, its *gorsedd*, its myriad publications, proclamations and exhortations, that new 'nation' reached out to its half-aware adherents in the tense and brittle parishes of a Wales going under the harrow of industrial capitalism. It was precisely at that point of essential contact that the *Jacobin* nation encountered a constellation of contradictions so brutal as to constitute a structural fault running through a society.

On the one hand, the half-formed ideology of the London-Welsh ran into head-on collision not only with the Welsh *ancien régime* but with new structures of values and sentiments which were beginning to emerge from the alternative society forming in opposition. On the other hand, at a climax of their campaign, they found, and themselves succumbed to, a mobilising myth which enabled them, at least in part, to effect a breach in that wall.

This myth, too, was a product of the Atlantic connection.[11] At their third eisteddfod at Llanrwst in 1791, the winning ode was devoted to the Christian conversion of the Madogwys, the Madoc Indians, the Lost Brothers in America. At that eisteddfod, William Jones, the Voltairean from Llangadfan, circulated an Address, *To All Indigenous Cambro-Britons*, announcing the brave news that the Madoc Indians had been found on the far Missouri and summoning the Welsh to quit the bondage of Egyptian taskmasters and find their promised land alongside these Lost Brothers.[12] This ignited the first outbreak of America fever in north Wales. For earlier in 1791, Dr John Williams, a learned Welsh divine who lived in Sydenham, had published a no less learned volume, an *Enquiry* into the truth of the tradition that America had first been discovered in 1170 by the Welsh prince Madoc, son of Owain Gwynedd. This sudden reappearance of Madoc triggered what was, in fact, a crisis of identity in Wales.

Madoc was reborn in a conflict of Atlantic imperialism. This was appropriate; he had first entered history as an instrument of imperialism and for three hundred years his story followed the trajectory of imperial conflict, trade rivalry and colonial settlement with hypnotic precision.

Stories about a Welsh seafarer Madoc, credited with the discovery of magic islands, had passed into European discourse through the agency of a Flemish poet by the thirteenth century. Though probably based on historical personages, possibly the Welsh half-Vikings who emerged in the twelfth century, such stories had left no trace in the Welsh historical record before the fifteenth century, when there are hints of a revival, probably associated with the quickening of Atlantic enterprise in that century. By the sixteenth century they had transmuted into a myth of a Welsh discovery of America. Dr John Dee, the amazing polymath who was the brains behind many of the overseas ventures of Elizabethan England, particularly at the critical juncture of 1575-83 and the onset of the Spanish Armada, came across the story during his researches into British claims to Atlantic dominion, grounded in the mythical exploits of British King Arthur, whose 'history' under Elizabeth had become virtually official doctrine. In 1580, Dee launched Madoc at the world; he was avidly seized on by a whole generation of imperialists as a weapon against the Spanish monopoly of the New World, lodged securely in Richard Hakluyt's great compilation, the *Principall Navigations . . . of the English Nation* and swept into European literature.

In the seventeenth century, the story went into eclipse, though it lived on in the margins of British and European writing, but thanks to a farrago perpetrated by Morgan Jones, one of the early Welsh settlers in America who claimed to have lived for a while among Welsh-speaking Indians, it suffered its sea-change into a myth of Welsh Indians. An elaborate 'history' was constructed tracing the migrations of the Madoc Indians from the Gulf of Mexico to the White Padoucas of the upper Missouri. Morgan Jones's fantastic story, however, failed to register for seventy years. It was finally broadcast by Theophilus Evans, in public correspondence and in the second edition of his influential history *Drych y Prif Oesoedd* (*Mirror of the Early Ages*) in 1740, on the traditional occasion of an American War with Spain. From that point, triggered by a search for Welsh Indians by Welsh-American Baptists and a report in 1752 that they had been discovered beyond the Mississippi, stories on the Morgan Jones model began to come in, at first in a trickle, later in a flood. The myth swept to its second great transatlantic climax.

Once more the key was imperial conflict, this time the rivalry over the lucrative fur trade of the far west of America between the British out of Canada, the Americans and the Spaniards who had acquired the vast and unknown continent of Louisiana from France in 1763. For years there had been stories of White Padoucas with a superior civilisation living on the headwaters of the unknown Missouri and in 1792 a French fur trader out of Spanish St Louis had come across a remarkable tribe on the upper Missouri, the Mandans, and reported them to be 'white like Europeans'. The Mandans were in fact lighter-skinned than most Indians, cherished legends of origins on the Mississippi mouth; there was much in their cosmology to give white minds pause. The oldest of a cluster of three tribes who shared an earth-lodge culture, they were unlike any other Indians the whites had encountered and were situated at the strategic cross-roads of the continent. The Spaniards, like everyone else, were working to a mythical geography of that continent which, in ignorance of the real character of the Rocky Mountains, considered that all that lay between the advance guard of the fur trade in the west and the Pacific Ocean was a single mountain chain with an easy portage. The British from the north had reached the Mandans in the 1780s and in a spasm of alarm, the Spaniards in St Louis organised a Company for the Discovery of the Nations of the Missouri led by Jacques Clamorgan, a West Indian adventurer of Welsh descent, and sent expedition after expedition up the difficult river in an effort to secure the Mandans and the fur trade and break through to the Pacific ahead of those British and Americans who posed such a fearful threat to Louisiana and the silver of Mexico to the south.

The tension had been immeasurably sharpened by the Nootka Sound crisis of 1790. Nootka on the Pacific, the fur trade with China and the dream of a global trading empire had been opened up by Captain James Cook (with David Samwell, Iolo's friend, in tow) in the 1770s. Given the notions on American geography then current, the Cook expedition's success implied that a quick land passage to the Pacific and Nootka would confer on its projectors a world empire based on the fur trade. In 1789, resurrecting their ancient papal monopoly, the Spaniards tried to expel the oncoming British from Nootka. Britain, already perturbed by the Spanish economic recovery which was beginning to loosen the foreigners' grip on South America, was far more ready to go to war with Spain over Nootka than with the French Revolution, and in the ensuing crisis, the multiple tensions of the American continent, the struggle for control of the new US republic, the conflict on the frontiers between Spain, Britain and the USA and the competition for the far west shuddered into a crisis which threatened a world war. Although the Spaniards gave way in 1790, the years which followed were years of tension in the west, as Alexander Mackenzie for the Canadians made the first land crossing to the Pacific, as Americans tried to get men up the Spanish Missouri, as the French under British control pressed down on the Mandans from the north, raising the Union flag in Spanish territory and as the Spaniards, led by their empire-building Welsh West Indian, organised the most scientific and dramatic exploration of the west before Lewis and Clark.

Second-in-command to that expedition and companion to its leader, the Scotsman James McKay, in one of the most effective (if forgotten) partnerships in western exploration was a young Welshman, John Evans. A Methodist turned Baptist turned Freemason and a *Jacobin*, he had been precipitated into this field of conflicting forces precisely by the outbreak of Madoc fever in Wales after 1791.[13]

For as imperial eyes riveted on the Missouri with its miraculous Mandans, the White Padouca traditions filtered back east to fuse with the multiplying stories on the Morgan Jones model and the growth in speculation as settlers pushing west encountered more strange tribes with strange languages. In the 1780s, the Americans discovered traditions among the Cherokee Indians of battles they had fought with Welsh intruders migrating from Mobile Bay on the Gulf of Mexico (which a Spaniard in the sixteenth century had once labelled *Tierra de los Gales*, the land of the Welsh) towards the Missouri. Only the Welsh had behind them those confident and semi-official Elizabethan pronunciamentos on Madoc. By the 1780s a tidal wave of Welsh Indian stories was breaking on English-speaking America. Literally scores of people reported direct conversations in Welsh with Indians, several Indian chiefs swore that their ancestors had been Welsh; many men told tales of saving their lives by talking in Welsh to Indians. There were stories of old Welsh Bibles and mysterious books among them; what appeared to be ancient forts strung out from Mobile to the Ohio were attributed to them. At least thirteen real tribes were identified as Welsh Indians, eight other tribes invented to fit. By the late eighteenth century, people realised that they had gone up the Missouri of mystery to enjoy their golden age as the Mandans. In the last years of the century, something of a Madoc fever broke in the USA and belief in Welsh Indians became universal.

The Madoc fever broke on Wales, to tap this vast and growing reservoir of folklore, in strictly traditional manner, in the wake of the Nootka

Sound crisis with Spain. It was unleashed by Dr John Williams's learned study of 1791. Williams was already heavily involved in the eisteddfods of the London-Welsh and in Iolo's *gorsedd*. Hard on his heels came 'General' Bowles, an Irishman sponsored by commercial interests in the Bahamas in deadly rivalry with a Scottish Loyalist firm which buttressed the Spaniards in New Orleans; Bowles had made himself a chief among the Creek Indians and cherished empire-building schemes for which he sought British support. He confirmed the stories of Welsh Indians and offered to help a missionary get to them. In a spasm of enthusiasm, the London-Welsh organised an expedition, Iolo Morganwg offered himself as agent and propagandist, constructed a comprehensive *Padouca Gazette Extraordinary* and, in 1792, read a paper to the Royal and Antiquarian Societies. To the Welsh he proposed an eleven-point plan to establish a Welsh colony near the Illinois in renewed contact with the Lost Brothers. This project had been taken up by William Jones, who circulated his *Address* at the Llanrwst eisteddfod in 1791. The first shudder of America fever ran through north Wales. Out of it came John Evans from Waunfawr near Caernarvon, into a circle of Welsh *Jacobins* in London and across the Atlantic.

Madoc was revived at a singularly apt moment, in the first flush of zeal over the French Revolution and the new liberty eisteddfods and in the first spasm of reaction in the Birmingham riots against *Jacobins* of 1791 and the royal proclamation against seditious writing of the spring of 1792. Overnight this new Madoc became the most miraculous Madoc of them all — a *Jacobin* Madoc.

It is not difficult to see why. In its vision of a resurrected Wales of noble savages in a new world, it offered Welsh *Jacobins* a living myth of Original Cambrian Freedom strictly parallel to that of the Freeborn Saxons and the Norman Yoke of their English comrades. It chimed perfectly with the millenarianism which was raising the voices of Welsh *Jacobins* several octaves. Above all, it reinforced a sense of identity, added something to the flavour of an Israel to be created in the wilderness. The Madoc myth ran as an insistent descant to the Welsh diaspora of the 1790s; John Evans was slogging his way up the Missouri in quest of the Madoc Indians even as projectors were scouring the American frontier for the site of a *Gwladfa* or National Home; the two missions were one in many migrants' minds, fusing in particular in the minds of Dissenters disaffected from British polity and dedicated to missionary enterprise. They were building a *Kingdom of Wales*, as many a Welsh applicant for American citizenship told the clerks in Philadelphia.[14]

What the Madoc myth offered was some *connection* between the

excitements of intellectuals and the hopes and fears of a people in
travail and in particular of their leaders, drawn from Dissent and to a
lesser degree from Methodism. The people who responded to the
challenge with direct and forceful action were distinctive. They were
hardly 'peasants'; the first organised migration from Montgomeryshire,
for example, was stopped under the law against the emigration of
artisans.[15] The countryside of upland Wales was peopled not only by
smallholders but by weavers, spinners, stockingers, clusters of craftsmen.
The people in Llŷn tended to move independently, building up communities in upper New York state in a coral-growth, but it was as
communities that they moved. This was even more true of the great
arc of migration country stretching from Cardiganshire and the south-
west up through the cloth country of Montgomeryshire and Merioneth
into a belt of mountain poverty running along the Berwyn mountains
to Corwen and north and west to Conway and the armpit of Llŷn. Over
the winter whole families from this lively, imaginative, intensely Welsh
and intensely poor people would meet to knit *en masse*, cheered on by
the poets and singers who turned the district into a heartland of Welsh
culture and, in due course, a stronghold of preachers and Sunday
Schools. Stocking sales at Bala and Llanrwst could reach 200,000 pairs
and £18,000 a year. Merioneth's rougher, cheaper web cloth went out
to the Gulf of Mexico through the busy little port of Barmouth to serve
British soldiers and American slaves.[16] Through the centre, centre-north
and stretching to the English border was the better-quality flannel trade
of Montgomeryshire, its farm-based industry subjected to the Drapers
of Shrewsbury.

In the late eighteenth century, the whole area drove into its first crisis
of modernisation.[17] The acceleration of industrial growth in England
brought cloth factors from Liverpool and Lancashire, a quickening in
the commercialisation of agriculture, the intrusion of the annual lease
into traditional community and the first factories along the Severn at
Welshpool, Llanidloes and Newtown, even in Dolgellau in Merioneth.
The consequences were complex: the emergence of some shoestring
native entrepreneurs, the reduction of poor but independent producers
to proletarians and, during the war years, a massive increase in pauper-
isation. Parallel to it, there was an explosive acceleration in the growth
of Methodism and Dissent, the former often mushrooming out from
strongholds earlier established by the latter. The weavers of Llanbrynmair, for example, were a recalcitrant bunch who never rode to Welshpool
market on a Sunday. They were Independents; they were to lead not
only the mass protest meetings of the 1790s with their demands for a

government of the poor not the rich, but the parties threading their way through the food rioters and the press gangs to the America boats. It was they who were to produce the man who was to father the first native-born governor of the state of Ohio in the USA.

Throughout the area, the accelerated modernisation of the war years brought crisis, worsened by taxes, levies, enclosures, the press gangs and militia lists, inflation and the virtual closure of the port of Barmouth. At the paroxysms of 1795-6 and 1799-1801, during the terrible sub-sistence crises with their famine prices, thousands were in disaffection. Those who could, those with some means and spirit, as most Dissenters and many Methodists were, voted with their feet. Their migration was peculiarly Dissenter in spirit and *Jacobin* in tone, and they went under the banner of Madoc.

This social crisis turned the quirky old Voltairean in Llangadfan, on the border of web and flannel country, into a spokesman for militant Dissent.[18] William Jones, born around 1729 and trapped at home by poverty and a large family, his yearning to travel stifled, became a spiritual American and one of the best-informed men on the Land of Freedom in Wales. Clawing his way up into self-taught knowledge and frustrated talent, he made himself into an accomplished poet and musician, learned Latin to translate Horace and Ovid, became a skilled antiquarian and an effective country healer until he was crippled by the Medicine Act. Amateur astronomer and physicist, as so many of his temper were, he was a credulous addict of any 'Celtic' and antique-romantic anthropology. A 'hot-arsed' Welshman (to quote the discreet Welsh of a friend)[19] he was a dedicated hater of Saxons, landowners and Methodists and read the history of the Welsh as one long struggle against English oppression. Their only hope lay in the New World alongside the Lost Brothers. No one did more than William Jones to focus Welsh minds on the idea of a *Gwladfa*, on the organisation of joint-stock companies for emigration and on the communal financing of vanguard groups and he did it through the medium of Madoc. The *Address* he circulated at the Llanrwst eisteddfod in 1791 started the America fever in the north and captured the mind of the young John Evans who was to become a pioneer of American exploration and the last of the Spanish conquistadors. William Jones never went himself, was seen off by a schizophrenic and dismissive obituary from Walter Davies and was rewarded by a century's scorn as an 'eccentric'. But it was his voice which rang in the heads of the hundreds moving on Liverpool and Bristol and which echoed hopelessly through thousands more.

William Richards was a more polished but no less prickly variant of the same species.[20] He became a Baptist minister in Lynn, Norfolk, whose history he wrote, but his heart and very often his person were in his beloved south-west Wales. Compiler of dictionaries in the style of Horne Tooke's *Diversions of Purley*, Enlightenment man and restorer of the original purity of the New Testament Church, millenarian in the manner of Priestley, he published a defence of the atheism of the French Revolution. Above all he was a dedicated, if often caustic, friend of America. He invested £800 of his money in the Republic and left his books to Rhode Island College. His copious correspondence with American Baptists was one of the axes of the migration movement and he was as active in organising Madoc hunts as in negotiating with ship-captains for communal transfers to the Ohio. No less than William Jones in the north, he was a 'contagious individual' to his bailiwick.

For the south-west was, if anything, even more of a heartland of Welsh America and its Madocian *Gwladfa* than the cloth country.[21] The sister societies of Cardiganshire, upland Carmarthenshire and north Pembrokeshire were also a nest of singing birds, country poets, Dissenter preachers and craggy polemicists over Biblical texts; around Tregaron and Llandovery, there was another stocking-trade concentration of Bala intensity. Though its little ports were flourishing and the decay of its small lead industry not yet too visible, Cardiganshire was hit harder by the population explosion than any county in Wales. With its smallholders, hill farmers, frustrated artisans and squatters encroaching without cease on the two-thirds of its stubborn soil owned by the Crown, it became a community of land-hunger and inching self-improvement, a land of seasonal migrants. It was also a land of contrasts. To the south-west, the Methodist father Daniel Rowland had thrown crowds into those public ecstasies which earned them the nickname of Jumpers, but a few miles away to the south-east was the *Black Spot* of the orthodox, a tight but potent fistful of Unitarians. From this district came the migrants who peopled the mushrooming industrial complex in south-east Wales, splitting chapel after chapel there with demands for 'vital religion', even as it nourished the Unitarians and *Jacobins* of so different a temper. Even more striking, it was the *ceffyl pren* of the south-west — the wooden cock-horse with its 'rough music' of an extra-legal village discipline — which helped to shape the *Scotch Cattle* workers' guerrilla movement of Monmouthshire.[22]

For it was during this time of travail that the region ground into a quasi-permanent disaffection from the Anglican magistracy which within a generation was to produce that classic guerrilla of the small farmer, the Rebecca Riots. This tension had begun to find a focus in the already turbulent town of Carmarthen with its small-scale industries and active press, its tribes of bloody-minded artisans, focus for the fertile vale of Towy and a cluster of small ports in contact with Bristol. Over the next generation, Carmarthen, a by-word for riot, locked into its insulating feuds which nevertheless came increasingly to reflect the Anglican-Dissenter tension of its hinterland, virtually seceded from public order.[23] And further west along the coast into Pembrokeshire, there were ports, coal-mines, an English population and the town of Haverfordwest, one of the most notoriously *Jacobin* centres in Wales. When the French staged their landing at Fishguard in 1797, the immediate response of Establishment and respectability was a witch-hunt against Dissenters which enmeshed William Richards Lynn in its McCarthyite toils. This was bilious prejudice but it was by no means lunacy. Authority knew who its enemies were.

For this was one of the early bastions of a peculiarly intransigent Dissent, one of the first breeding grounds of a disconcerting form of Methodism. Some of the greatest of the old chapels were there. William Williams of Cardigan was one of the rare Nonconformists to serve as a JP. A friend of Morgan John Rhys and William Richards, he, too, was an 'American'; his kinsfolk were as numerous in Pennsylvania as in Cardiganshire. From the river Teifi and its hinterland had gone one of the earliest and most distinctive of the Welsh migrations. Samuel Jones Pennepek himself had roots in this land which in its *Cardis* — the Galicians of Wales — supplied the most successful of the emigrants.

Madoc, then, playing on the minds of Dissenter leaders of the migrations, could turn emigrants into Children of a Cymric Israel. Morgan John Rhys, who was to appoint himself their Moses, brought out the first political periodical in the Welsh language in 1793. In it, he blazoned an Exhortation from Madoc to the renaissant Welsh: 'dyma ni yn awr ar daith ein gobaith.' Here we are now on the journey of our hope.

Note, however, the nature and function of this Madoc myth. It was essentially *connective* rather than *constitutive*. The thrust for migration had its own objective reality. Its leaders and its personnel were shaped no less by objective reality at its harshest. No contradiction is so painful in the 1790s as that, revealed by the voluminous Welsh-American correspondence of those years, between the evident, indeed desperate desire to emigrate among thousands upon thousands and their failure to do so from sheer brute poverty; shipping rates doubled between 1793 and 1799.[24] It was those with some competence who went and they were overpoweringly Dissenters of small property, with a complement of Methodists. All the efforts to bridge the gap by subscription, joint-stock companies, appeals to the American consuls, failed; when Morgan John Rhys finally launched the *Gwladfa*, his advertising in Wales was directed explicitly at a 'middle class'.[25] The role of Dissent was therefore crucial and while economic motives were without doubt central, the general *political* temper of the movement, its millenarian and missionary character, were just as significant. It was here that the Madoc myth, linking the preoccupations of nation-makers and religion-purifiers with the exigencies of community and survival, could work its magic. After a ragged and unorganised beginning, the migrations were consciously directed towards the creation of a new, free, 'restored' Wales in the west.

This connection between the obsessions of *Jacobin* intellectuals and the mind of Welsh Nonconformity was, however, something of a historical accident. In its interaction with the world of Dissent, the new *nation* failed to become a *constitutive myth*.

For it ran into a bewildering maze of contradictions.[26] The London-Welsh, themselves a minority among Welsh Londoners, were beginning to figure as national leaders; the first of their eisteddfods, at Corwen in 1789, they ran in response to an appeal from the locality. The men in Wales with such cultural interests, however, were themselves a minority, particularly in regions where Methodism was beginning to affect the social tone. They were moreover a very mixed bunch. Gentlemen like Thomas Pennant of Flintshire or Paul Panton of Anglesey were patrons of culture. Old Tory parsons could be devotees of matters Welsh. The natural contacts of the Gwyneddigion and their kin were without doubt the organic intellectuals emerging from the popular classes of Wales under the crust of a gentry-parson oligarchy. Such an organic intelligentsia was certainly beginning to emerge, but its characteristic representative was to be the Nonconformist preacher-journalist. Here the contradiction in the predicament of Welsh *Jacobins* proved to be crippling. By 1799, Iolo Morganwg was writing to William Owen from north Wales in angry despair — 'North Wales is now as methodistical as South Wales and South Wales as Hell!'[27]

Iolo's geography was correct. In the late eighteenth century, north and west began to follow south and east under the Calvinist harrow. Purist northerners, whose language and literature had developed in greater autonomy within what was for long a relatively immobile society, often scorned the 'Hottentot' Welsh of the more open south, heavily influenced by English, while southerners in turn often despised the 'hermetic backwardness' of the north. In terms of social structure and climate, the real dichotomy was east-west. In the early eighteenth century, of some seventy or so Dissenting chapels on record, each often serving a broad hinterland, only ten were in the north and they were in the north-east. The strongholds of Dissent were in the south and the east. The Methodist revival itself took its origins from Breconshire and south Cardiganshire. Methodism and Dissent together advanced into north and west, often in parallel with Griffith Jones's circulating schools, geared to adults, the Bible and evangelical purpose. Thomas Charles, the great Methodist leader who gave the celebrated Welsh Sunday Schools their characteristic form, made Bala in Merioneth into the capital of his sect, but he had come up from Carmarthenshire. At the great Baptist *gymanfa* or preaching festival at Nefyn in the Llŷn peninsula in 1792, a high point of the crusade, seven of the nine preachers were from the south.

These men, Methodists and Dissenters together, though riding the wave of the future, were in the late eighteenth century still a minority. Even when the Methodists became officially Nonconformist in 1811, it is doubtful whether Dissent, old and new, accounted for as much as 15-20 per cent of the population. So effectively did Nonconformity colonise the historiography of the modern Welsh that this brute fact has to be reasserted. That colonisation, however, was symptomatic. For these men were men of the Word, particularly the printed word. The book production of Wales was dominated by them. They turned the *cofiant*, the minister's autobiography in the style of Bunyan, into a new Welsh literary genre. The lyric poetry of Wales, especially that of the master William Williams Pantycelyn, found one major outlet in hymns.

In one way this *was* a link with the Gwyneddigion. Much of their correspondence reflects the agonies of authorship. It was during these years that the Welsh words for *dictionary* and *subscribe* were coined, to serve as presiding deities! These men moved through a blizzard of proof sheets, printers' errors (particularly if they tried to use William Owen's orthography!), awkward publishers, endless subscription lists. They exemplify what was to become a national obsession with the printing press. What they wrote, however, their style, was often remote indeed from that of the London-Welsh and their scattered allies in the parishes. Their celebrated Nonconformist triumph (it was virtually complete within two generations) was itself riddled with contradiction. The evangelical style, exemplified most clearly but not exclusively in Methodism, without doubt made all the running. For generations, most literate Welsh people were to live their lives within it or in reaction to it. It was complex. It bred generations to the discipline of a close and disputatious reading of texts, to the practice of criticism, to self-expression, to the social disciplines of self-management, the Sunday School, committee work, organisation. For Methodists were 'precisians' as well as 'jumpers'. It built on and bred a literate people. Griffith Jones's circulating schools – so effective that they caught the interest of a Russian Tsar – had held nearly 3,500 classes by his death in 1761, had taught (on a narrow reading and Biblical curriculum) over 150,000 pupils and by his estimate, two or three times that number of adult evening students. The schools carried on for a while under the patronage of Madam Bevan, a supporter. She left £10,000 in 1779 to maintain the impetus, but her will was contested and the money remained in Chancery for thirty years. The schools came to an end. But they had sustained the advance of Welsh literacy and evangelical religion, whose own schools were to resume the effort.

This religion itself, however, while nourishing a literate people, giving it voice, creating a powerful literature for it, producing its own brand of mysticism and dedication, could also show the seamy underside of its populism, an undercurrent of anti-intellectualism, a theatrical preaching style vulnerable to the charlatan and the mountebank, a close, inbred sectarianism which could be stifling. The Calvinism of the movement, in truth largely accidental in origin, became a tribal identity, with witch-hunts, sectarian fragmentation, orthodoxy-peddling. When the Arminian Wesleyan Methodists penetrated the Calvinist fief of Wales at the end of the century, the theological controversy which ensued deafened Welsh ears (and has since populated the dusty shelves of Welsh second-hand book shops).

These characteristics affected also large numbers of adherents to the denominations of Old Dissent, particularly the newer ones from the newly conquered areas. Baptists in the south-west were in some turmoil and in the shift of population towards the industrial areas, located in earlier centres of Dissenting penetration, there were crises in the chapels. One minister in Merthyr was hooted in the streets for trying to introduce hymns into chapel. Old Dissent, however, while often 'methodised' in its style, could never wholly shake off its origins. Their founding fathers, after all, had cut a king's head off, on principle. They laboured under disabilities, they looked to America and for a while, to France. However respectable they became, their stance had necessarily to be at least somewhat 'political'. Methodism, though virtually a distinct body for a whole generation before formal separation from the Anglican Church in 1811, was officially reluctant to separate; for years it remained deferential. It was essentially quietist and apolitical; it could easily become quite biliously Tory. This profound difference in quality remained important. Sometimes the line, in the nineteenth century, ran between brothers who were preacher-journalists. To put it crudely, the Baptist/Independent was a 'politician'; the Methodist a 'pietist'. That is why the complex phenomenon known by the shorthand phrase 'the radicalising of the Methodists' was so important to nineteenth-century Welsh politics.

One would hardly think so, however, from the correspondence of the gentry and magistrates of north Wales in the late eighteenth century. Its tone towards Methodists was often hysterical; the preachers were denounced as *Jacobins* and levellers (which tends to induce a state of shock in historians familiar with their official attitudes). In early days, Methodist missionaries to the north went through hell; they were attacked by mobs, ducked in ponds; one was thrown into a gentleman's dog kennels. This hostility remained sharp well into the nineteenth century. There were, quite probably, local exhorters whose denunciations of sin carried some social bite, but one has to note that both Methodist advance and conservative hysteria marched in step with the accelerating pace of economic and social change in the north and the west. Some historians have suggested that there is a connection between the displacement of the lesser gentry of Wales from the wider official life of the eighteenth century and both the growth of Methodism and to a lesser extent Dissent as an alternative social leadership, *and* an intensification of interest in native culture. Men of long pedigree and short purses cultivated roots and cherished an alternative system of values. Certainly, sociological research on later times has shown the close connection between Nonconformity and its sects and the social imperatives of local community. The Old Dissent, it is true, had its roots in people of some substance and independence and while its popular following began to grow, parallel to that of Methodism, particularly among the Baptists, it retained something of that character.

This was precisely the social area in which alternative local leaderships could and did emerge. But the consequences for the half-formed ideology which was emerging from the efforts of Welsh revivalists were complex. Much of Methodism and Dissent in its more evangelical forms was elaborating a 'Welshness' which was quite different from that of Iolo and the Gwyneddigion; much of it was blank, if not hostile, towards any *political* expression. On the other hand, among the popular classes which were being disrupted by the very social travail which was offering them Methodists and Dissenters as alternative leaders, responses could at least in part be consonant. The first painful emergence of a 'nation' in the modern sense within Wales was, then, contradictory and confusing. In a Wales in which all such groups were minorities, in which a colonial economy was yielding to a more modern form of capitalism, and in which political life, still firmly under gentry control, was blanketed by the violent conservative reaction to the French Revolution, it is perhaps not surprising that the most visible response was a surge of emigration under the banner of Madoc.

There *were* men, however, particularly within Old Dissent, whose intellectual odyssey could bring them within hailing distance of the unorthodox, the Deists, the radicals in London and scattered here and there through Wales. 'There are palpable and dreadful heresies in the country,' wrote the Methodist hymn-writer William Williams Pantycelyn in 1790, 'They say that some of the Baptists deny the divinity of Christ.'[28]

Against the rigours of Calvinism, with its rigid doctrine of the Elect, Arminianism, with its admission of free will and human agency – and the fuller humanist commitment it brought in its wake – had periodically rebelled.[29] A different train of controversies, equally ancient in their roots, centred on the question of the Trinity and the status of Christ. A multiplicity of variant attitudes found a focus in Arianism, which was a partial denial of the divinity of Christ and in Socinianism, a total denial. Nuances and shades of difference were legion, but the ultimate destination of many of these trends of thinking and feeling were Unitarianism, on the very frontier of Christianity, and the Deisms which lay beyond it. Theological commitment carried with it a complex of other attitudes, informed by Newtonian science, the politics and cosmology of the Enlightenment and the struggle to win full civic and religious liberty. In the third quarter of the eighteenth century, the democratic doctrine sprang full-grown from the Old Cause of True Whiggism and the Commonwealthmen in England; the first democratic pronunciamentos in England accompany the American Declaration of Independence. And one central force was personified in Joseph Priestley, scientist, political theorist, millenarian – and Unitarian.

The Welsh denominations, closely intertwined with their parent English bodies and given to (sometimes aridly obsessive) intellectual debate, particularly during their un-evangelical self-absorption in the mid-eighteenth century, were affected early, in particular within their often excellent and celebrated academies. The Independent academy at Carmarthen succumbed to Arminianism in the 1720s. It was moved about Wales in an effort to break the heresy, but soon after it returned to Carmarthen in 1743 it split again, this time over Arianism. In 1755, the Congregational Board in London excommunicated it. In 1726, Jenkin Jones, from Carmarthen, founded the first Arminian church in Wales in south Cardiganshire. From this nucleus, an Arian core was built up in that distinctive region, which moved remorselessly towards Unitarianism. Its great schoolmaster-ministers (the sect tended to produce mathematicians and scientists) exercised an influence out of all proportion to the group's tiny numbers; the small Presbyterian denomination went over *en bloc*; its very name came to mean simply liberalism in theology. Independent churches, in particular, with their congregational autonomy, were vulnerable. Into the last years of the eighteenth century, chapel after chapel was split among the Welsh Independents. A particular conquest was Glamorgan and its hill conventicles. Merthyr Independency was won early and as the population mushroomed, the Presbyterian families of the Vale tended to be drawn there. In the next generation, the small but highly influential knot of Unitarian radicals, although heavily outnumbered by orthodox Dissent, captured local control of Wales's first industrial town.

In the late eighteenth century, as numbers and the pressures of the new populist evangelicalism increased, the orthodox Independent academy moved, significantly enough, to the north, as part of the crusade, but the tensions between 'methodised' styles and 'unitarian', between Calvinism and Arminianism, between doctrinal purity and political commitment persisted. The Baptists, whose central assembly, the *gymanfa*, imposed a measure of federal control, after a succession of internal quarrels over baptism, entered a prolonged crisis from 1779.[30] One basic cause was sheer growth. Sermons at the *gymanfa* doubled in number and length. In the great drive to the north, the new converts proved insatiable addicts of the new pulpit oratory. In 1788, the Baptist *gymanfa* moved into the heart of what had been infidel country in Anglesey; there were nine sermons there, as at Nefyn four years later. Those sermons, and the style of worship generally, were rapidly 'methodised'. The new generation of preachers which emerged found their model in Christmas Evans who made Anglesey his fief, and rivalled Methodist John Elias himself as a giant in that particular mode of pulpit oratory which came to be regarded as typical of the Welsh. This grated horribly on the nerves of Baptists like William Richards of Lynn, Morgan John Rhys, the trenchant J.R. Jones, Ramoth, who ran a celebrated chapel in the north-east and was to lead a secession against the trend. Men like William Richards preached a non-sectarian liberal religion: 'our name is Christians and Christians only,' a creed based on the New Testament rather than that Old Testament much favoured by the brimstone brethren, open and quick to political commitment, which opponents denounced as Unitarianism or even Deism. Throughout the 1790s, the Baptists were locked in controversy; after 1799, there was a schism and the anti-Methodist radicals formed a short-lived General Baptist denomination. Its brief strongholds were in the Towy valley, the Vale of Glamorgan and its eastern hills.

Not even the Methodists with their rigorous central control and discipline were immune. One of their founding fathers, Peter Williams, brought out a translation of the Bible in 1770 with notes which questioned the doctrine of the Trinity. For this, he was to be expelled. Once again, it was a small group in the Vale of Glamorgan, Thomas Williams of Bethesda'r Fro and John Williams of St Athan, who took up his cause. Both were friends of Iolo Morganwg. In 1790, Peter Williams and David Jones translated the old Puritan Bible of John Canne, annotated it in unorthodox style and, horror of horrors, launched a cheap pocket edition. It was the Baptist minister Morgan John Rhys who went on tour with it, advertised it in the first Welsh political periodical and even took it to the France which had just seen the light of liberty. Joseph Priestley's simultaneously rationalist and millenarian *History of the Corruptions of Christianity* and *History of Early Opinions of Jesus Christ* sent ripples of controversy through all the sects even as James Bicheno's dramatically millenarian *Signs of the Times* captured minds set racing by the French Revolution following so hard on the heels of the American.

This millenarian tone was one point of contact between liberal Dissenters and men like William Owen and Iolo Morganwg — there were so many Witnesses to Resurrect! Another was the education of the Welsh. Welsh and Sunday schools were needed, the ordinary Welshman's command over his own language was often oral, dictionaries were an urgent necessity. The ambition to 'raise up the old homeland', 'codi'r hen wlad', could unite such people around practical issues. The Welsh had to be put in possession of their patrimony. Their religion had to be pure and rational, as close as possible to the primitive simplicity of the Early Church. This kind of thinking and feeling brought such men, indirectly, close to the Gwyneddigion's obsession with a purified orthography, their universalism of a Welsh language, close to Iolo's Druidism. It was the crisis of war and revolution, governmental repression and Methodist advance which shuffled liberal Dissenters and Druidic revivalists into a loosely united intelligentsia which, while often denounced as 'cosmopolitan', was in fact much more 'nationalist' than the deeply Welsh evangelicals.

The pattern is one made familiar by European experience, that of the Czechs in particular. Antiquarians, poets, philologists, the radical and rational religious, in an atmosphere of millenarian myth, were conjuring a nation out of a past they had made usable and, as people's remembrancers, reached out to a corrupted people without memory. By 1789, such men had an eisteddfod once more, by 1792, a *gorsedd*. One enterprise remained to complete the pattern, a journal to carry the word to the unregenerate. In 1793, it appeared. William Owen, the London-Welsh and their friends put their weight behind it. Its motto was the creed Iolo Morganwg had bestowed on his Bards: 'Y gwir yn erbyn y byd', Truth against the World. In its first number it announced that proceeds were going towards finding the Lost Brothers; it praised republican France and preached republican America. And its editor was Morgan John Rhys, a Baptist minister who did not object to Voltaire and published the French free thinker Volney. Within eighteen months, Morgan John was leading the Elect out of a barren Egyptian desert towards a Canaan they were to build from their own bones.

Notes

1. The basic text for the London-Welsh is R.T. Jenkins and H.T. Ramage, *A History of the Honourable Society of Cymmrodorion and of the Gwyneddigion and Cymreigyddion Societies 1751-1951* (Hon. Soc. Cymmrodorion, London, 1951).

2. My picture of Denbighshire is derived from D.J.V. Jones, *Before Rebecca: Popular Protest in Wales 1793-1835* (Allen Lane, London, 1973) and A.H. Dodd, *The Industrial Revolution in North Wales*, 3rd edn (University of Wales Press, Cardiff, 1971) and a number of specialised works, more particularly those of J. Geraint Jenkins, *The Welsh Woollen Industry* (National Museum of Wales, Cardiff, 1969) and 'The Woollen Industry' in Donald Moore (ed.), *Wales in the Eighteenth Century* (Christopher Davies, Swansea, 1976).

3. The basic material comes from R.T. Jenkins and H.T. Ramage's history of the London societies, the work of David Williams and my own work; rather fuller portraits of these people in my *Madoc: the Making of a Myth* (Eyre Methuen, London, 1980).

4. David Samwell's journal of the Cook expedition is printed in J.C. Beaglehole (ed.), *The Journals of Captain James Cook on his Voyages of Discovery: the Voyage of the Resolution and the Discovery 1776-80* (Hakluyt Society, Cambridge University Press, Cambridge, 1967), Vol. III, Part 2, Appendix 2, pp. 987-1300; see also E.G. Bowen, *David Samwell* (University of Wales Press, Cardiff, 1974).

5. E. Williams—W. Owen, 7 March 1797, NLW 13222, fo. 131-4.

6. *Merthyr Guardian*, 3 January 1835, letter from Taliesin, Iolo's son, with retrospective reference; the 'Buonapartism' of many popular and working-class militants (e.g. Thomas Hardy, leader of the LCS) needs study.

7. The best source for this transatlantic release of Jacobinism is the manuscript

journal of Morgan John Rhys of his grand tour of the republic in 1794-5; see below, Chapters 4 and 5.

8. My friend and research student Hywel M. Davies is producing a PhD thesis on this theme, which is more central than many of us have imagined.

9. For all that follows on Iolo Morganwg, the basic source is the magnificent scholarship of Griffith John Williams, notably his *Iolo Morganwg* (University of Wales Press, Cardiff, 1956); unfortunately Professor Williams died before he could produce his long-awaited second volume, but he has a brilliant essay (in English) in his *Iolo Morganwg* (BBC Annual Lecture, Cardiff, 1963); there is an excellent short critical essay (in English) in the Welsh Arts Council Writers of Wales series, Prys Morgan, *Iolo Morganwg* (University of Wales Press for Welsh Arts Council, Cardiff, 1975) and a biographical essay in Ceri W. Lewis, 'Edward Williams, Iolo Morganwg' in Dyfnallt Morgan (ed.), *Gwŷr Llên y Ddeunawfed Ganrif* (Llyfrau'r Dryw, Llandybie, 1966: collection on literary men of the eighteenth century); relevant here is the splendid Stuart Piggott, *The Druids* (Thames and Hudson, London, 1968).

10. I give a fuller portrait of Iolo in my *Madoc: the Making of a Myth*.

11. For all that follows on the Madoc tradition and its multiple forms, see the detailed account in my *Madoc: the Making of a Myth* which, on this period, serves as a companion volume to this.

12. This address, which like everything William Jones wrote, is worth reading (if not worth always believing!) may be found in W. Jones–W. Owen, 6-7 August 1791, NLW 13221, fo. 341-342-339, 340-3.

13. I give a full account of John Evans and his mission in *Madoc: the Making of a Myth*.

14. This statement is based on the naturalisation records of the federal district court and county courts of Pennsylvania: Federal Records Centre, Veterans' Building and City Hall, Philadelphia, and fifteen counties.

15. W. Jones–W. Owen, 1 July 1793, 5 May 1794 and n.d. (1794) NLW 13224, fo. 109, NLW 13221, fo. 301-5.

16. There is a brilliant essay on this society in R.T. Jenkins, *Hanes Cymru yn y Ddeunawfed Ganrif* (University of Wales paperback reprint, Cardiff, 1972), especially Chapter 5 and pp. 104-8.

17. On this critical theme, I have used Jones, *Before Rebecca*, Dodd, *The Industrial Revolution in North Wales*, Geraint Jenkins's work on the cloth industry (see footnote 2) and Jenkins, *Hanes Cymru yn y Ddeunawfed Ganrif*.

18. The major source is a contemporary life written by Walter Davies in *Cambrian Register 1796*, vol. ii (1799), pp. 237-51, supplemented by his voluminous correspondence among the William Owen papers, mainly in NLW 13221; I give a fuller picture in *Madoc: the Making of a Myth*.

19. 'Tin-boeth' was the expression: T. Jones–W. Owen, 20 October 1795, NLW 13221, fo. 256.

20. A contemporary life, John Evans, *Memoirs of the Life and Writings of the Rev. William Richards, Ll.D.* (London, 1819), a penetrating essay in R.T. Jenkins, 'William Richards o Lynn', *Trafodion Cymdeithas Hanes Bedyddwyr Cymru* (Welsh Baptist Historical Society, 1930) and a mass of correspondence with Samuel Jones in Pennepek; his own work is discussed by David Williams (*Welsh History Review*, 1967).

21. On the south-west, the superb essay, David Williams, *The Rebecca Riots* (University of Wales Press, Cardiff, 1955), Jones, *Before Rebecca*, and Jenkins, *Hanes Cymru yn y Ddeunawfed Ganrif*.

22. See the brilliant essay on the Scotch Cattle in Jones, *Before Rebecca*, and my *The Merthyr Rising*.

23. My mind is influenced by the work of David Williams and D.J.V. Jones on

the town and the working-class parallel suggested in John Foster's work on Oldham in *Class Struggle and the Industrial Revolution* (Weidenfeld and Nicolson, London, 1974).

24. W. Richards—S. Jones, 3 April 1801 and 1800-1 *passim*: Pennepek.

25. Prospectus of the Cambrian Company 1796: several copies in Cambria Historical Society, Ebensburg, Pennsylvania, the Historical Society of Pennsylvania and William Owen papers, NLW; printed in J.T. Griffith, *Morgan John Rhys*, (USA, 1899 and W.M. Evans, Carmarthen, 1910), p. 248.

26. What follows on Welsh Dissent and Methodism is based on twenty years' reading; the works of David Williams (*Welsh History Review*, 1967) and *A Bibliography of the History of Wales* (University of Wales Press, Cardiff, 1962); supplements in the *Bulletin of the Board of Celtic Studies* will provide an entry; I find myself much influenced by the work of R.T. Jenkins.

27. Quoted in Jenkins and Ramage, *History of the Cymmrodorion*, p. 123.

28. Quoted in J.J. Evans, *Morgan John Rhys a'i Amserau* (University of Wales Press, Cardiff, 1935), p. 143.

29. The best general survey of these themes is Jenkins, *Hanes Cymru yn y Ddeunawfed Ganrif*, Chapter 3, and his particular studies, *Bardd a'i Gefndir, Edward Ifan o'r Ton Coch* (Cymmrodorion, Cardiff, 1949) and 'William Richards o Lynn'.

30. The best treatment is R.T. Jenkins's essay, 'William Richards o Lynn', especially the section entitled 'Y Rhwyg yn Salem' (The schism in Salem).

3 DAGON'S COUNTRY

Morgan John Rhys burns in the mind like a sudden flame, all warmth and brilliance and brevity.[1] In a generation of concentrated individuality and creative eccentricity, he marked himself out as boldly as he marked out the bounds of his Beula in the west. Popular journalism, negro emancipation, civil liberty, rational religion, there was scarcely one liberal, and often deeply unpopular, cause he did not adopt. He carried a crusade for Protestant liberty into revolutionary France and preached Indian property rights to a victorious American army beyond the Ohio. He was a visionary and there was a dreamer in him, though this was not the impression he made on such American hardheads as the Quaker speculator Henry Drinker and the tough and conventional Richard Rush. He rarely carried anything to completion. He was a precursor born. He let himself be trapped by his times, his friends, his loyalties. He could not come to a sharp enough focus in time; he was dead before he was 45 and forgotten for a century. Yet in himself he mirrors the aspirations, the achievements, the frustrations and the contradictions of the Welsh in the Atlantic Revolution.

Born on the Glamorgan-Monmouth border into a family of small freeholders who were members of the old Baptist cause of Hengoed, a characteristic stronghold of Welsh Cromwellian Dissent in its new liberal persona, Morgan John opened a school in the district at the age of twenty and taught for two years. It was a notable success and he was to publish handbooks on the running of Welsh and Sunday schools, of which he was a pioneer. In 1782, Hengoed invited him to preach. After three years of this, he made the characteristic decision to go to America, on missionary work. He had booked passage to Charleston and was within three days of sailing when his brother brought him news of his mother's death. In the following year, he entered the Baptist academy at Bristol and, in 1787, was ordained minister at Penygarn chapel, Pontypool in Monmouthshire. An immediate success, he was at once swept up into the great Baptist campaigns in the troubled north of Wales which, like those of the Methodists and Independents, were assuming the character of highly successful, indeed rather alarming mass evangelical movements. Other missions caught his mind. He threw himself into the first large-scale anti-slavery movements, published his first pamphlets in that cause and argued for the Christianisation of the

American Indians. Committed to civil and religious liberty, he tried to get to America again.

This time, he was distracted by a mission nearer home. For in 1790, a pocket version of the heterodox John Canne Bible came out, a marvellous instrument for his revivalist and now increasingly millenarian purpose. He travelled with the Canne Bible, setting up Sunday schools and seminars. But these were also the first, and to liberal Dissenters, ecstatic months of the French Revolution. In a striking demonstration of the unexpected in him, he gave up his chapel and crossed to Paris to preach the rational religion of liberty and work for the Conversion of the Last Days. Nothing is known of this startling mission, but it must have been an amazing winter. It seems also to have been rather more successful than might have been expected. For when he was driven home by the outbreak of war in Europe, he began to organise an association to translate the Canne Bible into French and to promote its distribution. William Williams of Cardigan and William Richards Lynn rallied and a Baptist *gymanfa* in the south-west committed itself to the project. It was said that in his travels to promote this enterprise, Rhys also began to create political societies; it was certainly during 1792 that he began to assimilate Iolo Morganwg's teaching on the Bards and the Druids, to establish close contact with the London-Welsh.

He had returned to find that the regeneration of the Welsh had assumed a new dimension of reality in the mission to find the Madoc Indians.[2] The intensive work of Iolo Morganwg reached a climax in the spring of 1792 in a second edition of Dr John Williams's study and in Iolo's own papers to the Royal and Antiquarian Societies. His original intention to travel by a southern route and go up the Arkansas with the help of 'General' Bowles had been abandoned after his encounter with Charles Gratiot, one of the pioneer traders of St Louis who had been introduced to the Londoners by a New Orleans merchant of Welsh descent. Gratiot shifted the mission bodily into Spanish territory. On his recommendation, a crowded meeting in the Prince of Wales coffee house in April 1792 adopted a hard, practical plan which at last won the support of influential patrons. The expedition was to make its way through Philadelphia to the Ohio, take a flatboat to St Louis, where Gratiot, using his own bank and the London-Welsh house of Mackworth, would equip them with boats and furs. Setting off as a trading venture, with Spanish licence, they were to make their way up the Missouri, trading from tribe to tribe until they reached the White Padoucas. In their first flush of enthusiasm, the Madocians, who had already approached the African Association and the Missionary Society in the same cause, suspended their subscription in the hope of getting support from the British government which was still, at this point, publicly anticipating many years of peace.

To this end, Iolo had read his paper to the Royal Society the previous month, though publication was postponed to keep the affair a secret from the Spaniards. Given its initial commitment to the Madoc myth, Iolo's essay was cogent and persuasive. It was couched in imperial no less than Welsh or missionary terms, arguing the case, which Alexander Mackenzie would press nine years later, for a line of British posts stretching through the Madoc Indians to Nootka Sound: 'a hundred well-disposed Welshmen there (being of the same language with them) would do more towards acquiring a considerable accession of Territory to *Great Britain* than a hundred thousand scoundrels in *Botany Bay*.'[3]

Those 'hundred well-disposed Welshmen' turn up, however, in a very different context: an eleven-point plan which Iolo drafted at the same time and circulated among his friends in London and Wales. This was a draft petition to the Congress of the USA asking for their assistance in the purchase of land 'near the Mississippi between the Ohio and the Illinois'. An emigrants' company was to be formed and as soon as 100 men, exclusive of women and children, had signed on, was to ship the vanguard party to the selected site. All who could contribute £5 towards the land purchase money were to form a Company of Colonists who, on settlement, were to provide land at a low rental to a Company of Mechanics, the latter travelling free at the Company's expense. The settlement was to be run on the 'purest principles of Justice, Peace and Liberty . . . assented to by solemn affirmation and manual signature by every emigrant before he can be admitted of the party'. The Library, however, which was to include five copies of William Owen's Dictionary as well as encyclopaedias and technical treatises, was reserved for a 'select society', the directive elite of the colony, in which 'the legal language shall be Welsh and all pleadings in Law, all Religious worship etc shall be in it, the English also to be taught as a learned language and source of knowledge.' No one was to be admitted to the Colony who could not speak Welsh unless he had a wife who could.[4]

This was the first serious attempt to translate the dream of William Jones Llangadfan into reality; at that moment the Voltairean himself was bombarding the American representatives in Britain with requests for assistance. The locale of the *Gwladfa* was skilfully chosen, in an area which was to be the target of several such state-building schemes, in the orbit but out of the power of Spanish authority and within striking distance of the Madoc Indians on the upper Missouri. Nor was the idea a pipe-dream. Dissenters in the cloth villages of Montgomeryshire were already organising and in the May of 1792, a volunteer to accompany Iolo appeared in the person of John Evans, a 22-year-old Methodist from Waunfawr outside Caernarvon, friend and protégé of the poet David Thomas, 'Dafydd Ddu Eryri' (Black David of Snowdon) one of the few Methodists who were *persona grata* with the Gwyneddigion since he had won a prize at the Llanrwst eisteddfod.

It was in that spring of 1792, however, that this buoyant movement ran into its first jarring shock. It was the cruel impact of recalcitrant old reality which had driven Morgan John home from Paris. In April the threat of war became actuality. The disintegration of the French armies, the advance of the Prussians and Austrians over the border and on Paris, the surge of counter-revolution and the radicalisation of the Revolution in response suddenly tightened nerves in Britain. Church and King had already mobilised against dissent — and Dissent — in many localities; the great debate over Burke and the Revolution was becoming sharper. The Priestley riots in Birmingham the previous year had been a warning. The dramatic and seminal Part Two of Thomas Paine's *Rights of Man* had come out in February and the first, unprecedented popular political societies began to register on official awareness. On 21 May came the first royal proclamation against seditious literature and the earliest stirrings of a witch-hunt.

By July, William Jones was seriously alarmed. The Spaniards had captured 'General' Bowles on his return to Creek country. This was bad enough, but conditions in Wales were worse; in Montgomeryshire, machines were eating people and pauperism was sprouting. Voltaire was right: soon there'd be nothing left but tyrants and slaves. On the other hand, news of the Madoc Indians was spreading through Wales. An immediate, planned emigration was essential. Already, William Jones told William Owen, a young man from his district was looking for a Philadelphia ship in Liverpool; he meant to get to the USA, rally friends and put a petition to Congress. This was almost certainly Ezekiel Hughes, a young man of energy and initiative from the old Independent community of Llanbrynmair who in the next year was to undertake just such a mission as Iolo and William Jones prescribed.[5]

What had really frightened the Voltairean, however, were rumours he'd picked up that Iolo was pulling out of the Madoc project and that the mission was on the point of collapse. From May onwards, certainly, Iolo slumped into an agonising personal crisis and a surrender to the enervation which episodically conquered him. During that summer he was up to his eyes in the Jacobinism and millenarianism which bubbled up in London as the news from France got more and more dramatic; in the autumn of 1792, there was a sudden spurt of growth among the new artisan clubs in the teeth of a reaction which was itself becoming alarmist to the point of hysteria; Iolo was busy helping William Owen with his dictionary and on his own exposition of Druidism. His letters to his wife Peggy, however, were a catalogue of disaster: he had been ill with inflammation of the liver, followed by a quinsy and a bilious fever. For a fortnight he had been unable to speak. He went for weeks without a proper meal and was living on laudanum; by mid-summer he became convinced that all his children had died and his letters were hysterical with wild talk of Chatterton's suicide.[6]

The suspension of the Madoc subscription no doubt discouraged him; 46 years old, he had a wife and three children. As much as any personal difficulty, however, it was the abrupt change in the political climate which was decisive. Morgan John Rhys found himself driven in a new direction. The French Bible project lost impetus. Morgan John was busy all over Wales, forming societies. At the end of June, he was at the massive *gymanfa* at Nefyn in the uneasy Llŷn peninsula. But there was so much to do: the struggle against slavery, Sunday schools.

Taking precedence over all other commitments, however, was the increasingly desperate necessity to resist the drift to war and reaction. More and more men thought of the Apocalypse, listened to Prophets, tried to read the Signs of the Times. Morgan John made contact with the Londoners, read Iolo on the Druids. Throughout Wales there are signs that an embryonic intelligentsia was shuffling into shape. The looming threat of reaction demonstrated that scholarship and faith were not enough. The French, defending Humanity against the Beast, had a word for it – *propagande*. Truth against the World. What the Welsh needed was the Word. Morgan John, Will Owen, Iolo and their friends began to talk of journals and printing presses.

Young John Evans of Waunfawr, however, no one and nothing could divert.[7] A man of bold rhetorical temper and high-minded boasting, who tended to refer to himself in the third person, he was evidently seized with a sense of mission. 'Is there one thing in the possession of Ieuan ab Ivan that he would not sacrifice in the cause of the Madogion?' he wrote to Iolo, 'No, not one: even my precious life would I lay down for their sake!'[8] He moved abruptly out of Waunfawr, to the shock of his family, and into London. There he found a place, in a stint of harsh poverty and deprivation, among a troop of young Welsh bucks, chafing in their articles and their apprenticeships, full of America and its 'Brave Citizens' and *Jacobins* to a man. He shared their threadbare days and nights loud with talk. Full of dreams, a bunch of them crossed the Atlantic after him in 1793, hoping to buy land from Dr Samuel Jones. As soon as Evans had done his duty, one of them wrote to the good doctor, 'thousands would emigrate to join their Old Brethren in your climes' — a sentiment echoed by every single Welshman who wrote to Dr Jones in those years of iron.[9]

John Evans found himself at a loss. William Owen seemed obsessed with other matters. The suspension of the Madoc subscription proved futile; government was in no mood to listen to *Jacobins*. Iolo told a friend in Philadelphia that the British government knew nothing of the mission; the Welsh were talking of an approach to the American minister.[10] John Evans lost patience. Ever ready to launch himself into implausible enterprises with a near-lunatic insouciance, he abandoned Iolo, despite their close friendship. When Thomas Charles, leader of his denomination, reached London at the end of July, John got a letter from him to a Welsh minister in Baltimore. Iolo wrote him a note for a bookseller in Philadelphia on 15 August. Five days earlier, the crisis had reached its paroxysm in France with the popular assault on the Tuileries. In the days of blood and exaltation in Paris, through the streets of a London rocking to the news, John Evans beat the bounds of his friends, borrowed £20 from another hungry young man, booked immediate and hideous passage in the steerage and slipped out of England like a thief in the night. On 10 October, after a ghastly crossing, he was in Baltimore.

Behind him, Britain plunged into its first convulsive crisis of the revolutionary years.[11] For on 10 August 1792, the French monarchy went down before plebeian democrats in Paris and the *féderés* led by those Marseillais who had manhandled their guns across France, singing their marching song. A new nation of Citizens summoned its manhood-suffrage Convention, massacred its prisoners, and to the trumpet of Danton's speeches, stopped the 'uniformed butchers' of the old regime in their tracks at the 'miracle' of Valmy, threw them back at Jemappes and sent its armies into the Low Countries, calling on the cottages to rise against the palaces. A new political man confronted a startled Europe, in the *sans-culottes*, democrat, militant and terrorist. The new political man of the Anglo-American world, Thomas Paine, hooted by the Dover crowd, crossed the Channel to take his seat in the French Convention.

In England, as a new wave of refugees came washing ashore, thousands of respectable sympathisers with France recoiled in horror even as thousands more flocked into their unprecedented clubs, 'tradesmen, shopkeepers, and mechanics', their mouths full of the transatlantic insolence of Thomas Paine, calling each other Citizens, organising for democracy. In response, a gale of 'loyalism' blew across the land. John Reeves, a cynical and authoritarian lawyer, organised loyalist associations with covert government support, the inquisitorial Freeling in the postal service, Evan Nepean in the Home Office. In city, town, corporation and parish, loyalist associations mobilised the conservative, the patriotic, the sycophantic, the prejudiced, the repentant and the maliciously lunatic. Addresses denouncing *Jacobins* poured in. In some places there were house-to-house canvasses of 'loyalty'; in some, a heresy hunt. Paine-burnings lit the sky, for it was in 1792 that they hanged and burned 'poor Tommy' (in Cardiff, the corporation paid for the *auto-da-fé*). Hannah More produced her Will Chip series of right-thinking pamphlets for the plebs, much admired by the middle class and promptly translated into Welsh. Loyalists sent in furious scrawls denouncing Dissent in terms which would have gladdened the shade of Charles I. 'Did not their sires of old murder their king?' William Wilberforce marched his men to the guns and an avalanche of denunciation thundered into the Home Office. Arrests, prosecutions, persecutions multiplied. In November, in another 'alarm', the government mobilised the militia and summoned Parliament. And after the execution of Louis XVI, with French armies menacing the Scheldt and French principles menacing the glorious constitution, Britain went to war with the revolution.

The gale blew across Wales and its London intellectuals. Dr John Williams, in a fright, called for the *Gorsedd* of Bards planned for Primrose Hill to be postponed, government would surely suppress it as Jacobinical.[12] 'For God's sake have nothing to say to them,' wrote Peggy to Iolo Morganwg, as all the malice of Glamorgan spat at her husband's head,

> nothing never grieved me so much as to discover that you have wrote an ode in favour of Pain's opinion more warm than wise, forever all ways running from one extreme to the other ... what will become of you afterwards friendless or supported by such as is likely to be the cause of drenching theyr cuntery with blood.[13]

Too late. The Bard of Liberty, whose natural religion of a Welsh Druidism had just been published in William Owen's *Heroic Elegies of Llywarch Hen*, to win praise in France, went headlong into conflict with enemies, rivals, friends and patrons in showers of mutual abuse. Walter Davies, *Gwallter Mechain*, was mandarin in his All Souls conservatism; he was to charge even the genial William Owen with *Jacobin* notions in his

Cambrian Register of later years. David Thomas slammed his door in the face of Jac Glan-y-Gors, the Welsh Paine.

If friends and allies were divided, what could be expected from the serried ranks of the 'loyal'? Methodists, hordes of whom, according to one distraught curate in Anglesey (whose remarks Nepean promptly reported to the King) had been overrunning north Wales and 'descanting on the rights of man', shuddered into loud conformity. The ballad-mongers indulged their taste for timpany jingoism. Even the representatives of the Three Denominations of the Old Dissent in west Wales, under the chairmanship of that William Williams who had been so strong on French Bibles, were quick to proclaim their faith in the ancient constitution (though government was loath to believe them and had good reason not to). In many localities life was made unpleasant for dissenters and the unorthodox of every stripe.[14]

But the storm passed. By the early summer of 1793, as the troubles of war began to bite, the popular movement came clambering into the light again. The war in particular affronted many, within and without the ranks of Dissent. And some had never faltered even at the height of the loyalist spasm. Morgan John Rhys came out of his corner fighting. Appalled by what had happened, he was seized by the urgent necessity to awaken his benighted countrymen with the Word. He moved relentlessly on the printing press at the little Methodist community at Trefecca, in Breconshire. Its 'father', the quietist old tailor Evan Moses, was terrified. This man would be a curse on the Godly; his rage against government was hair-raising. But many at Trefecca liked Morgan John. A company was organised to launch a journal. In the cause of Wales, Rhys was able to rally William Owen and his friends, Iolo, even some of those most disgusted at Jacobinism, and a scatter of earnest, dedicated men in the parishes. A loosely united Welsh intelligentsia formed around the press. And in February 1793, the very month when Britain went to war with France, even as Daniel Isaac Eaton started a new English tradition with his *Hog's Wash; politics for the people*, Morgan John Rhys published the first number of the *Cylchgrawn Cymraeg* (*Welsh Journal*) the first political periodical in the Welsh language.[15]

Until the third number appeared in August, the politics of the journal were indirect, allusive, rather than overt — though sufficiently audible to provoke charges of 'subversion' at once. For as his motto, Morgan John took the slogan of Iolo's Bards — 'Y Gwir yn erbyn y Byd': 'Truth against the World'. In the first number, he announced that all profits would go 'to open a door' to the Old Welsh in America, the Madogwys. In the second he published his exhortation from Madoc to the Welsh:

'Dyma ni yn awr ar daith ein gobaith . . . Here we are now on the Journey of our Hope' — to that land which the springtime of creation had made gentle. For the aim of the journal was to *purify*.

It was to purify the language. Rhys tried to use William Owen's new and 'authentic' orthography, but could get neither letters nor support. He advertised Owen's dictionary, with its 100,000 words, many of them 'rediscovered'. He printed the Welsh literary classics, ran essays on how to read correctly, how to run Welsh language schools. It was to purify religion. There were essays on divinity, establishment, persecution and degeneration — which provoked violent responses, for Calvin was clearly under threat. It was to purify thought and action. The pivot of the journal's ideology was science married to a correct reading of the Signs of the Times. Rhys promised full exposition of Isaac Newton on Prophecy, the Revelation of Daniel, the prophecies of John. The eisteddfod was propagated; there was plenty of verse, quizzes on theology and science, 'calculations', titbits of useful knowledge — an essay on the orang-utang. The shadow of that future which was falling across the Welsh no less than their cousins across the Irish sea darkened the article on the cultivation of the potato, the poor's bread. The journal certainly lived up to its promise to display 'various things never seen by the monoglot Welsh before'.

It began in fine style, with a dozen named distributors in London, Bristol and key centres in north, mid- and south Wales. From the beginning it evoked response, but from the beginning it ran into distribution problems. From the beginning, opinion polarised. The storm did not break over its head until August. In the second number published, over Evan Moses's muttered protests, from Trefecca in May, the radical thrust was stronger. It splashed Bishop Watson's reformist charge to his clergy, quoted Benjamin Franklin, detected Natural Reason among the inhabitants of Greenland. In this number, however, the missionary impulse was strong. There were powerful articles on the emancipation of the blacks, the conversion of Hindus and the assembly of Indian chiefs at Nazareth, Pennsylvania. More striking, this was the issue which printed a letter from John Evans in Baltimore to his brother.[16] The literate Welsh, struggling for Enlightenment, labouring to raise up their despised and neglected people, at last learned that one of their number, at that moment, was on his way to their Lost Brothers.

Within a week of his arrival in Baltimore, John Evans had walked through Philadelphia to Lower Dublin and then to the Welsh Tract and the Welsh churches in the Great Valley.[17] He moved from Baptist to Baptist; Dr William Rogers offered him house-room in Philadelphia. 'My conscience tells me I must be a Baptist,' he wrote to Dr Samuel Jones in November 1792. His mission soon began to crumble in the face of transatlantic reality. Samuel Jones urged him to stay put for a while and learn surveying; a chorus of voices in Baltimore and Philadelphia warned him off; one adviser told him to go back to Britain and return as a trader. In the end, two merchant patrons found him a job as a clerk in a counting-house, offered him facilities to trade on his own account and arranged for him to learn surveying.

At that point, his mind was fixed on Kentucky, promised land for so many, and he was hoping for official American support. In November, there was a sudden rush of Canada to his head. He told Iolo Morganwg that he meant to make his way to the far British post of Detroit which was clandestinely supporting the Ohio Indians in their war against the oncoming Americans. He would not fail to let Iolo know 'that I am still without *losing my hair*'. The Madogion or Death! he added, in a variant on the official oath of the French Republic. When he wrote to his brother on Boxing Day, however, he was back on the Ohio—St Louis track. But by the time his first letters were coming into London and Waunfawr and Flemingston, he had lost patience again. David Jones, minister of Great Valley Baptist and a celebrated frontiersman himself, tried to dissuade him; back home William Jones Llangadfan was agonising over possible Spanish treachery at New Madrid. Once more, nothing and no one could stop John Evans. As soon as the first shoots of spring were out, he was off, to a chorus of despair from his friends. His last stop was Dr Samuel Jones's house; the doctor was appalled at the thought of his setting forth alone ... the distance ... the wilderness ... the Indians ... the Spaniards ... 'God is my shield and my recompense in a just cause,' replied John. Shortly after St David's Day 1793, the young man from Waunfawr started to walk towards the wilderness. In his pocket he had one dollar and seventy-five cents.

On this first incredible venture, he went to Pittsburgh, waited for a month for 'the high waters' and was carried to Limestone, the Ohio station in Kentucky. He struck inland through Kentucky at this, one of the critical moments in its history, with settlers flooding in and Indians out of Spanish territory harassing the villages and the Wilderness Trail. He moved through the wilderness from Bourbon to Cincinatti. At that frontier outpost of the Indian war which was raging, Evans was taken up by an engaging Irish scoundrel, Brigadier-General Wilkinson. Wilkinson was deep in a conspiracy with the Spaniards, offering to take Kentucky, sour at neglect of its interests on the Mississippi by an American government apparently more concerned to effect a trade opening into the

Spanish colonies, into secession and annexation to Spain. John Evans found the old charmer friendly and helpful. He may have given the Welshman some useful advice, for when he left after a few days he headed not for St Louis but for New Madrid, a good deal further south.

New Madrid was the only successful immigrant centre in Spanish Louisiana. It had been founded in 1789, with Spanish permission, by Colonel George Morgan and was full of Americans. John came down the Ohio and out into the great Mississippi, scudding south to the settlement, where after taking an oath of allegiance to Spain, he was permitted to land (the ferry was run by a man called Jones). At last he set foot on the sparse and savage territory he and Iolo and the others had brooded so long over back home.

Even on this remote frontier, the Chosen Race were present: 'Here I was kindly received by Mr. and Mrs. Rees my countrypeople.' This was Azor Rees, a slaveholder in New Madrid and a prominent local figure, granted a lieutenant's commission in the second company of the militia about the time of John's arrival, given to 'Don Azor Rees for his courage, zeal and good conduct'. Azor's wife was a celebrated frontier character, Dinah Martin, born of a Welsh mother and a German father in Pennsylvania and renowned as a woman of rare culture and learning. It was lucky for John Evans that she was there, for ten days after his arrival he went down with fever and was laid out for two months. Dinah Rees nursed him back to health.

But by early July, the Madoc fever was on him again: 'My resolution and anxiety for proceeding on my voyage being hightened to such a pitch that I was determined to start for the Illinois with one man only'. In his report, John Evans does not give his companion's name nor give any hint of the sheer lunatic bravado of this sortie. For the whole district was gripped by fear of an Indian war. The Osage Indians to the west of St Louis, the Imperial Osages, had cut loose on their raids again, those raids which ranged right up to the steps of government house in St Louis. In March hostile Indians had tried to massacre Osage chiefs in St Louis itself and the Lieutenant Governor Trudeau had to protect them in person for ten days on end, smuggling the Osages out when their enemies were dead drunk. Baron Carondelet, the belligerent Governor down in New Orleans, had ordered the Osages destroyed and Louis Lorimier, a French trader and part-time spy who had set up an outpost at Cap Girardeau, half-way between New Madrid and St Louis, where he tried to settle Indians fleeing across the Mississippi from the Americans, was instructed to deploy his Lobos and Shawnees against the Osages. News of the decision for war had leaked out and there was a general and deadly fear of retaliatory massacre.

It was through this appalling menace that John Evans and his companion set out, cutting north behind Cap Girardeau, ironically enough in the very place where, ten years later, the first Baptist church was to rise west of the Mississippi. Their expedition was a disaster. By the evening of the first day, they lost the trail, such as it was: 'Now lost in the infinite wilderness of America. Oh unsufferable Thirst and hunger is an amusement in comparison to this . . . The parent sun . . . has turned my Enemy and threatens to beak my brains like a cake and withdraw from me my Pressuous Eye Sight.' On his third blundering day, John Evans's fever returned. They came through floods: 'Travelled several miles in water from the hip to the Arm Pitt amongst a numerous crowd of the bigest water reptiles I ever saw.' On the seventh day they got within sight of a Spanish post, but John Evans, unable to go a hundred yards without rest, flaked out five miles short of it. It took him nearly the whole of the following day to get to the village, 'bear foot, bear legged and bear headed'. After resting for a day, he gave up and tottered across the Mississippi to Kaskaskia, the American outpost opposite.

The luck of the Welsh stayed with him. In Kaskaskia there was a John Rice Jones, Esq. John Jones, born in Merioneth, had emigrated in 1776 itself. He had fought with George Rogers Clark, the frontier hero, and had settled in Vincennes before moving to Kaskaskia. He was a well known frontier lawyer and an agent of the great Canadian fur-trading firm of Todd and McGill. With this man, John Evans spent the days of his recuperation. For eighteen months, he vanishes from sight. When he comes back into the light of evidence, he emerges as a close friend of William Arundel, a frontier merchant of Cahokia nearby. A letter which Arundel wrote to John in August 1795 — 'My level and your Square must strike the Necessary Balance and Best Rules in the World be the Guide amongst friends' — strongly suggests not only friendship but fraternity in Freemasonry. Arundel was also a favoured client of Todd and McGill, who at that point were locked in secret negotiations with Jacques Clamorgan, moving spirit of the Spanish Missouri Company, over the latter's plans for ambitious expeditions up the river in search of the Mandans and the Pacific. It is probable that John Evans was found a job by Arundel and John Rice Jones and spent those eighteen months as a servant of the Todd fur trade empire.

They were tense months. The rivalries of Europe and America intersected at that frontier. In a USA torn by sectional disaffection and fierce struggle between pro-English Federalists and pro-French Republicans, George Rogers Clark had been appointed a French general by the Girondin envoy of the new republic and was trying to mobilise an army to attack Louisiana, even as a federal army under Anthony Wayne was massing for a campaign against the Ohio Indians and their occult British backers. Further south, Lorimier at Cap Girardeau was directing his Indians against Kentucky even as speculators and private empire-builders in Tennessee and along the southern borders were throwing their own Indians against the Spaniards'. To the north, British traders, in control of the terrible Sioux, were encroaching hand over fist on Spanish land and Spanish fur and to the far west, the Canadians were still pressing hard on those Mandans who were Clamorgan's objective. On this remote frontier, the missionary to the Madogwys was trapped in the multiple tensions of the Atlantic crisis precipitated by the French Revolution.

For many of his fellow-countrymen back home in Wales, those tensions were now becoming unbearable. The third number of the *Cylchgrawn* came out in August 1793. The strain at Trefecca had proved too much; to the infinite relief of Evan Moses, Morgan Rhys had to finish it on a press in Machynlleth. Titus Evans, the printer, was promptly dismissed from his job in the excise as a consequence and the journal had to migrate again, to Carmarthen.[18] For in that August number, the *Cylchgrawn* lurched decisively into an overt and combative radicalism.

The pages bristled with controversy — over an established Church, over William Owen's orthography, over the generally 'subversive' tone of the publication. Rhys had to rebut charges that he was hell-bent on demolishing the immortal John Calvin, spiritual father of Welsh Dissent. It is 'the persecuting spirit' which is the enemy, answered Morgan John (in the second number he had printed an account of the burning of Servetus) and he denounced sectarianism in every shape and form. Many readers, however, were weary of theological dispute and demanded hard news and comment. Rhys promised them a monthly digest at threepence and promptly printed the first news column to appear in the journal.

Its tone was unmistakable. The first item reported massive American grain shipments to heroic France, testimony to both the humanity and the success of the great republic. The next talked of the persecution of Paine's *Rights of Man* and alleged that the war was costing £1,500 an hour. The execution of Louis XVI and the assassination of Marat were reported in similar terms. Violence and cruelty were abhorrent, but Louis could hardly be called a martyr and Marat quite possibly had wished well to his country. With all Europe gathering to crush her and with civil war raging within, France was resisting heroically. If she could but win time enough to reunite, no despotic alliance could stop the sun from rising.

Vibrant sympathy with the French republic throbbed from every line and the violence was explained, indeed explained away, in global terms, in a very long and remarkable extract from Bicheno's *Signs of the Times*, a highly influential millenarian tract which explained the convulsion in terms of The Beast, the overthrow of Anti-Christ and the Last Days. Morgan John Rhys was careful not to commit himself to every detail of Bicheno's creed, but he cited John Knox's curse on the French monarchy and argued that the turmoil was part of God's purpose. By November, he was asserting that the cruelty (Marie Antoinette's execution had been reported) was God's instrument for uprooting the blight of Papism from the world. Priests and Jews were converting in droves. It was not the duty of Britons to denounce and curse the French but to eradicate their own ignorance and renounce their sins, lest the judgement of God fall on them, too. They must learn to read the Signs of the Times.

What is very striking, however, in this number, is that this message was linked *directly* to a eulogy of the American republic. It printed a long and favourable history of religion in the USA, quoted fulsome extracts from Gilbert Imley's euphoric essay on Kentucky and – more immediately to the point – published Samuel Jones's May letter to John Evans's brother, which called on the Welsh to come over in their thousands and reported that the man from Waunfawr had set off for the Madogwys.

There is evidence that this August *Cylchgrawn* had a direct effect on the migration movement. For about the same time, Dr Enoch Edwards, the courier of the great American merchant and landowner Robert Morris, financier of the revolution, came to Wales on his European mission and he preached a New Cambria on Morris's lands.[19] The first economic dislocations of war had succeeded the poor harvest of 1792. Already, there had been the first riots against the cost of living around Swansea. The *Cylchgrawn* talked of an amusing poem it had received about the mass flight of the men of Merthyr to the hills on the approach of the press gang.[20] It was in mid- and north Wales that the strain registered first and most sharply. 'There is a humming in some parts already,' wrote William Jones in the July, reporting that the Egyptian taskmasters in Merioneth were demanding more bricks. It may well have been at his prompting that the *Cylchgrawn* printed Imley's *Kentucky*, for he added, 'they are like bees in winter, afraid of the weather.' This was a very proper time therefore to 'publish a description of the *land of promise*'.[21] By September, George Lewis in Caernarvon was telling Samuel Jones of plans to transfer the Independents of north Wales *en masse* to the Ohio and Kentucky. And there was a political bite to the enterprise. Timothy Thomas, son of Joshua the Baptist historian, called his brother, who was about to emigrate, 'a downright Sans-culotte Republican' and the phrase had become commonplace.[22] William Jones was almost certainly correct when he reported the following year that a serious emigration movement was starting in 1793, with a particular focus in Bala and Merioneth. It was stopped, he said, by the unofficial sea war between Britain and America, the wholesale seizure of American ships and the pressing of male passengers into the British navy, and by that outbreak of Algerian piracy against United States vessels which was to send the newly formed US Marines to the shores of Tripoli.[23]

During this year, the first individuals and small groups made their way to the ports and it was about this time that Llanbrynmair, in William Jones's country, generated the first organised movement for a *Gwladfa*. The leader was Ezekiel Hughes, then 26 years old. Characteristically, he came from one of the most rooted families of the district. Nor was he a 'peasant'. His family had once held three farms, though their base now was the big traditional *tyddyn* at Cwmcarnedd Uchaf on the Wynnstay estate. Ezekiel had been sent to school at Shrewsbury to learn English and was apprenticed to a clockmaker and jeweller at Machynlleth. With his father's hearty agreement and the support of his cousins the Bebbs, and friends like the Roberts family, themselves no less typical of the straitened but still substantial ranks of Old Dissent in this, one of the first strongholds of Nonconformity, Hughes assumed the leadership of an organised group around Llanbrynmair, with its mixed rural-industrial population, already seething with disaffection. He took a group of a dozen or so to Liverpool to find an American ship. Their objective was Kentucky. And it was evidently a communal movement. They were prepared to lay out £2,000-3,000 and Ezekiel was to return to fetch the rest of the people once the vanguard had established itself. They got nowhere. They were taken off the ship in Liverpool under the law forbidding the emigration of skilled craftsmen, the 'seduction of artists'. 'There is your boasted British liberty!' shouted the American captain as they were frog-marched ashore, the American consul having played a pusillanimous role. William Jones was beside himself. He had failed to get any response out of the American minister Pinckney; he and Ezekiel were now writing direct to America. He knew that Iolo Morganwg had seen Pinckney in Oxford but he'd had no response either. And what was Iolo doing wasting his time on Tom Paine politics? Edward Jones had told him that Iolo didn't dare show his face in London because of his Jacobinism.[24]

By the spring of 1794, indeed, Jacobinism had become more risky than ever. As the radical movement revived, authority went into action against it. The Scottish judiciary launched its merciless attack on the first attempt to hold a *Convention* (dread word!); in August and September, Muir and Palmer were given their savage sentences after appalling trials. Government refused to disown the Scottish judges. Barracks were rising on every hand. The scare about Hessian mercenaries (with their echoes of the American war) grew into a real fear over the winter. The days of English liberty seemed numbered as *Jacobins* waited for a suspension of Habeas Corpus and mass repression. The popular societies, in defiance, organised a new campaign for a British Convention, the London Corresponding Society came out into the open, sent delegates north; the Society for Constitutional Information and even the aristocratic Friends of the People mobilised behind them. In stormy mass meetings in the north and in London, something like a national campaign got under way, even as the French won through to military success. In Paris that spring, streets and prints were loud with 'the British Convention and its 90,000 men'; on stage, Fox was portrayed as the leader of a British revolution. Church and King loyalism once more came growling into action and the witch-hunt against *Jacobins* got under way again in many regions. In April 1794, a mass meeting in London threatened civil disobedience and 'the dissolution of the social compact' if English liberties were annulled. At that very moment, William Jackson, passing himself off as an American, moved through Britain on a secret mission to the United Irishmen, carrying even more secret letters to the 'friends of liberty' from the British *émigré* colony in Paris. On 24 April he was arrested. In rapid sequence man after man was hauled before an obsessed Privy Council. Finally, on 12 May, confused police raids went out against twelve leaders of the LCS and the SCI. Pitt got a Committee of Secrecy from the Commons and convinced it that 'a traitorous conspiracy' was on foot. On 17 May, Habeas Corpus was suspended. There were arrests, pursuits, witch-hunts all over the country. Not a society or a group escaped. There were rumours of 800 warrants. Fox professed himself in fear of the Tower. There was a minor stampede for the America boats and in October, amid crowd actions and riots against *Jacobins*, Thomas Hardy, John Thelwall, Horne Tooke and their friends were formally charged with High Treason.[25]

All the whores and thieves of London are assembled about the fellow called *Reeves* and his *fiddlers* and *faddlers* in a mighty band, *bawling* and *squawling* like the Songs of Caterwauling, *God-save-the-king* — *Church and King for ever!* They press every one that passes by into this infernal service, crying to him — *Blast your eyes!* Cry *Church and King! Church and King, damn your soul!* I jabber'd Welsh, squeaked out *Church SANS King*, in as broken a manner as I could, and passed for a *Dutchman.*

Iolo Morganwg in the summer of 1794 had good cause to blast the eyes of 'Reeves, Jones the Harper . . . and those very loyal Sons of Bitches'. His papers were seized and he was one of the many summoned before the Privy Council:

They confessed I was too *prudent* for them. They are satisfied they say that I have seditious papers somewhere. I told them I should be obliged to them for finding them out. I will put you, said one, in Custody of the Messengers. Do so, said I, and after you have done so, ask the laws of England for what.

He accused Edward Jones of denouncing him to the Council, with the aid of 'the Billingsgate Bitch', Mrs Nicholl, out of jealousy of his Druidic history of the Bards. When the first attempt failed, his enemies contrived a second raid, but by that time, Iolo had packed off his material to Bath, Bristol and Flemingston. The *Gorsedd*, however, now ranked as a seditious society in the eyes of government and half the patrons of Iolo and many of his Gwyneddigion friends turned icy. The 'Billingsgate Bitch' wrote:

Had Mrs. Nicholl *then* known Edward Williams's principles, she would not have subscribed to any of his writings, for she would not purchase poetry fine as Homer's, were it written by a Republican, and her inducements to put her name to his verses were the accounts she had *formerly* heard of Edward Williams's morality and general good character, not his merit as a poet, which (even before she perused these last specimens) she knew to be very small. She admits no Jacobins under her roof.

The impact of repression in 1794 was harsh; it banished reformers, and the popular movement in particular, into a half-world of semi-legality. But it was in no sense decisive. On the contrary, Jacobinism grew in strength throughout the terrible year of 1795. By the May of that year, Iolo had bounced back again, to address his 'writ' to that William Owen who had originally been disconcerted by the bloody advent of democracy in France:

> Be it known unto all men by these presents that, on Wednesday the 20th day of May, *one thousand seven hundred and eight o'clock* and exactly at five o'clock in the evening, *Citizens* and *Sans-Culottes George Dyer* and *Iolo Morganwg*, being instigated thereto by the Devil, intend to set out from Chancery Lane thence to proceed to Pratt Place, Camden Town and there, with force of arms, to enter the house of Gwilym Owain, *Bardd wrth fraint a defod Beirdd Ynys Prydain*, otherwise known by the *Bardic* names of *Gwilym Fardd Glas*, *Gwilym Meirion* and y *Bardd Glas o Feirion*, then and there to drink tea and to eat bread and butter till they
>   'can eat and drink no more-o!'
> and after that, to talk of *Politics, republicanism, Jacobinism, Carmagnolism, Sans-culottism* and a number of other wicked and trayterous *isms* against the peace of the Lords *Kingism* and *Parsonism*, their crowns and dignities.[26]

In Wales, manners had to be less metropolitan. The power of local establishments, which could be terrifying, was turned massively against dissent in the sparse and bitter parishes. Only in places where the social order, or some liberal gentleman out of step, could offer protection — the ironworks settlements of Merthyr Tydfil, where the *Jacobin Cambridge Intelligencer* circulated, where the local Presbyterian farmers and shopkeepers were 'sturdy old Republicans', where the Cyfarthfa Philosophical Society was later to offer a refuge, or that tight little Llys-wen in Breconshire, where an eccentric local bigwig protected John Thelwall in his 'exile', or the close and occult clan networks of alienated Llanbrynmair or southern Merioneth — could a man of questioning temper open his mouth with impunity. William Jones Llangadfan had his letters opened, was officially warned by magistrates and threatened by more shadowy figures. Men were sacked, discriminated against, leaned on. Often a hint was enough. Methodists, particularly perhaps those who *might* once have 'descanted on the rights of man', rallied convulsively around their quietist and often High Tory leaders; the official spokesmen even of Dissent recollected the virtues of a *measured* Whiggism. Friendships were broken, doors slammed in faces. Welsh response to the repression and the *alarm* rehearsed the experience of the earlier loyalist explosion of 1792-3: massive hostility to anything which could be labelled *Jacobin* by many, a fastidious shrinking by the fainter friends of liberty; on the other hand, a toughening of spirit among the committed — y gwir *yn erbyn* y byd — and more striking, louder and louder echoes from a hitherto non-political plebs, going through the mill of population pressure, social change and war — hungry for *room* and freedom.

The *Cylchgrawn* had in fact gone under before the repression was unleashed in May. Morgan John Rhys went down fighting. The fourth number, in November 1793, struck a resonant Welsh nationalist note. Were the Welsh forever condemned to be hewers of wood and drawers of water for other peoples? Why did they, alone among the peoples of this world, learn an alien language first and scorn their own? This in itself made them, historically, a nation of 'bunglers'. Morgan John demanded a national campaign to secure the £10,000 of Madam Bevan's charity for Welsh-language schools. He'd been printing primers for such schools for some time. In the November number, he was defiant. He published Edward Charles's satire on preaching styles (which provoked fury), printed a poetic attack on Dumouriez the traitor by a Merthyr minister and coined the Welsh word *gwladwriaethwyr* for 'republicans' (interestingly enough, the Welsh version of *Sunday Schools* had also to be explained in English!). Most striking of all, Morgan John published the celebrated fifteenth chapter, a Dialogue between the People and Privilege, of *The Ruins of Empires* by the French Deist Volney, which was to become a standard text of working-class movements over the next two generations. He said he had taken it from the Sheffield *Patriot*, but it was evidently a direct, personal translation.[27]

But by this time, the *Cylchgrawn* was butting its way through storms. In north Wales, even William Owen's name was mud because of his association with this 'sedition'. Rhys, in November, repeated that his journal was open to all opinions, but he refused to print 'slander'. He begged for support. Money was drying up; subscriptions were slow, problems of distribution, particularly in north Wales, were crippling. For many, however, the *Cylchgrawn* had become an addiction. They demanded that it be turned into a monthly. Rhys promised a bi-monthly. The fifth number, in fact, *did* cover January-February 1794. But it was the last.

It printed a millenarian commentary on the times and Ben Franklin on the Indians. It reported at length on the King's Speech and the replies by Sheridan and Stanhope. It supported the *patriots'* campaign for a Convention, eulogised the Martyrs of Botany Bay and denounced the window tax. But Rhys's editorial was a valedictory. He thanked the generality for their 'no help'; his November appeal for prompt payment had been ignored; he could not get the journal circulated quickly enough. He drew up a list — it was almost a liturgy — of the pieces he had failed to print: Isaac Newton's thoughts on prophecy, Daniel and John, Revelation. The printers had refused to publish a *cywydd* (ode) on the state of Britain, William Owen's defence of his orthography and Voltaire on war, 'because the Deist told too much of the truth about Christian illusions'.

Morgan John, at least in print, was not giving up. He said that if he could find a way to distribute speedily throughout north and south, he would bring out a *Welsh Remembrancer, Cofiadur Cymreig*: threepence fortnightly in the south, sixpence monthly in the north. And he added what was evidently a heart-felt warning — 'na fydd dim dadleuon crefyddol i gael lle ynddo' — there will be no place for religious controversy in it.' Its purpose would be to alert the monoglot Welsh to the Signs of the Times.[28]

This was whistling in the dark. As his letters to William Owen and others make clear, he had already decided to go to America.

This journey, however, was to be no scuttling for cover, no personal search for security. A young lad like Ezekiel Hughes was one thing. Morgan John Rhys, hammer of slavery, preacher of Sunday and Welsh schools, promoter of the John Canne Bible, missionary to the French, editor of Wales's first political journal in its own language, was something else again.

In April, he was back in his old place at Pontypool, probably to say goodbye. He wrote to William Owen to tell him he was leaving in midsummer for America, though he was not sure whether from London or Bristol. He was going back to Carmarthen that month to bring out his last publications. These included not only a gazetteer of the world and its religions, but the important *Y Drefn o Gynnal Crefydd yn Unol Daleithiau America*, an essay on the organisation of religion in the USA, which carried sketches of Kentucky and arguments in favour of emigration. A collection of hymns, also full of America, accompanied it.[29]

He then moved north and clearly with a purpose. The significant evidence comes, as usual, from William Jones Llangadfan, now in the last year of his battling life and shortly to be finally seen off by a clever, witty and repulsive obituary from Walter Davies, *Gwallter Mechain*, who was evidently at home in All Souls.[30] 'Emigration', wrote William Jones to William Owen on 7 May, 'is now become almost epidemical,' despite the threat of the law against artisan movement and the propaganda of press and landowners. Certainly, early in 1794, a tremor seems to have run through north Wales. Even the Methodists were affected. Robert Jones of Rhoslan had reported to his son in March that the mania to emigrate had hit some districts 'like a sudden thunderstorm'; the Monthly Meeting had to take account of it — if the skies were 'a little cloudy at the moment', this was the consequence of sin; it was folly to think that chastisement could be dodged in America.[31] In Anglesey, the Independents reported that leading figures were on the move. Joshua Thomas was telling Samuel Jones in June that a massive migration, akin to a folk-movement, was preparing. The famous chapel of Ramoth was about to lose a good proportion of its membership and a score or more were leaving Bala. North-eastern Wales was affected; Jenkin David was taking many of his congregation.[32]

Morgan Rhys quite evidently rode this tide. William Jones reported in May that an important conference on emigration had just been held in Bala.[33] He was appalled at the unorganised character of the movement. People were setting off at random, at great expense, in ignorance. It was essential that immigrant societies in the USA be contacted and some discipline drilled into the migrants. William Owen had suggested a joint-stock company. William Jones had prepared a plan

for incorporating the adventurers into a Company on pretence of Trade in order to avoid the obstacles which government may possibly throw in the way. The chief object we should have in view is to gain a separate settlement for our countrymen on some of the Western Waters in order to keep up a friendly correspondence with our cousins the Padoucas.

The lands which Enoch Edwards had proposed were 'out of the line to our relations the Madogwys' and exposed to Canadian attack in the event of war. The old Voltairean was well aware of the southward drift of people from the northern and middle states, favoured Kentucky and suggested that Pennsylvania would be a good base, perhaps Dr Samuel Jones's lands? 'People should unite like a trading company, have agents, trustees and other necessary managers to provide temporary settlements in a line from Philadelphia to the Ohio' and thence to the Madogwys. In a few years they ought to be able to raise a fund to bring the poor over from Wales, 'on an easy redemption, without exciting the jealousy of our government, because the laws of Pennsylvania allow strangers to make purchases and keep their allegiance.' William Jones showed himself no less well informed on the costs of transplantation within the

States and he announced the formation of a society, with graded subscriptions, to finance the project.

This plan, more elaborate and relatively well thought out than Iolo's first sketch for a *Gwladfa*, in fact foreshadowed Morgan John Rhys's activities in America. For, significantly enough, in the very next sentence, William Jones reported: 'Morgan John Rhys . . . was taking his leave with his friends in Llanbrynmair going to Columbia.' Rhys was in the big meetings in Anglesey and Bala in May and June; the next month he was at Ramoth and in Glyn Ceiriog and everywhere the talk was of America. Jenkin David, from the Wrexham area, who sailed with Rhys, told Samuel Jones, quite specifically, that Morgan John meant to explore America, particularly the north-west, Kentucky and the south and return to the old country. However loose-textured, some plan for a *national* movement was under way and Rhys was to be its pioneer. In America, Moses, The Cloud and the Promised Land were for ever on his lips.[34]

William Jones said that Rhys had meant to sail almost at once, but had missed the American ships because they were full (one can well believe it; to judge from Pennsylvania records, the first serious migration of *Jacobins* heading for safety and the Jeffersonian Republicans took place in this summer). He was then going to take any ship, even a British one, which became available.

Almost at once, the storm of repression broke. A story current in later years had Rhys and his friend Joshua Watkins staying in Carmarthen, when a stranger arrived with a warrant looking for him. Morgan John, assisted by friends, promptly fled to Liverpool. There was no question of 'flight' to America; his mind was already made up. But there is nothing implausible in the story. This sort of thing was happening all over the country in the summer of 1794. At all events, Morgan John Rhys, picking up Jenkin David and his people from north-east Wales and the Bala contingent, moved to Liverpool and sailed on the *Port Mary* on 1 August 1794. The journey was frightful; one of Jenkin David's children was among those who died on the ten-week crossing. It was 12 October before they reached New York.[35]

On arrival, they were greeted by Dr William Rogers, provost of Philadelphia College, and passed smoothly along the Baptist network. Jenkin David moved out into the Great Valley where he took the place of David Jones, off as chaplain to Anthony Wayne's army in the west.[36] Morgan John got himself a horse and rode the whole span of the Union, from Vermont to Georgia. From the first day, he kept a diary, a rough, on-the-spot daily journal which he later wrote up in the form of letters home.[37]

His mission clearly weighed on him heavily at first. His first letter gave a long list of the goods needed for the crossing. Within a matter of days, he had spotted a likely place for a settlement between New York and Philadelphia, but suspended judgement until he had seen more of the country. He visited Sparta on the Hudson, a liberty settlement launched by British *Jacobin émigrés*, but thought even less of its chances than he did of the Llŷn projects in upstate New York. His letters are full of precise detail — the 11,000 houses raised in New York that year, the number of churches, the quality of the soil. Marylanders looked sickly; the yeomanry of New York were too buckish. In the northern and central states, however, his diary is formal, self-consciously literary and rather unrevealing.

Occasionally, the individual breaks through. He began to spell his name Rhees. He was struck by the New York ladies, even though fine feathers hardly suited Republicans. They certainly had spirit. 'What! Great Britain conquer America!' cried one, during one of the endless discussions of the war crisis, 'No! we might take up that Little Island and plunge her into one of our Lakes!' The 'fair', in fact, rather pressed on him. 'This poor widower', he wrote of a Baptist brother in Wilmington, 'keeps a very smart young lass for his housekeeper and has nobody else to live with him. I would certainly pray if I did not mean to marry her. Let me not be led into temptation!'[38] It was a prayer he felt compelled to repeat at regular intervals, not least on the Boston coach —

Left Providence; I hope Providence will not leave me ... strange commotions in my mind this morning; an American fair, yes, one of the fairest I ever saw, sat at my side in the coach — meekness and modesty sat on her cheek; everything spoke here the virtuous maid, what heart would not be attracted to her? Full-dressed with caring, snow balls etc! But alas, she is the coachman's wife!

The Philadelphia ladies were far less dazzling — 'painting, plumes and feathers they leave to Indians and barbarians,' preferring to cultivate the mind and a family economy. 'The mind — the mind is the standard of the man, and why not of the woman?' It was as well he thought so. He was to marry one, of ironclad piety.

Food and drink occupied him a great deal, too. American taverns were much the same as English, though the service was less prompt — no man called anyone master in this country. Several times, he conducts an earnest but lively discussion of the virtues of American cider and beer as antidotes to the 'stinking God', whisky. Always an open-minded man, however, he seems to have achieved a more balanced view in the end, since his executor noted among his property in 1804 one barrel which held 250 gallons of the stuff and another of the same size which was empty.

The release of political inhibitions is tangible. He often roars like a *sans-culotte*. He took offence at Washington's attack on the Democratic Societies as 'self-created'. The President was, no doubt, too much affected by the excesses in France. There was, after all,

> a long arrear of Protestant blood to be avenged — so many ignoble despots and vagabond priests to be reduced to men, or else banished or destroyed. The divine thunder, which had long been reserved must be tremendous and the electrical shocks which purified the air of such vermin, rapid and severe.

But the process would be speedy. The men of Delaware, for example, had as much chance of stopping the Hessian fly as despots an army of *sans-culottes*: 'What are improperly called French Principles pervade the universe and universal emancipation must be the result.'

The first two months of his diary, however, are generally jejune. The pages read like an official handbook. All the major sights are duly noted, the expected comments made, but the writing is lifeless. October he spent in New York state. In November he was through New Jersey into Pennsylvania, moving easily from Baptist chapel to Baptist chapel. He visited Samuel Jones in Lower Dublin and listened to the debates in Congress. Philadelphia was properly commemorated as the Mecca of men of his mind. The open pulpit of so many American churches warmed him: 'in America there are no dissenters . . . Free Enquiry is the Fountain of Freedom,' though he was affronted by the exclusion of ministers from the legislature in so many states.

In December, he passed on through Wilmington, duly stopping to admire the ingenious conveyor-belt mills of Oliver Evans — good name, that! Old Pencader, however, was now drained of Cambro-Britons. At Baltimore, he found an old man who remembered the place when it was nothing but 'an Irishman and his hut'. Rhees found it beautiful. Marylanders in general, however, were lazy. Tobacco was draining them. Though he was bucked at the splendid sight of the citizen militia returning from the Whisky Rebellion. Republicans would batter down these feudal castles yet!

In Washington, the walls of the Capitol stood only a few feet above the ground, though the President's house was 280 feet by 275 and the

grand hotel would soon be done. Fortunately, the dingles of Georgetown with its 260 houses were agreeable and the inhabitants looked
cheerful. It is in Virginia, however, that the diary starts to come to life.
The reason is clear – 'This is a Land of Liberty full of slaves.' The
countryside was dazzling, the towns commodious, but slavery affronted
the eye. At Mount Vernon, he composed a prayer to Washington to free
his blacks. He was invited to address the House of Representatives in
Richmond. These Virginians, 'free, friendly and volatile', had done so
much to abolish feudalism and promote equality. Why could they not
take the final step and free the slaves?

Even here, however, there is something conventional about his
phrasing. The first real break comes on the Virginia-North Carolina
border, when half the congregation walked out on one of his sermons.
After this shock his eye becomes sharper, his pen more pointed. A whiff
of reality begins to come off the pages. For he was now approaching
that deep South where both slaves and democrats were plentiful. By the
time he crossed the Tar and New Rivers into Raleigh, North Carolina,
on the last day of 1794, he was spurring his horse.

And at that very moment, hundreds of miles to the west, the man
Morgan John and his fellow Welsh had lost sight of for nearly two years
also began to move. What eighteen months of waiting in Kaskaskia and
Cahokia had done to John Evans can only be guessed at. The speed of his
response when an opportunity presented itself speaks for itself.[39] About
Christmas 1794, he reported three years later, 'I was informed of a gent
at St. Louis who was engaged to go up the aforesaid River [the Missouri]
for three years.' John had evidently heard some rumour through the
Todd network of Clamorgan's plans for a great expedition up the
Missouri to the Mandans, to be supplied by the Todds and captained by
James McKay, an experienced frontiersman formerly with the Canadian
Norwesters. 'Now or never as I thought,' John Evans reported, 'it was
time to make aplication.' So, in the depth of winter, he crossed the icy
Mississippi into suspicious little St Louis.

He knew he had chosen a bad time. 'I thought within myself that it
was rather a ridiculous busyness as it was a Critical time on Spanish side
on account of the report of Clark's armie and I not able to speak one
word with any body, they speaking French. However I went.' and his
fears proved all too correct: 'and was taken for a Spy, Imprisoned,
loaded with iron and put in the Stoks besides, in the dead of winter.'

Notes

1. The only serious life of Morgan John Rhys to date is J.J. Evans, *Morgan John Rhys a'i Amserau* (University of Wales Press, Cardiff, 1935: a life and times). There is a memoir in J.T. Griffith, *Morgan John Rhys* (USA, 1899 and W.M. Evans, Carmarthen, 1910); my own studies, 'Morgan John Rhys and Volney's *Ruins of Empires*', *Bulletin of the Board of Celtic Studies*, vol. xx (1962), and 'Morgan John Rhees and his Beula', *Welsh History Review*, vol. iii (1967) are developed more fully here, using in particular a great deal of new evidence from the USA: the manuscript of his 1794-5 journal, photocopies of which were kindly supplied me by Mrs Mary Murray Brown of Mount Kisco, New York, a descendant of Rhys, and Brown University, Rhode Island; his correspondence with Dr Benjamin Rush in the Rush papers at the Historical Society of Pennsylvania, and the copious material in Cambria County Historical Society, Ebensburg, Pennsylvania, on the Beula settlement, where I was greatly assisted by Ms Edna Lehman, the curator.

2. I have covered this phase of the Madoc history in great detail in my *Madoc: the Making of a Myth* (Eyre Methuen, London, 1980) and give precise references in 'John Evans's mission to the Madogwys, 1792-99', *Bulletin of the Board of Celtic Studies*, vol. xxvii (1978), a development of the article by David Williams, 'John Evans's Strange Journey', *American Historical Review*, vol. liv (1949), and *Transactions of the Honourable Society of Cymmrodorion* (1948).

3. The final draft of Iolo's paper is in NLW 13104, fo. 28-62.

4. Iolo's Plan of Welsh Colony, among his notes in NLW 13104, fo. 255-6.

5. W. Jones–W. Owen, 15 July 1792 and n.d. (1794), NLW 13221, fo. 311-12, 301; Samuel Roberts' reprint, with comments, of the memoir of Ezekiel Hughes in the American *Cambrian* of 1882 is in NLW 491, fo. 20.

6. E. Williams–M. Williams, May-December 1792, NLW, Iolo Letters (henceforth Iolo) 807-14; see my *Artisans and Sans-culottes; Popular Movements in Britain and France during the French Revolution* (E. Arnold, London, 1968; reprinted 1973).

7. For a detailed account of John Evans's actions, my *Madoc: the Making of a Myth*, Chapters 7 and 8, and 'John Evans's mission to the Madogwys, 1792-99'.

8. J. Evans–E. Williams, 22 November 1792, NLW, Iolo 158; this is the original and reveals the identity of the recipient, concealed under the 'Dear Friend' of the English translation among William Owen's papers, NLW 13222, fo. 315-16.

9. J. Williams–S. Jones, 10 August 1793; Pennepek.

10. E. Williams–W. Pritchard, 15 August 1792; this letter, with others in John Evans's possession, passed to the Archives of the Indies in Seville: Archivo General de Indias, Papeles de Cuba, legajo 213: they are reprinted in A.P. Nasatir, 'John Evans, explorer and surveyor', *Missouri Historical Review*, vol. xxv (1931), with other material in Nasatir's superb edition of Spanish documents on the Missouri, *Before Lewis and Clark* (2 vols., St Louis Historical Documents Foundation, St Louis, 1952).

11. My *Artisans and Sans-culottes*, pp. 3-4, 58-74; E.P. Thompson, *The Making of the English Working Class* (Gollancz, London, 1963; revised edn, Penguin, Harmondsworth, 1968), Part 1.

12. J. Williams–W. Owen, 5 December 1792, NLW 13222, fo. 291.

13. M. Williams–E. Williams, 7 January 1793, NLW Iolo 604.

14. J.J. Evans, *Dylanwad y Chwyldro Ffrengig ar Lenyddiaeth Cymru* (Hugh Evans, Liverpool, 1928), pp. 112-34; my *Artisans and Sans-culottes*, pp. 74-6.

15. On the journal, see the publication itself *Cylchgrawn Cymraeg* (or *Cyn-Mraeg*

at first in Owen's orthography), 1793-4; M.J. Rhys–W. Owen, 9, 11 January, 6, 25 April, 26 October 1793, 2 April 1794 in NLW 13222, fo. 381, 375, 341, 361, NLW 13221, fo. 277-9; fo. 131-4; Evans, *Morgan John Rhys a'i Amserau*, pp. 26-9, 153-7.

16. J. Evans–E. Evans, 26 December 1792, in *Cylchgrawn Cymraeg*, vol. ii (May 1793), pp. 114-16.

17. For all that follows on J. Evans, my *Madoc: the Making of a Myth*, Chapter 8 and 'John Evans's mission to the Madogwys, 1792-99'.

18. Evans, *Morgan John Rhys a'i Amserau*, pp. 26-8.

19. E. Edwards, M. Jones, W. Richards–S. Jones, 1793-4: Pennepek; W. Jones–W. Owen, 7 May 1794, NLW 13221, fo. 302-5; Norman B. Wilkinson, 'Land Policy and Speculation in Pennsylvania 1779-1800' (unpublished PhD thesis, University of Pennsylvania, 1958).

20. *Cylchgrawn Cymraeg*, vol. iv (November 1793); D.J.V. Jones, *Before Rebecca: Popular Protest in Wales, 1793-1835* (Allen Lane, London, 1973), Chapters 1 and 2.

21. W. Jones–W. Owen, 1 July 1793, NLW 13224, fo. 109.

22. G. Lewis–S. Jones, 3 September 1793; T. Thomas–S. Jones, 22 September 1793: Pennepek.

23. W. Jones–W. Owen, 7 May 1794, NLW 13221, fo. 302-5.

24. W. Jones–W. Owen, n.d. (1794) NLW 13221, fo. 301.

25. *Artisans and Sans-culottes*, pp. 76-80.

26. For this Iolo correspondence, see E. Williams–H. Jones, 4 June 1794; Mrs W. Nicholl–E. Williams, 19 May 1794 in NLW Iolo 837, 297; E. Williams–W. Owen, 20 May 1795, NLW 13221, fo. 49.

27. I have argued this point, from Welsh and English translations of the French original, in 'Morgan John Rhys and Volney's *Ruins of Empires*', *Bulletin of the Board of Celtic Studies*, vol. xx (1962).

28. *Cylchgrawn Cymraeg*, vol. iv (November 1793) and vol. v (March 1794).

29. M.J. Rhys–W. Owen, 2 April 1794, NLW 13224, fo. 131-4 and Evans, *Morgan John Rhys a'i Amserau*, pp. 33-7.

30. *Cambrian Register 1796*, vol. ii (1799), pp. 237-51: William Jones died in August 1795, at a wretched moment in a wretched year. Walter Davies alleges that the Voltairean had a deathbed conversion to Christianity, but I don't believe him.

31. Quoted in Evans, *Morgan John Rhys a'i Amserau*, p. 38.

32. J. Thomas–S. Jones, June 1794; J. David–S. Jones, 8 November 1794: Pennepek, and the evidence cited in Evans, *Morgan John Rhys a'i Amserau*, pp. 37-40.

33. For this important letter, see W. Jones–W. Owen, 7 May-10 July 1794, NLW 13221, fo. 302-5 and the supplementary evidence in Walter Davies's obituary, *Cambrian Register 1796*, vol. ii (1799), pp. 247-50.

34. J. David–S. Jones, 8 November 1794: Pennepek and M.J. Rhys's journal, see below.

35. Evans, *Morgan John Rhys a'i Amserau*, pp. 33-5, 40; J. David–S. Jones, 8 November 1794: Pennepek; journal of M.J. Rhys.

36. Great Valley Baptist Church Pennsylvania: Monthly Meeting Register 1790-1823; J. David–S. Jones, 8 November 1794: Pennepek; see below, Chapters 4, 6, 7.

37. The Journal of Morgan John Rhys: Rhys kept a day-by-day rough record and then wrote it up formally, at first in the guise of letters home, later as a diary. From 12 October to 31 December 1794, only the letter-form survives. From 1 January 1795, both the rough daily notes and the formal record survive; from 16 April, the formal record ceases, except for an unfinished letter composed in Washington, Kentucky, on 30 April 1795. The journal ends on 30 October 1795.

J.T. Griffith in his memoir (I have used the Carmarthen 1910 edition) printed a version of the diary as a fifteenth chapter (pp. 118-229). He used only the formal record and censored that. For some unaccountable reason (perhaps the difficulty of the handwriting) Griffith broke off at 29 March at a most interesting moment and did not resume until 6 July.

I have used a photocopy supplied me by Mrs Mary Murray Brown and the remainder of this chapter is based on the journal, in letter form, from 12 October to 31 December 1794.

38. This comment, like others of similar character, was omitted by J.T. Griffith from his published version. Griffith was sent the Journal by Rhys's grandson, W.J. Rhees, secretary and archivist of the Smithsonian, who commented, 'You may not like some of his liberal sentiments, but they suit me very well. He was 100 years ahead of his time.' This, however, refers to religious sectarianism, not housekeepers. J.T. Griffith (see his memoir, p. 229) was evidently perfectly adapted to his (time, of course, not housekeeper!).

39. Remainder of the text taken from John Evans's original report on his return from the Missouri: J. Evans–S. Jones, 15 July 1797: Pennepek; I have printed this letter in 'John Evans's mission to the Madogwys, 1792-99'.

4 WESTWARD THE COURSE OF CAMBRIA

On New Year's Day 1795, while John Evans went slouching miserably into his cell in St Louis, Morgan John Rhees was proudly rising to address the House of Representatives of North Carolina.[1] The town of Raleigh he found promising, scarcely a hundred houses as yet and not a single mansion two years ago, but level, healthy and happily remote from the corruptions of commerce. In its spacious Capitol, he spoke on 'the heavenly themes of liberty and confraternity, annexing thereto the Signs of the Times', and summoning the legislators to the emancipation of the human race, 'the very Africans not excepted'. It went down well. Hats were raised and money thrown. It was vain to insist that he did not preach for lucre. The members thought ('with reason', Morgan John informed his diary before deleting the comment) that ministers could not travel without money.

He certainly needed it:

> A shoemaker charged me for putting a few stitches in my boot. This was worse than paying a shilling, Virginia money, *for a twopenny lash to my whip*, at Alexandria. O for a million of good British mechanicks in this country!

Rhees was evidently half-hypnotised by the South, by that uneasy coexistence of a slave society with the radical democratic movement he found so congenial. From Raleigh southwards, the shadow of Moses falls longer and longer across his journal. Let The Cloud move before! But so many missions now jostled each other in his mind. He developed an eye for country, a feeling for resource and potential. He was on the watch for Cambro-Britons, indeed cultivated a nose for them in the most unlikely places. He knew of the old Welsh settlements in the Carolinas and moved remorselessly on to the very rim of the southern frontier, punctuating his progress with peppery comments on tavern-keepers and brother Baptists. But he missed no opportunity to sing *Ça Ira* with the crews of French privateers in the ports and to drink toasts to the irresistible *sans-culottes*. Above all, it was slavery which took possession of his appalled spirit; the desperate need of the black brethren began to drive all other ideas out of his head. In Georgetown, he suffered the first of those personal crises which threatened to unhinge him from his original purpose.

He had threaded his way there along the now familiar network of meeting-houses and generally atrocious taverns. He moved towards the coast, into the pine barrens. Over Cape Fear River and its cheating land-ladies he went, through Fayetteville, named, he duly noted, after that unfortunate Lafayette who had begun so well, but 'split his Bark on the Rock of Royalty', into the Scotsmen around Lumberton who worked their plantations with their own hands and used no slaves. The preaching was strictly Trinitarian in Lumberton court-house and Morgan John preferred to lodge out of town, with a Baptist blacksmith who had cleared 40 of his 2,000 acres and lived off his own cloth, beef, pork, poultry, bread, butter, cider, wine and brandy. In thanks, he had raised a meeting house and Rhees preached there to the country people, many of whom, sick of swamps and marsh, were migrating to the backlands of Georgia. The Welshman found them feckless. In England, Pitt would have slapped the window tax on the gaping cracks in their ill-fitting log cabins!

He crossed the Little Peedee into South Carolina and ran into a sequence of Welshmen.[2] David Owen summoned the neighbours for miles around to hear Rhees preach in the woods. 'They were attentive, but Achan (I mean Slavery) must be removed out of the Camp before there is any prosperity in the country.' Administering as many 'Abolition Pills' as he thought could be easily digested, Rhees rode on by way of another descendant of the Ancient Britons, to cross the Great Peedee at Davies's Tavern, run by a Welshman and his French wife. Moving now through savannahs and under lofty pines, he was struck by the virtues of Indian corn and promptly despatched a sermon on the subject to Wales. Would that 20,000 acres of this woodland (nine or ten dollars was thought a good price for a thousand feet of board in America) could be exchanged for one rocky mountain in Wales! After an ideologically and gastronomically encouraging breakfast on Black River with Mrs White, a good old republican lady who'd been burned out by the British in the war and couldn't stand aristocrats, Rhees crossed into Georgetown on 8 January. Burned by the British and the Tories in their 'infamous cause', it then numbered about 150 houses and got most of its goods from Charleston (at a hundred per cent profit to its shopkeepers, according to Morgan John). An English Baptist recently arrived found the town congenial, however, and Rhees put up at the only tavern in the place, run (inevitably one feels) by Roberts from Bala, yet another Welshman.

It was in Georgetown that Rhees first felt the full shock of slavery.

'My God! is this the land thou has consecrated to liberty?' White girls, who could not stoop to pick up a handkerchief or move a chair, flogged negroes mercilessly in the street, handling a cowskin better than most gaolers in England. The whites were initiated from birth into a system of barbarous cruelty. They ruined black girls before they were fourteen, drove them on to the streets on a Monday, to earn at least six shillings sterling clear money by the Saturday. The white militia turned out 'all gentlemen', poor as they might be, greater tyrants than lords and dukes in the Old World. Rhees was horrified to hear that the education of blacks was forbidden under pain of a £50 fine. On each of the four days he spent in Georgetown, he preached violently against slavery. 'It seems all the human race are *Negroes*, without flogging, they will do nothing.' He encountered a polite but icy resistance. All the ministers of the place gathered around him. They had been losing their congregations through preaching against slavery. 'Who will run the risk of their lives to preach against it? Jesus Christ spoke in parables and so will I.'

The coming of Morgan John evidently revitalised the cause in George-town, for the ministers begged him to stay. There were other attractions. His English brother was making £200 from preaching and his school would bring in another £200. And there was a French privateer in the bay, which had brought in a Spanish Letter of Marque valued at 40,000 dollars. The action had lasted six hours, 'but the Sans Culottes are desperate. They sing, fight and conquer . . . *Ca Ira, Ca Ira!* Godspeed to them all in their crusade to overturn all tyrants and emancipate all slaves.'

It took a real 'battle of the heart' for Morgan John to turn down his friends and move on, following The Cloud. He could no longer escape, however, what was fast becoming an obsession. On the first day out from Georgetown, over the Sampit River and along Push-and-Go Creek, where they spent four and a half miles shuttling from one ferry house to the next, he and Bishop Meredith reached the Shackleford plantation, where no white man was at home. What was to be done? They called the blacks together and preached to them: 'I tried to talk to them in their own language. They were remarkably attentive. Sang hymns as well. We found a few of them serious and rational . . . They only want instruction.' After a charming meal of roast potatoes, all the poor negroes could give them, they lay down to rest three in a bed, happy in a day well spent.

The next day, however, was Charleston:

Dirty streets, houses some of them elegant, other so-so. Hai! Ho! what is this? A negroe girl carrying one of my countrymen (asquat)

on her back, poor fellow, he cries out Bo ho ho as if he was going to
the slaughter house and I cannot save his life.

The tension of Georgetown was here redoubled, for Charleston had
been the original objective of Rhees's two abortive attempts to reach
America over the last ten years. He duly noted its population of 16,400,
7,700 of them slaves, its exports of $3,846,392; its regular city plan,
neat streets of well built houses (though too narrow for this climate),
its piazzas and balconies. There were several colleges, the library was 'a
good shell' which lacked only books, and religion was crippled by the
barriers between black and white. 'Had it not been for the old British
curse of Slavery, the South Carolinians would be a brave people.'

That curse, however, was black beyond measure. Rhees's view of
slavery was simple, direct and uncompromising: 'The Information I had
this day concerning Slavery', he wrote in his journal for 17 January,

> proves to a demonstration that too many of the Planters in this
> country are a set of the most dissipated, barbarous and unprincipled
> wretches under Heaven. They treat their negroes worse than the
> West India planters. In the midst of winter they work them without
> a rag to cover their nakedness and flog them till there is hardly an
> inch of their bodies without a scar or a wound. If any of the poor
> negroes turn religious and learn to read a little in their bibles so as to
> instruct the others, some of their cruel masters will take them up for
> this and endeavour to flog them to silence. But as it is impossible for
> them to shut the mouth which God has opened, they may sell the
> poor creatures to other masters still more cruel if they can meet with
> them. The Bablers are sold and banished from their friends in order
> to get rid of their Impertinences. But it is too late, the seed is sown.

On the other hand, but for 'the old British curse' (an intriguing
shift!) the Carolinians *were* a brave people, generous and friendly. Their
criminal laws needed revision, but at least their judge was genial. Sentenc-
ing one man to be hanged, he added that 'they should all soon follow in
the same way,' while another was instructed that the Lord would have
mercy on his soul between twelve and one o'clock: 'I need not inform
you what countryman the Gentleman is.' The celebrated Dr Ramsay
welcomed Morgan John as did many of the clergy of the place, reading
through the drafts of the essay he began to write in answer to John
Lawrence's defence of slavery. On 21 January, the French in the city
celebrated the execution of Louis XVI with a grand procession to an

Altar of Liberty on Bocquet's Green and the Welshman preached a suitable evening address. It was once more with reluctance that Rhees quit Charleston after twelve days, hopeful that at least some of its people would remember his call to instruct and emancipate their negroes.

'If in theory we are obliged to admit the doctrine of free agency,' he wrote a few days later in Savannah, 'experience daily evinces that it is not altogether in man to direct his steps.' For in that city, the passion for the negro cause gripped him by the throat and threatened never to let go.

Escorted out of Charleston by a goodly company and a concert of frogs, Rhees ran into the first serious trouble of his journey. Though he had known only six days of rain and one of snow since landing in October 1794, he now met torrents and floods. The party forded the Edistow River with difficulty and had to wade through creeks for a mile before Rhees could preach at the house of a man who had come to Carolina without hat, shirt or shoes worth wearing at the end of the war and now owned five thousand acres and scores of negroes at Coosawhatchie. Colonel Scriven sent a man to guide them to his place on May River, where they were weatherbound for a couple of days. Rhees's horse was ailing and had to be left behind as the Welshman braced himself for the canoe trip into Georgia.

The social climate was getting rougher, too, as he penetrated into the newer frontier state. The abominable practice of duelling had occupied them at Judge Bee's; the lawman wanted offenders deprived of citizenship for life. 'This would stab their cursed, contemptuous and dastardly honour to the quick,' snorted Rhees. A few days later, a gentleman was called out from a dinner he attended in Savannah and promptly 'knocked on the head'; there was a gunfight. This evil suited slaveholders, Rhees was quick to note. One of them boasted of having shot a black in the public highway. Certainly, the stories about slavery got worse as he approached Georgia; pregnant women driven out to deliver in the fields, a black given 600 lashes for appearing decently dressed in public. Wet and wilting at the river prospect, Rhees exploded in anger – 'O God of love and compassion how long shall these tormentors of the human race exist on thy earth? . . . consume such vermin from the creation.'

It was in a black mood, then, that he set off in a canoe with four oars down the May river, through the narrow cut into Savannah Bay. It was thirty miles, hard rowing against wind and tide in some places and his arms stiff from the steering. The oyster shoals and pomadum trees made a pleasant prospect, but once in the Savannah, huge waves threatened to swamp them. For the first time, Rhees feared for his life. It was an exhausted man who battled in under Savannah bluff, immediately to succumb to weakness, bad headaches, 'an obstructed perspiration', which left him unable to walk, read or write.

It was in this city, however, that he was transfixed. He found Savannah captivating, with its high bluff, pleasing plan, its many squares which let the air blow free — 'How do you do, Brother Dust?' — to tyrant and slave alike. There was the 'beautiful and never-fading verdure', the myrtle, the fan pomadum, the orange, peach and lime, the biggest bay trees he had ever seen. And troops of friends clustered around, Mr McColl the Independent minister whose meeting-house was open to all denominations, and that rare specimen, an honest lawyer, in the amiable person of Citizen Clay. He met Citizen S., an English republican refugee from Manchester. They pressed the claims of Savannah upon him, dinning its salubrity and the longevity of its inhabitants into his surprised and half-incredulous ear. Rhees, in totally congenial company, was stopped in his tracks.

For there was challenge, too. On 2 February, he went out with some friends to visit the ruins of the Orphanage which the English leader of the Calvinistic Methodists, George Whitefield, had established. This was the spiritual godfather of the Welsh Methodists at home and his enterprise, to Rhees, reeked of ambiguity. Not only had he planted his institution in a remote and barren spot; to maintain orphans and divinity students, he had used charitable funds to buy a slave plantation! The Lord, very properly, had destroyed college and chapel by lightning. The Countess of Huntington, who had set up the Welsh Methodist leader, Howell Harris, in a settlement of his own back in Wales, took over this one, but after her death, Whitefield's will was contested and the intrepid tutor Johnson was forced out with a sword to his heart. There was much talk of reviving the place, but nothing had been done. All Rhees found at the site were three or four cows, two or three blacks, Mr Evans a tailor, a massive nine-foot portrait of the Countess of Huntington in a gilt frame and an old map-screen torn to pieces 'and further your deponent saith not,' save to remark that most of the students had since turned Baptist or Presbyterian.

The experience evidently set Rhees's brain furiously to work. It was reinforced by the urgings of lawyer Clay, who battled for the poor, and of the *Jacobin* from Manchester whose capital schemes had been blocked by the men in power in Georgia, vile Aristocrats whose only purpose was to prey on the vitals of the public. There were too many English and Scots in Georgia, hell-bent on quick profit. 'They do all they can to veil the glory of the rising empire; but rise it must in spite of slave-holders and Aristocrats.'

The decisive impact, however, was that of the black church. The negroes had built a Baptist meeting-house, where Rhees preached on his second day. He was moved beyond words. The singing, in particular, — 'their music is far superior to anything I have yet heard on this continent' — touched a Welsh chord. Prostrate in fever a week later — 'My head! My head! I am full of heaviness' — his one thought was — 'I'll strive to go and hear them sing.' There were more compelling reasons. On the very day of his arrival in Savannah, he had been visited by 'poor Andrew', the black preacher. Andrew Bryan had launched a black church in 1788. Several of his flock had been taken up and flogged in public. They began with Andrew himself, who stripped and stood the whipping without a murmur, followed by his congregation. This savagery had faded, but Bryan's mouth was now stopped. Although the blacks claimed a congregation of four hundred, with twice that number of potential members, they had been warranted to hold a service for only two days in the year and were subjected to constant harassment.

Morgan John boiled over. 'The slave holders are such poor blind devils that they will keep these men in ignorance, that they may cut their throats one day or other.' He threw himself into the enterprise, preached around the town, rallied friends and allies and launched a petition at the stubborn heads of authority. Once more, it seems to have been his presence, his zest, which energised a fading cause. It was he who drafted the constitution of the new church, which was pure Rhees.

1. Jesus Christ is the only head of the church.
2. Believers in him are the only members.
3. They are to choose their own officers.
4. The Bible is their only rule of faith and practice.

He named the church Beth-Shalom and rallied friends like Ebenezer Hills, John Hamilton and Evan Clay to the cause. They raised £200 on the first day, contracting to build a meeting-house sixty feet by fifty, with galleries all round, the pulpit open to any who subscribed towards the £1,000 needed.

There was more. For Rhees determined to succeed where Whitefield had failed. He would set up a school, open to the poor children of free blacks, to those of the slaves their masters would permit and to poor whites. Books and clothes would be provided free until the children were apprenticed and the school was to be run by a committee of annually elected citizens.

In the cause, he spent weeks in Savannah, working in a kind of fury, in the teeth of resistance from nobs and mobs. A brief trip out to David Fox's place on the Little Ogeechie brought momentary relief. Game was so plentiful that one brother claimed to have bagged 93 blackbirds with a single discharge. The men carried lanterns at night to hypnotise the deer, who lined up to be shot, one after the other. Undeterred by these epic feats, Rhees chose a likely spot for settlement, but the idyll was brief. An urgent call sent him back post-haste to Savannah where the crusade, apparently, could not be sustained without his presence.

Quite clearly, Rhees was tempted to stay. His friend Robert Roberts of Bala, who had accompanied him all the way from Baltimore, went back north, but Rhees could not.

> I must stop here to preach three Sundays more at least, Providence having opened a door of usefulness. I dare not go on unless the cloud moves before me . . . I have reasoned and remonstrated all the way from Virginia here. But now I cannot go much further unless I enter the dominions of Spain. Here then, where slavery abounds, I will make a stand.

For a few weeks in February 1795, it looked as though the New Cambria would arise in Georgia, on mission not to the Welsh Indians, but to the Savannah blacks.

He was running into rough weather. The powerful snubbed him and crowds of drunks heckled the black services. The close-knit circle of friends closed tighter. Lawyer Clay took him out to his place on the Great Ogeechie. The phaeton stuck in the mud and had to be hauled out by main force, to cross a two-mile causeway, 'the perfection of bad roads in America'. The myrtle and game, however, were abundant, the inhabitants comfortable. How tempting it would be, were it not for those rice plantations and their slave gangs! 'Much as I formerly admired rice, I shall eat no more while it is cultivated by slaves.'

At the Midway meeting-house, all the men came armed. This was the edge of disputed Spanish territory, the fief of Creek and Cherokee, lethal hunting ground of spy and counter-spy, chosen arena of that ambiguous 'General' Bowles who had so impressed the Welsh brethren in London. Rhees suspected that the arms were directed as much against the blacks as the Indians. On the night after the thanksgiving service, he had a dream-vision of George Washington's conversion to the abolitionist cause, which he promptly wrote up in prose reminiscent of Volney's *Ruins of Empires*.[3]

The Welshman had to resolve the dilemma. He went on to Sunbury and was offered free passage to the Spanish frontier by a fellow-countryman. But what was the point? Was he to go to Kentucky, to the north-west? His horse was fetched over from Carolina – 'half-starved'. But would Beth-Shalom church survive without him? Several citizens presented him with a memorial, begging him to stay or at least to return. By the end of February, he came to something of a decision. He had to renew the search for a site for Cambria. Could that newborn Wales ever flourish among slaves? He promised to return and certainly meant to. It may have been in Savannah that he freed Robert Stewart, Pompey the mulatto, who was later to make the bricks for the Welsh settlement.[4] But, rather half-heartedly, he decided to move out of Savannah, up the river, to the Baptist settlements in the back country beyond Augusta.

His doubts must have been reinforced by the influenza which laid him low as soon as he left town. He made slow progress. They were burning the wire-grass and he advanced in company with a running blaze which sometimes swept across the road. Augusta, with its long street of 200 houses along the Savannah, was ablaze, too, very hot against the Yazoo speculators and a bought assembly. Infidels flourished there, a Theist preached every Sunday and young bucks heckled the orthodox. They were trying to build a steamboat to beat the current which sometimes delayed river traffic from Savannah for three weeks, but the inventor's design was too complex. Rhees struggled on beyond Bedford, but was forced to turn for shelter to Colonel Sanders.

Here, the older obsession began to return. Sanders was very knowledgeable about Creeks and Cherokees, assured Rhees that many of the chiefs and warriors were men of principle. He offered the Welshman a pony valued at £25. The old horse, who had travelled over 1,500 miles from Vermont without a change of shoes, was even less ready for the mountains than his rider. Rhees accepted and baptised the pony 'Primrose'. He pushed on slowly, still plagued by influenza, and came out among his Baptist confrères near Ray's Mills.

At this point, Kentucky fever hit him. He met family after family getting ready for the Wilderness Trail to the 'paradise of America'. A kind of mania seemed to have seized the people. Two of the prime movers were the Baptist ministers Sanders Walker and Peter Smith. The latter, with nine children and a hatred of slavery, was heartbroken at the thought of leaving the Georgia-South Carolina border country, but he was 'a northward man', as he told Dr Samuel Jones of Philadelphia when he reported Morgan Rhees's arrival, and he could do no other.[5]

Rhees spent several days riding about the meeting houses, visiting the little town of Washington and its mineral spring, holding long and earnest discussions on settlement and Indians with the Reverend Stringer and Colonel Henricks, only jewel in the Georgia assembly, who lodged him in a charming little room like a thrush's nest. The Baptists hereabouts in the foothills of the great mountains pleased him; their government was 'purely republican'.

It was there that he finally made his decision. It took him two days. The people were all 'mad for going to Kentucky'; four Baptist ministers were taking their flocks. To escape the pressure, Rhees locked himself up in a cabin, still suffering from his influenza, though the peaches were already in bloom. It seems to have been Peter Smith who finally settled his mind. Smith had been through Kentucky to the Miami on the Ohio the previous September and he supplied Rhees with copious memoranda on the Holston, Kentucky and Ohio rivers. Through 11 March Morgan John 'travelled the Western Territory on maps and in history'. Another day's brooding and the writing of a commentary on the 118th Psalm settled it. 'Would it not be a capital piece of Quixotism to go and form a settlement on the Mississippi in Latitude 44?' The empire of the earth, after all, was travelling westward.

He went to see Smith on the 13th. The influenza had gone, to be succeeded by an agonising toothache. He told his friend that he intended to go to the Ohio, to spy out land for the Welsh come and coming to America. About May or June, he would go up the Ohio to Redstone and so back to the eastern states. The following winter he'd spend in Savannah, to settle the black church and to ready himself for the establishment of Cambria in the spring.[6]

It had been a 'hard contest', but scorning the toothache and trusting that The Cloud would move before him, Morgan John Rhees pointed Primrose's nose resolutely towards Golden Grove on the Seluda, rallying point for the emigrant trains of the Wilderness Trail.

It took him a week, slowed as he was by rain and his own weakness and he had another ten days to wait at the Grove. The journey was tedious; for twenty miles on end he travelled alone through the woods. But as soon as he crossed the Savannah into South Carolina, he felt the whole countryside astir. He ran into wagon trains moving south into Georgia even as Georgians were heading north to the promised land of Kentucky. What a country, with its good folk ebbing and flowing like the sea to all points of the compass! Colonel Baird at Abbeville, surrounded by Irish and threatened by a Quaker immigration, was moving to Kentucky 'for want of good society'! Morgan John saved a black from a flogging and a gunsmith from corruption, but had to take to his bed at Golden Grove in sheriff Carter Torrents's house. The good sheriff was out half the night after negro thieves, kidnappers who sold black girls to other states and the Spaniards. Most of the people Rhees met in the back country favoured emancipation, provided the blacks were settled elsewhere, and the Welshman felt the government should indulge their 'strange prejudice'. Happily, he had recovered by the time of the great three-day preaching conference which launched the migrants. Many of the ministers failed to appear and it was a Welsh Jonah who had to preach repentance to them. Many were in tears, for they were leaving a pleasant country.

On 30 March, the company assembled. The whole neighbourhood was in motion. Parents parted with children, friends embraced as at a last farewell. Packhorses laden with pots, kettles, kitchen gear, together with the women and children, formed the centre of the battalion. The men rode front and rear, armed with rifles. At nine in the morning, they set out, after the final blessing, to cross a fine ridge of iron ore and to camp a hundred strong at Macbeth's store, where Morgan preached the word. The next day, after the first twelve miles to a Baptist chapel, they plunged into the hill country, crossing the Seluda twice and halting by the beautiful 600-foot cascade at Fall Creek, where Rhees, too tired to describe 'the august architecture of God', unrolled his blanket with dozens of others in Dillingham's log house.

On the first day into the mountains, the little hills seemed to have been 'skipping and dancing for joy when the Almighty formed this part of creation'. Within three days, they had become dreary little tyrants and the great Bald Mountain, 'three miles high', a positive relief. The going was tough. They entered North Carolina on April Fools' Day, along endless streams with a 'kind of evergreen laurel' growing on the banks like a hedge. Over Green River and into the Blue Ridge they trudged, the mountains truly grotesque, lacking only cultivated plateaux to make them sublime. They camped at Cane Creek, where settlers were raising their cabins, and at Craig's Blockhouse were entertained by a ballad-singer who addressed himself to the Yazoo swindlers:

Take the speculating statesmen
And drown them in the sea,
As did the bold Bostonian men
Once serve the British tea.

Thus cheered, they passed on through heavy rain and Buncum county town. A miserable place Rhees found it, a few wretched huts on a stony hill without a garden: 'But I suppose it suits the inhabitants.' On along the French Broad River for a while, to cross the Ridge and sleep at Dillon's, a tolerable pigsty whose inhabitants lived like pigs. The North Carolina pastimes of whisky and eye-gouging made sleep a little difficult.

The next day, they had to cross Ivy River eighteen times, with hardly a patch of level ground, a couple of cabins in 25 miles, good cattle country without a drop of milk and corn four times as dear as fifty miles below. But at last, at about three in the afternoon, they approached the majestic Bald Mountain and their spirits rose. Over 150 people and 200 horses went Indian file up a narrow ridge, many lashing themselves to the saddle, many hanging on to the horses' tails. Halfway up great vistas opened up before them and they camped, dry at last, under a full moon. Morgan John, stretched out beside a spring, enriched his journal with classical metaphors.

In the morning, his vocabulary was stretched still further, as they reached the summit of the Bald and a glorious sweep of mountains burst on their sight. The land near the summit he thought the best he had seen in America. At their feet was Tennessee, an attractive tapestry, with the forests ready marked with the girdling axe and fire clearing the ground for maize and summer grain. The famished horses scrabbled down the slope. But the descent was hair-raising, a four-mile plummet over terrific precipices. Only the trees stopped them slithering head over rump. The worst path he had ever seen, it would have been deemed impassable in Europe. And at the foot, there were eight more miles of ferociously bad road, crossing and recrossing Indian Creek, up another hill and down another sheer slope. They were lucky to arrive with no bones broken at that Nolichucky River which gave John Sevier his nickname. Here, the Indians had killed one family and driven off another a few months back, but the settlers now felt strong enough to give the migrants a welcome. They crossed the rough river at a bad ford, but found haven in a fertile vale, thick with people and sugar trees. That baneful beverage whisky again made the night hideous, but Rhees, least closed of Baptists, took a little of the stuff, with milk and sugar, to stimulate the system before settling down to sleep.

While the party rested on the morrow, Rhees with some others pressed on down Devil Steps and up Winding Stairs, where several horses broke their necks, to attend service at Keele's meeting house. And on the next day, they entered the last settled region before the Wilderness, the little towns of Jonesborough (a court-house, a few stores and fifteen houses) and Greenville (25 houses) where, thank God, a man could get a cup of coffee. After crossing the Holston, Rhees broke off to visit Colonel Cocks, a lawyer counted the greatest man in the territory. 'No religion, no, but very civil, polite company.' Cocks was one of those patriots, stimulated by the anti-British boycott, who would not consume or wear any article which was foreign. Small wonder, for he could live off his own on his plantation, a roasting pig every day of the year and droves of cattle sent off annually as far as Philadelphia. The cattle Rhees found stunted and ill-bred, however. Americans, he asserted, and he was to repeat it in Kentucky, were unsuited to experiment and innovation. 'Strangers to Want and no ambition to excel, they still pursue the old beaten track.'

Having delivered himself of this, to say the least, unconventional judgement, and stocked up with Cocks's ham, fowl and biscuit, he joined the company as they entered the Wilderness, the lawyer's hymns of praise for the Cumberland country still echoing in their ears. On Clinch Mountain, they met a party of Kentuckians out hunting. There was a scatter of hunters' cabins along the route, though Indians made frequent inroads upon them. After the Clinch River came Powell's, and then it was up Cumberland Mountain to the Kentucky frontier at the summit. At that point, they stopped and mustered their arms. For ahead lay Dagon's Country, black as night.

This was the dark and bloody killing ground, which Indians and renegades prowled. Only a few weeks back Lorimier's Lobos out of Cap Girardeau had been raiding the Kentucky valley. Ravaged camp sites and whitened bones they had already passed. A tension gripped them and would not leave them for four days and nights. Men, women and children, they numbered 155 souls. A party almost as large was coming up behind. They organised a vanguard of a dozen, grouped the women and children centre, elected officers and made Morgan John their chaplain. With arms at the ready and after a prayer from Morgan, they marched ten miles into the woods and camped. Eight sentinels took two-hour turns through the night. After prayer and a hymn, they lay down in the open like the Patriarchs of old. The women were fearful, but Rhees knew that God was encamped about them.

Over Cumberland River in the morning, they ran into way-stations run by renegades and runaways. Game was easy to come by for these, but not for the emigrant company, whose noise sent the deer scurrying for cover, though they were lucky when the vanguard snatched a turkey from the jaws of a 'panther' who had winkled it out of a tree. The stations were sheer robbery, nothing but salt bacon and twopence a

pint for milk! Though Rhees caught his first glimpse of bear meat —
'astonishing fat'.

There was worse than poor fodder. Near Broad Lick, Cherokee
tracks ran across the path and they found that Middleton's store had
been broken up because he had joined the Indians in plundering travellers.
They passed a deserted camp where there had been a massacre and saw
the graves of four Baptist ministers who had been scalped the previous
year. Rhees preached an oration over them which they were perhaps
fortunate not to hear:

> But all in vain they are putrefied
> Their labour ended in this place
> Death like an arrow stopped their race
> But could not rob them of their grace.

Whether in consequence of this experience or of the general tension,
discipline began to give way. Rhees and the officers had to call the
company to order, before they camped in the thick cane brakes, which
the ravenous horses tore into.

A rain-soaked night heralded the worst Sunday Rhees was ever to
experience. The morning was very wet and the road a quagmire as they
crossed Racoon Creek and Laurel River and many streams. At last they
reached a station with soldiers, but there was nothing to be had but
peach brandy and whisky and stale bread at fourpence a pound. They
thought to stop there, but the weather brightened a little and the officers
ordered them to march on. It was a Sunday and Morgan's stomach
sickened with foreboding. They scarcely made eight miles, when men
and beasts half-starving were engulfed in a dreadful thunderstorm.
Thunder reverberated from the rocks and lightning lit a lurid scene as
men, women and children without shelter huddled against the rain.
Suddenly there were shouts from the rear and four of the men who had
tarried at the station came running in a fever. An Indian had fired at
them from the woods but his musket had flashed in the pan. Panic.
Women screamed, fainted, hid the children. Men rushed aimlessly to
and fro, shouting. The officers rallied them. They fired off a volley
and recharged, that their guns might be in order. A double watch was
mounted and men stoked bonfires through the night. 'I expect it was
the lightning,' said Rhees, though not until the morning, huddled on a
tree stump over his stained and tattered journal in a dripping forest.[7]

That morning, they were up early, tense and strained. They saddled
and packed in double time and, soaked to the skin, passed through

Hazel Patch with its deserted cabins, over several flooded creeks, endlessly up and down barren hills, until, topping a steep slope, they found themselves ringed by the great horseshoe of the Rock-Castle River, in flood and twenty feet deep. The officers ordered a halt for the flood to subside, but the panic was still on some of them. They hurled logs into the river and clung to them, others swam their horses. Makeshift rafts were thrown together. Rhees himself was one who could not wait. He swam Primrose over and reeled exhausted into Cookham's Cabin, the only white man's booth in the country. In the morning, the rest came over, many splashing helplessly in the swift current, to be rescued by human chains from the shore.

But once over the river, the fear lifted. 'Every one begins to scamper.' At Logan's Station they reached the land of the living and breakfasted on venison, turkey and bear flesh. The latter Rhees found sweeter than mutton, its fat more agreeable than pork. At last, they reached their destination, the Crab Orchard in Lincoln county, where the settled part of Kentucky began and the company dispersed. After such deserts, mused the bone-weary and waterlogged Welshman, no wonder Kentucky seemed such a paradise. An Elysium it certainly was on that luxuriant April day, even though the inevitable Baptist brother, Moses Bledsoe, kept him up talking until midnight.

A fortnight later, Rhees was writing in different vein: 'I have not yet seen Imlay's "eternal verdure",' ran his report to the eager listeners back home in Wales,

> nor does 'the brilliant sun of latitude 69, piercing through the azure heavens produce such an early maturity as is truly astonishing'. Flowers full and perfect as if they had been cultivated by the Hand of the Florist have not yet made their appearance ... Thy soft zephyrs have not yet breathed on sweets and the inhaled air has not given a voluptuous glow of health and vigour to ravish the intoxicated senses! The sweet songsters of the forest no doubt warble their tender notes in unison with Love and Nature but they do not appear to feel the influence of this genial clime more than any other equally salubrious

and so on for several paragraphs of heavy-handed irony at the expense of Imley and his tribe of enthusiastic promoters.[8]

When a country had assumed the magic character of a veritable Land of Cockayne as Kentucky had in the crabbed mountain parishes of Wales, a degree of disenchantment at the reality was perhaps to be expected. Not that Rhees denied its fertility and wealth. On the contrary, two weeks of his journal are punctuated by multiple exclamation marks. He once rode 28 miles without seeing a foot of bad land. The principal city, Lexington, had more trade than any city its size on the Continent. It teemed with hatters, saddlers, tailors and tradesmen who were too well paid (they picked his pockets, he complained). Two or three hundred dwellings, many of them fine buildings of stone and brick, jostled the three churches, the court-house, two printing offices turning out weekly newspapers, the prison and the college administered by the excellent Dr Henry Toulmin from England, who had crossed with Thomas Cooper and Priestley's son.[9] As for Judge Lewis's home three miles outside the town — 'This is England, a veritable palace!'

Moses Bledsoe lent him a horse while Primrose rested and Morgan John rode out to Georgetown, where Craig the Baptist minister not only ran a store but had erected grist, hemp, fulling and saw mills, a still and the first paper manufactory in the commonwealth. The town already had 70 houses, a court-house and a chapel. Frankfort, the capital, nestling by the Kentucky river in a dazzling countryside, was beautifully laid out; its capital would have done honour to an old-established realm, let alone this infant state. Two years ago, there were but two roof houses in the place, now there were thirty of the fine local stone, 'bordering on the marble kind', besides cabins. The rate at which population was increasing, accelerated by the overpowering presence of the federal army for Wayne's campaign, was startling. Fifteen thousand men could be mobilised at Lexington in a matter of hours. Already, flour, beef, pork were moving in bulk down the river to New Orleans and the Kentuckians confidently awaited the Spanish opening of the Mississippi. Their horses and livestock were equal to any in the Union. At Bourbon town, he heard of a ewe who brought forth four ewe lambs in the spring, who themselves produced two lambs apiece, while the mother gave birth to four more in the fall, thus springing sixteen lambs from her loins in a single year! Not even Georgia's 93 blackbirds at a stroke could equal this, particularly as he had the word of a reputable minister for it! Iron ore, coal, salt and mineral springs were to be found everywhere; furnaces and forges were sprouting. Kentucky was clearly destined for glory.

But there was a worm in the bud. 'I have not seen in my travels a place where religious worship is treated with more contempt than Lexington.' Most of the inhabitants were a contemptible, proud, ignorant and vicious set — fine Republicans! All his congregations were small, desultory and O Lord, how heavy! Within a week his voice was gone, his sermons hoarse and weak. 'All the churches are gone to sleep.' Moreover, this ebb of principle, this slough of short-sighted materialism were inherent in the very bounty of their hard-won commonwealth. 'I am really afraid that Nature has done too much for Kentucky'; already many farmers could sit back at their ease. Would the next generation need to work at all? Elegant stone houses everywhere, ladies as full-feathered and fashionable as in European cities — what sort of newfoundland of freedom was this in an infant state which a few years ago was inhabited only by Indians? And the rot was going deeper:

> They have deprived the preachers of Christianity of the privilege of a seat in their Legislatures and not only tolerate but encourage slavery! They are aware that the benign system of juries is inimical to their dark deeds. They boast of an attachment to France and bawl for liberty, at the same time as they keep in Egyptian bondage a great proportion of their fellow creatures.

It was a morose Moses come down from the mountain who quit the idol-worshippers of the promised land and turned Primrose's nose towards the Ohio. As he neared the great river, his spirits revived — perhaps because the settlers thinned out. At May's Lick, there were newcomers from Jersey who shunned slavery — at long last, a decent congregation! Washington town was a thriving little place, only four miles from the river station at Limestone. It had 150 houses already, many of them of stone, and its Baptist meeting house was large. 'Here I raise mine Ebenezer, hither by Thine help I'm come.' And at the Blue Lick salt works, his mind was riveted by the great animal bones they were unearthing. He saw one tusk four and a half feet long, weighing 50 pounds, another was even longer. Part of the jaw survived, with terrible grinders, a snout as callous as steel, pincers powerful enough to cut a bar of iron in two. What huge race of extinct carnivores were these? More of those great brutes which had so taken the mind of that excellent Republican Thomas Jefferson perhaps? At the great debate between Priestley and Volney in the Philosophical Society in Philadelphia, Jefferson used a mammoth jawbone from Big Bone Lick as chairman's gavel, to the frustrated spleen of that irascible Tory William Cobbett. And how effectively had he marshalled their evidence to counter Buffon's assertion that everything decayed in the New World! What a perplexing place this Kentucky was! It was a troubled Welshman who set himself down in busy little Washington to write a report for the waiting Israelites back home. He never managed to finish it. As it was, it took him so long that when he reached Limestone on May Day he found the flatboat had gone. He had to gallop for several miles along the shore until they picked him up.

Once on the great river, however, he sloughed off Kentucky like a discarded skin. That sudden sense of liberation, that stretching of the mind, that sheer wonder, which seems to have swept over practically everybody who saw the Ohio country in these early years when the hand of the white man was still light upon it, took possession of his mind. From shore to shore, the company rolled down the majestic river. The water was remarkably still, the country beyond description. 'I was almost lost in amazement and love in contemplating the work of creation.' For thirteen hours they talked in their 'little wooden house'. Here and there, a hut rose on the bank; cocks crowed in the wilderness. In the night, it was harder going, with a lot of rowing, but on the second day, they came to the new settlement of Columbia at the mouth of the Little Miami, nestling under its hill among fine pastures.

Morgan John landed, set his foot, as he put it, on 'the unbroken grass' of the new frontier of freedom. He found Columbia delightful. Though troubled by the Ohio floods, its soil was as rich as Kentucky's and there were already 900 families in the settlement. He found the Baptist minister and preached to a fine congregation. The sonorous words nearly died on his lips. For some Indians, the first he had seen, turned up to listen. What an opportunity, he confided to his diary that night in a careful third person, for someone to make a great name for himself preaching among the heathen, 'that the bloody hatchet of the Indian may be buried within the earth, never to rise and scalp mankind any more'.

New aspiration jostled old dream in his singing head. For in the morning, a fine May morning, he climbed the hill and found it was an old, a very old fortification. Ringing the town in a semi-circle, it bore the marks of what he thought must have been streets and walls among the earth mounds. There in the rubbish, he found an old, broken stone and, *diwedd annwyl*, was the inscription in Welsh? He scrabbled among the rubble. The stones were too broken for him to make much sense of them, but some characters looked remarkably like the Welsh alphabet. He ran back to the town and they told him the region was full of such relics of a once-great people. Below the rapids, there was said to be a monument erected by them when they left Kentucky, pillars recording some great calamity which had befallen them. Everywhere around there were proofs 'of a race of men not altogether savage existing in this country'. Was he treading in the steps of the Madogwys?

It was with an old excitement quickening to new life in his veins that he rode the six miles into the frontier capital of Cincinatti. The town itself seemed in a fever. Drums were beating, companies mustering, Wayne's soldiers thronged the streets, prices were rocketing and, despite the peace talks at Greenville, everyone was uneasy, 'for the whites have taught the Indians treachery'. He made his way to Gordon's hotel, and there, on 5 May, at long last, he heard his first hard news of his compatriot John Evans.

An American captain told him that Judge Turner of the Western Circuit had introduced Evans to the Spanish commandant at St Louis, Zenon Trudeau. The Spaniards had taken the Welshman under their protection; any discoveries he made would accrue to the monarch of Spain. Only five weeks ago and a mere three hundred miles away, John Evans in St Louis had been getting ready to go up the Missouri in search of the Welsh Indians.

Notes

1. The whole of this chapter, except where otherwise stated, is based upon the entries in Morgan John Rhees's Diary from 1 January to 5 May 1795. I have used the original, on-the-spot record he made day by day, supplementing it where necessary by reference to the more formal report-letters and journal he made up later. From 16 April, this formal record ceases, except for a letter composed in Washington, Kentucky, on 30 April.

2. For a summary account of the Welsh settlements on the Peedee and Welsh Neck, see E.G. Hartmann *Americans from Wales* (Christopher, Boston, 1967), pp. 52-4.

3. On Rhees and Volney, see my 'Morgan John Rhys and Volney's *Ruins of Empires*', *Bulletin of the Board of Celtic Studies*, vol. xx (1962).

4. On Pompey, see *Cambria Freeman* (Pennsylvania), 20 January 1872, and Chapter 7.

5. P. Smith–S. Jones, 23 April 1795: Pennepek.

6. Ibid.

7. Rhees Diary, 12 April 1795.

8. Letter, Washington, Kentucky, 30 April 1795, included in Diary. The Imlay referred to would be Gilbert Imley, husband of Mary Wollstonecraft, author of *A Topographical Description of the Western Part of North America*; a second edition appeared in London in 1793.

9. J. Priestley–Jedidiah Morse, 24 August 1793, Gratz collection, case 12, box 12, Historical Society of Pennsylvania; see M.C. Park, *Joseph Priestley and the Problem of Pantisocracy*, (Philadelphia, 1947). Toulmin's father, Joshua, succeeded Priestley at the Birmingham meeting house.

5 CONTENTIOUS CANAAN

In fact, it was John Rice Jones of Kaskaskia who had secured John Evans's release.[1] He crossed the river and managed to convince the Lieutenant-Governor that the Welshman was not a spy. Trudeau was still suspicious, however, and held John in St Louis. It was when Judge Turner came up river on his circuit and Trudeau paid his customary courtesy visit that he was reassured. Turner had heard of Evans's mission and pointed out that, even if the Welshman failed to find Welsh Indians, he might find a great deal more. The consequence would have surprised William Jones Llangadfan; the Spaniards took over John's enterprise as an official Spanish mission. Trudeau issued Evans with letters-patent in Spanish, French and English, gave him some presents for the Indians and instructed him to get to the Mandans, explore the upper Missouri and penetrate to the Pacific, to win the prize of 2,000 pesos which Governor Carondelet in New Orleans was offering to the first Spanish subject to make the land crossing to the South Sea.

John, now settled in Cahokia across the river, still needed a companion. Gratiot, who had enthused the Madocians back home, was not in St Louis, but it was probably at this time that Jacques Clamorgan made contact with the Welshman. Clamorgan, whose real name was Charles Morgan, was an adventurer, almost certainly a West Indian of Welsh descent. 'Slave trader in the West Indies, merchant, land speculator, explorer, keeper of a negro harem, church warden and bachelor father of four children', he was an outsider and the driving force behind Spain's last imperial enterprise in North America. Louisiana's predicament was near desperate; ringed by a great arc of menace, from thrusting American speculators on the borders of Florida, endlessly threatening migrants pressing on the Mississippi, an army of freebooters massing in Kentucky even as the American federal army destroyed the Indians of the northwest and moved ominously forward, it was further harassed by British fur traders driving down into Spanish territory, manipulating the Sioux into a blockade of the Missouri and moving on the Mandans to pre-empt the fur trade and the route to the Pacific. While Carondelet down in New Orleans shuttled his gunboats up the river, negotiated with Wilkinson and Kentucky secessionists, turned Indians loose on the Americans and called for action on the Missouri, Trudeau, starved of resources and lurching from crisis to crisis, was ground down into an ineradicable pessimism.

Clamorgan's response was a bold imperial challenge. In 1794, he launched his Missouri Company with vaulting ambitions of Pacific dominion; the slow and sedate merchants of St Louis, following the lead of their patrons in the Chouteau family, recoiled in alarm, and there were only nine shareholders. In June 1794, however, Clamorgan sent two pirogues up the river under the schoolmaster of St Louis. The expedition was a disaster, pillaged without mercy by the Sioux and the Omahas under Black Bird, a murderous prairie Borgia, who through the skilful use of poison and bluff, had made himself a power among the lower Missouri tribes. An emergency boat sent out to help was itself plundered, and by June 1795, the full extent of the disaster was known in St Louis.

Totally unabashed, Clamorgan proposed a third expedition, twice as large as the others and vastly more ambitious. The bulk of the shareholders, together with Trudeau, resigned from the Company in horror and denounced Morgan as a megalomaniac to Carondelet. In fact, Clamorgan was working in secret with the great Canadian house of Todd and McGill, forced to transfer its base since the Jay Treaty between Britain and the USA had finally withdrawn the presence of the British in the lands north-west of the Ohio and handed them to the Americans. Todd and McGill were to pump supplies and young traders into the faltering Spanish enterprise and support Clamorgan in his bold plan to run a line of forts and trading missions up to the Mandans and beyond to the Pacific. The choice of James McKay as leader of the major fort-building expedition formed part of the deal.

When John Evans was released and permitted to move back to the American side of the river, McKay was away from St Louis, buying supplies in Canada and the eastern states. In August 1795 he was to take up the Missouri the greatest expedition Spain ever directed towards the Pacific and he took it out within a few weeks of his return to St Louis; he signed on John Evans as his deputy within days of his arrival. In all probability, Clamorgan and his team had already made contact with the Welshman; on his return from the Missouri, Evans lived for a while in Clamorgan's household.

In May 1795 the deal had not yet been clinched and Judge Turner left the area before any partner had been found for Evans. The judge gave the Welshman plenty of advice, however, urged him to keep a journal and asked him to look out for unusual elk and red-haired goats he had heard of in the west. He consulted Auguste Chouteau on Evans's behalf and could assure the Waunfawr man that the Pacific could lie at no great distance from the Missouri's source. With this cheering thought, the judge said goodbye to John and got into his official barge with its banners and buglers. He was not to escape from the Chosen Race so easily. A few days later, having turned into the Ohio, he ran into Morgan John Rhees.

On his first day in Cincinatti, Rhees had called on Brigadier-General Wilkinson.[2] The General was a busy man. After his services to the Spaniards during the George Rogers Clark scare of 1793-4, he had submitted a bill for $8,000 as well as the arrears of his pension. His monster, conspiratorial scheme for wholesale subversion in Kentucky, at the cost of $20,000, 20 pieces of artillery, 10,000 stand of arms and two Spanish regiments, had been rejected by the Spanish Council of State, but the Governor at New Orleans had been authorised to resume negotiations. It was at Wilkinson's prompting that he had occupied and fortified Chickasaw Bluffs and, when Morgan Rhees arrived, the General was in the middle of delicate transactions with the Spaniards, arranging for a safe-conduct to New Orleans for Benjamin Sebastian and his fellow-conspirators of 'the secret committee of the West', bearing a draft treaty between Spain and an independent Kentucky.

Nevertheless, Wilkinson found plenty of time for the Welshman and, like John Evans before him, Rhees succumbed to his charm: 'The General is without exception one of the most pleasing men in his manners I have ever been in company with.' Moreover, he seemed better acquainted with the Western Territory than any white man living. Wilkinson and Morgan John spent a whole day poring over the General's maps, looking for the most promising areas. The next day, Rhees duly set out with two companions in a canoe. They made slow progress at little over three miles an hour. A boat carrying flour from Buffalo to New Orleans passed them at three times that speed, but warmed by a cordial overnight welcome from the Independent minister, Captain Brown, they pushed off from the mouth of the Big Miami shortly after breakfast. And it was at this point that Morgan John's Cloud stopped.

The country on the west bank below the Big Miami caught his imagination. He landed at several places and found it

uncommon rich ... Fine prospect and plenty of level land all round, first-rate quality, well watered by the creeks running into the Ohio. The turkeys are so plentiful that a man may kill as many as he pleases of them. Deer and bear likewise in abundance, with some elk and buffalo, with plenty of wild geese, ducks etc. almost as tame as barn owls.

He took the fateful decision — 'Marked out a spot on the side of a hill to build a town.' To that spot he was to direct the searchers of his Cambrian Company a year later.

During the night, however, they floated on for another 75 miles to the mouth of the Kentucky. At that moment, he was within a few days' journey of John Evans. There were signs of Indians on the far bank – a war-party with stolen horses, perhaps some of Lorimier's braves out to disrupt the peace talks – and they found a fish no bigger than a trout, with a bill two and a half feet long, big enough to take a man's head. They witnessed the speedy marriage of several couples *en masse* from among the sparse American settlers (who lacked sobriety, in Morgan's view) but otherwise the trip was uneventful. The return up the Ohio was hard rowing, however, until a nomad breeze caught Morgan's cloak, hoisted as a sail. Rhees spotted the ruins of an old fort on the edge of the river which exactly resembled the old castles of Wales, and he dropped off at the Miami to inspect an ancient barrow formed by art into a perfect circle: 'If the Ancient Britons did not live here, people of similar custom have.' It was something to talk over with Judge Symmes, the New Jersey man who had first bought the land between the Miamis in 1787. They were still talking when Judge Turner came sweeping up-river in his official barge, accompanied by a thunderstorm.

Through a day and a night, stopped short of Cincinatti by wind and current, Morgan John and the judge talked. Turner confirmed the captain's story about John Evans and repeated the instructions he had given the young Welshman. But the judge was himself up to the hilt in a grandiose plan to establish a settlement on the Mississippi itself opposite the mouth of the Missouri (Iolo's chosen site for a *Gwladfa*), to the mingled hope and apprehension of the neighbouring Spaniards in St Louis. It was on this prospect that he held forth. The Illinois was beyond description. 'Was you to be transported from Wales into that country,' he said to Rhees, 'and opened your eyes, you would suppose yourself in a country designed by art, in every direction and proportionally, for a gentleman's seat on every spot.' Everything pointed to that place as the grand emporium of the West. There was plenty for Morgan John to mull over as Turner took him to see St Clair, the Governor of the Western Territory, and his Secretary Sargent.

This visit set the tone for Morgan Rhees's stay in Cincinatti. Night after night, he dined with the Governor, his staff and the military, or went on long intimate rides with Brigadier-General Wilkinson. Happy hours were spent with the army surgeons, Doctors Alison and McClure. He rode to the meeting-houses and settlements around Cincinatti and Columbia, finding everything congenial. The month he spent in Cincinatti was probably the happiest of Morgan's time in America. When he left, the inhabitants of the frontier city made him a handsome present, to which he responded in appropriately republican terms — 'Their voluntary present he esteems of greater value than ten thousand times the sum extorted from the pockets of the public by an Established Hierarchy.'

Nevertheless, he began to feel uneasy. Wilkinson had blithely responded to his habitual toast to the British *Jacobin* martyrs condemned to Botany Bay with a promise to go and hang the judges who'd condemned them, but had warned that 5,000 families would migrate from Kentucky as soon as a land office had been opened on the Ohio side. The Governor St Clair agreed, adding for good measure that the American people were the most corrupt on earth. Rhees came face to face with an Indian, 'a good specimen', in the company of Indian Wells, an American who had been taken prisoner by the tribes when a boy, had fought with them against St Clair, but later had gone over to Wayne's army to earn a captain's pay. Shortly afterwards, a letter from Fort Wayne talked of the Wabash as the American Garden of Eden, while the mail from Philadelphia brought the gloomiest news from Europe, England and Wales. Everything seemed to conspire to make him restless. He kept riding out alone — '"Take care of your night cap" (meaning my scalp)', they shouted after him. He found more barrows, flints, shaped stones, real polished crystal, all relics of some superior race which had once lived thereabouts. Despite his choice of the Miami site, Judge Turner and the news about John Evans had evidently unsettled him. By mid-June, he had decided to push on further west. He would make for Detroit, at that moment still in British hands. This was the gateway to the Illinois, the upper Mississippi and the fur-trade fiefs of the north-west. Perhaps he intended to follow John Evans into the land of mystery.

The inescapable first step was a journey north to the army headquarters at Greenville, where the Indians were coming in for parley. For this, he needed an army escort. He was still waiting for it when the chaplain to the army himself rode into town, in the person of that redoubtable Welsh-American David Jones. When Rhees finally left with his escort on 15 June, he encountered the chaplain lying ill at a station. 'If the old man does not get better soon', ran his jovially ferocious comment, 'he will be apt, according to the sailor's phrase, to kick the bucket.' Morgan John was optimistic. The 'old man' was then 59 to Rhees's 35; he lived till he was 84, outliving several of his eight children. Rhees kicked the bucket sixteen years before Jones did. And several times in his remaining span, he must have wished that his original prophecy had proved accurate. For it was from the moment he met David

Jones that the Welsh language creeps into Rhees's journal – in a sustained, but occult, running fire of sarcastic comment on both the army and its irascible chaplain.

For David Jones came straight out of a tradition which was simultaneously American, Welsh and Baptist in the strictest connotation of those terms.[3] He was a product of the remarkable Welsh migration in the early years of the century which had created what Morgan Edwards had called 'the emigrant church', the famous Baptist community in the Welsh Tract, Pencader, in Delaware, a few miles from Newark. Prime movers in the enterprise had been the family of Morgan ap Rhydderch of Llanwenog, Cardiganshire, in south-west Wales. Rhys ap Rhydderch had been an officer in the army of Oliver Cromwell, and went over to Delaware in 1701 at the age of 81, in company with the children of his brother Morgan; they took the name Morgan as a surname in America. A second wave in 1710 brought David Jones, who lived on the Teifi and married a Rhydderch girl. Their son Morgan was the father of David Jones, who was born in 1736 and studied at Hopewell and Middleton, New Jersey (under his Morgan kinsfolk) before entering the Baptist ministry in 1761. His wife, Ann Stillwell, came of even more rooted stock. She was descended from a man who in 1631 came over in the same ship as the celebrated founder of Rhode Island, Roger Williams, whom every Baptist in Wales erroneously counted a Welsh hero.

David Jones became the pastor of a chapel in New Jersey, but his flock saw little of him. Wilderness fever gripped him early. He made two trips to the Shawnees and the Delawares on the Ohio in 1772-3, one in the company of George Rogers Clark himself. His published journal became a minor frontier classic and, in all, he made more than a dozen horseback sorties into Kentucky and the Ohio country.[4] But it was the War of Independence which made him a hero. David Jones was very Welsh and very Baptist and felt intolerably oppressed by the British government in both capacities. His sermons during the crisis year of 1775 were so fierce that the Tories chased him out. He became the minister of the Baptist church in the Great Valley of Pennsylvania and a close friend of his neighbour, 'Mad Anthony' Wayne. He served throughout the war, at first under General Horatio Gates (he named a son after the general) at Ticonderoga; later under Wayne. He was at Brandywine, Germantown, Valley Forge; he narrowly missed death at the Paoli Massacre. His famous sermon, *Defensive War in a Just Cause Sinless*, and several others, were very popular and so angered the British that they put a price on his head and wrecked his church. His favourite text was from Nehemiah, iv, 14: 'Be not ye afraid of them, remember the

Lord which is great and terrible, *fight* for your brethren, your sons, your daughters, your wives and your houses.' Entrusted with a letter from Wayne to Benjamin Franklin, he threatened to blow out the brains of any man who came near it. Anthony Wayne reported, 'my chaplain, Dr. Jones, has a peculiar faculty of making the soldiers fight well.'

Many thought he ought to have been a soldier and a frontier soldier at that. His speech was peppered with eccentricities, 'plain words and queer illustrations'. He quarrelled with Thomas Paine, as he did with most people, but was radical enough to write for the *Aurora*. 'Pronounce your words shorter,' he told his son, 'Let your voice be masculine, for a thin, squeezed-out voice is the ruin of good oratory.' The man himself was as angular as his speech. Nearly six feet, with a great beak of a nose, the 'fighting pastor' of the Great Valley always wore breeches, buckles and his hair in a pigtail. His opinions were no less old-fashioned. He refused baptism to women and children at Greenville and was later to wage a fierce controversy with Samuel Jones in defence of the laying-on-of-hands. It is characteristic that he denounced Samuel's arguments as un-Welsh, denounced the new-fangled Welsh themselves as un-Welsh. Who was this 'liberal' flibbertigibbet Samuel Jones in comparison with good old Abel Morgan? 'We have been amused with some trifling details of his correspondence with one Joshua Thomas who by his name I suppose to be a Welshman.' (This was Joshua Thomas of Leominster, the greatly respected Baptist historian of Wales), clearly no wiser than the Welsh in America, if Sam Jones was representative. Many men had laid down their lives for the laying-on-of-hands, but he supposed they were just another bunch of superstitious Welshmen! David Jones feared nobody. He volunteered again for the war of 1812, at the age of 76, denounced his commander-in-chief as a drunken fool and got him replaced.

As soon as Wayne took command of the army for the 1794 Indian campaign, Jones was off to the west (it was Jenkin David who took his place in the Great Valley).[5] He found Morgan John Rhees insufferable. Two such Welsh Baptists as these would have been hard put to it to maintain fraternal relations on the banks of the Teifi. On the Ohio, quirky old David Jones was confronted with a Welshman claiming to be a Baptist, who wanted all denominations ground to a powder, favoured Freemasons and the French, was at that very moment devising a marriage service for the Baptist churches of the west which reduced the ceremony to a civil contract, refused to swear an oath in court and cherished disturbing notions about red and black brethren. And he was no less new-fangled as an American: scarcely eight months in the country and already teaching patriot grandmothers to suck republican eggs. The relationship between David Jones and Morgan Rhees, abrasive from the start, grew into a growling feud which had direct and damaging effects on the latter's fortunes at two critical moments in his life.

For the moment, however, Morgan John simply found David Jones a nuisance, as he rode north through magnificent country, which got busier and busier as he approached Greenville. 'Dadl', he entered in his diary on the second day of their acquaintance, 'argument' — over religious establishment in the army. 'Dadl' threatened to become as familiar a word in his bold hand as 'Cloud'. But there were other matters to occupy his mind. At Fort Jefferson, he met white men who had been prisoners of the Indians for years. Two boys were going home with their father. One had his squaw with him; another, aged 19, Indian jewellery in his nose and ears, had been a prisoner for 15 years and could speak no English. His father had recognised him from a mole on his back and they had fallen weeping on each other's necks. He saw haymakers out on the prairies and marvelled at the richness of the soil. 'To a man who never saw such a thing, it would be incredible to say that the grass was near as high as my head on a horse 19 hands high!' In some ways Greenville itself was just as impressive. The fort was laid out in an oblong 600 yards by 300, four bastions at the right angles of the cantonment, with four blockhouses in the middle of the curtain wall. In the centre was the citadel with four more blockhouses and a well providing 70,000 gallons of water a day. There were plenty of gardens and many of the officers had good houses. There were not more than 1,500 soldiers there, but the picket lines were organised so cleverly that they presented a truly formidable appearance to the Indians.

Rhees was welcomed by the Commander-in-Chief, Anthony Wayne, who drank tea with him. Henceforth he was a regular guest at dinner and was treated as an officer. His relations with the military, however, grew increasingly correct, rather than warm. 'Ond yn gyntaf, rhaid i mi sylwi at un camsyniad yn y gyfraith filwriaethol,' he entered in his diary on the morning of arrival on 18 June. A capital error in the army's regulations: sentries were not permitted communication with anybody. One of the Indian chiefs had held out his hands in friendship and a sentry had spun on his heel, to the Indian's visible dismay. Better to break a law than shame an innocent stranger in this way. How typical of military rigidity! 'The Commander-in-Chief has declared that there shall be no Sunday this side of the Ohio.' Even musicians were dismissed on a Sunday, when soldiers had to work. 'But if God will not watch, who will guard the city?' As for the chaplain, he never preached more than once or twice in six months. He could not even be present at the funeral of a poor soldier. 'A chaplain in this army is a mere cypher. He does nothing as far as I can see . . . the chaplainship is a real evil.' In the end, Rhees organised private preaching and Sunday services for the officers and men who wanted them.

But this was little more than a grumbling descant in the 'British Tongue'. What really occupied him were the Indians. The 'copper-coloured brethren' at Greenville soon colonised his mind as thoroughly as the blacks in Savannah. At Greenville, he was present at a peculiarly poignant moment in the history of the Indians of the north-west. By Jay's Treaty, the British government, overriding its own local officers, had virtually abandoned to their own devices the tribes it had manipulated for so long. With thousands of settlers pressing behind, the federal army, after its victory at Fallen Timbers, was calling them in to a peace settlement which was in practice a surrender. At Greenville began that erosion which was to expel these people from history. The moment itself, however, was peculiarly tense. As the Indians came in, halting, suspicious, conscious of defeat and betrayal, anxious to please but equally anxious over their dignity, all the skills of the frontier world were demanded, that peculiar blend of firmness and flattery, the giving of presents in the correct ritual, the measured tones, the finding of the right words, skills which Wayne had in abundance. At this one brief moment when, in effect, one civilisation yielded to another, a migrant Welsh observer watched, ignorant, ill-informed, patronising in good Enlightenment style, but fascinated, his comments moving from a clinical curiosity into a half-reluctant sympathy and ending in something near admiration.

On the first day, he was the prisoner of appearances. There they sprawled, the Indians, naked most of them, except for a little rag around the middle. Others were clad in fantastic dress and forever painting themselves. He watched for over an hour as one chief painted his face in all directions, constantly admiring himself in a glass. Some of the squaws looked well, but no wonder most of them did not, since Indian women did all the work. He saw two graves with white flags streaming over them; two chiefs had fallen in a duel. Suicide was no disgrace either, one of the Seneca chiefs had killed himself here last week. The Indians would 'suffer death sooner than submit to slavery or brook great disappointments. Would to God the Negroes had more of their disposition.' At dinner with Wayne, a band played and Indians crowded around the door – music hath charms . . .

As more and more of the tribes came in, Rhees's comments grew more rewarding. It was cold on the 20th. 'Such weather will not do for an Indian to deliver an oration, for he thinks the *Great Spirit* frowns upon him at such a time.' But the pipe of peace had been kindled since the 16th and there had been one or two talks at the council house already. 'They want more whisky, even the squaws are fond of this poisonous beverage,' but after all, in many respects these men were 'mere machines'; the highest bidder purchased their favour. The spirit of revenge was so initiated into them with their mother's milk that it would be difficult to extirpate it in this generation. But Rhees saw no reason why they could not be instructed. The complexion of the children seemed docile and 'some of the squaws we visited today are remarkable handy in making neat moccasins. If these people could but put off their laziness they would learn anything. Why not?'

But there was so much to be done! They killed off the stupid and deformed without compunction, buried live infants with their dead mothers, put down the aged. The hard labour of the women checked their population growth. If women became pregnant during the hunting season, there were abortions.

What first penetrated the preacher's mind, however, was Indian oratory and the ceremony of peace-making. At five o'clock on the 21st, the firing of guns, answered by the garrison cannon, announced the approach of a large company of Indians:

The Chiefs of the Delawares and Potowatomis entered the council house in the general's garden about six. They delivered their different speeches which on this occasion were very short, though they made a long harangue of it by way of repetition. After mentioning what their forefathers had done, they thanked the Great Spirit for bringing them here to salute their brother. They had cleared the way of brambles and thorns and not listened to the voice of bad birds. They prayed the Great Spirit to give them attentive ears, enlighten their eyes and purify their hearts, that the pending treaty might be a last blessing to them and us ... The C-in-C answered them by telling them he was glad to see them all, that the ways were all now open, that the pipe of peace had already been kindled, that the Miamis, Wabash, Delawares, Wyandots etc. had smoked out of it, that some of the Shawnees were come in, that in ten days he had information that about 7,000 more to be in. That then the fire should have fresh fuel added to it and that its sparks should enlighten the heavens from the rising to the setting sun, that as they had come a long way and were fatigued, he would order them plenty of provisions and some drink to make their hearts glad. After a hearty handshake and some explanations, they parted. Both Nations were obliged to have an interpreter and they no doubt must add or diminish according to their own humour. The Indians approbated the speeches of their chiefs and interpreters by saying *Yuch*.

After this dignified ceremony, they got drunk and stayed drunk all the next day, stabbing themselves and selling their wives for a bottle of whisky. Then the Miami and Potowatomi chiefs complained they were tired of eating beef. They all wanted mutton and pork. 'They hoped as they were brothers he would treat them with a glass of wine before they parted.' The Sun, chief of the Potowatomi, said he had a pain in his bowels; they were all idle. They wanted something to divert them, something uncommon.

No sooner had Wayne calmed them with a promise of whisky and wine, than more Potowatomi and Chippaways came in from as far away as Michilimackinac and Lake Huron.

They called General Wayne *The Wind* [from his impetuosity in battle]. As soon as the voice of The Wind reached us, we made no delay but hastened to this place, to see the Great Man. We have travelled a far way and we now want rest. We hope our brother will give us something that is good to eat and drink.

The noise they made in their dancing that night was so loud that Rhees could not sleep. The next morning, however, it was dwarfed by an explosion in the laboratory where rockets were being prepared for the Fourth of July. Only rapid action saved the powder magazine and all the troops rushed to arms. A special assembly of the Indians had to be summoned to calm their instant suspicion.

By this time, Rhees was visiting the Indian camps. He witnessed the entry of the great chief Little Turtle, who had defeated St Clair. He saw an Indian boy hit a sixpenny piece with his arrow at 117 yards. One chief, leading a band of half-breeds, could talk English fluently. He found an old Delaware of 110 years of age whose wife had been baptised in Philadelphia and could speak English. They were generally too shy to talk unless they were drunk, but gradually he began to make contact. He had a long conversation with a Potowatomi who could speak French. All his children, said the chief, prayed to and feared the Great Spirit! 'Upon close examination', commented the Welshman,

I believe the Indians will be found to have a greater sense of some

kind of religion than the whites. Pity their minds were not directed
to a proper channel. If anything the difficulty in convincing them
will be their readiness to give a formal assent to everything you say!

Their speech was more accessible. He thought the repetition of the
same sounds indicated a barrenness of words, but their idioms had fewer
gutturals than German. 'The ch and th sounds sometimes like the Welsh.'
The sequel was inevitable. On 26 June, he reported, 'Began a vocabulary
of the different Indian dialects.' By the time he left, he had compiled
a fairly large dictionary, mainly of the Delaware tongue. And Indian
oratory he found very impressive:

> The Indians use a pattern of oratory for all nations. Their address is
> bold and unaffected, their motions natural and expressive of what
> they say. They speak with great warmth but keep good time inasmuch
> as they can stop when they please, for the interpreter to translate. If
> such are the dictates of nature, let us follow nature in all our public
> speaking.

This professional appraisal he followed through; he modelled his Fourth
of July oration on the Indians.

But it was a shattering incident on the eve of the Fourth which really
transformed the Welshman's attitude. Unfortunately, part of his journal
is lost and some of the detail is missing. The experience, and it was
clearly a harrowing one, can, however, be reconstructed. The Indians had
captured and brought in some deserters from the American army, while
at the same time a number of soldiers were condemned to death for a
capital offence. The Indians were horrified. They apparently thought
that it was the men they had brought in who were to die. They assembled
in large numbers to protest, the troops were called to arms and General
Wayne faced a crisis.

> He assured them that those condemned men were not the same as
> those brought in but other, very bad men. He further said they
> would not die perhaps whilst the Indians were still here. He called
> for the chaplain and told the Indians he had committed those con-
> demned to the care of this man, to prepare and make them fit, by
> whitening their heads, to go to the Great Spirit. This is the only job
> the chaplain has had to do since I have been here and I am afraid
> without some superior assistance he has a hard task to begin with.
> Question: would it not be better to preach oftener to the soldiers

and endeavour to prevent crimes than to trust to the chaplain to send them well to the kingdom of heaven by preparing their heads and making them white with a few days' exhortation to repent?

But how I admired the Indians' oratory and argument! Whether it was out of superstition or humanity, it is not for me to determine. This I am sure of, that they have human feelings as well as other men. Perhaps it is not so much the love of cruelty but the barbarous customs of their nations that makes them brutalize prisoners so much in time of war. They have no idea of punishing in time of peace! but will share the last morsel of bread they have even with an enemy. O that the time, the set time has come to introduce the Gospel in its purity among them!

The experience, however patronising the terms in which he described it, obviously moved him. He spent a day reading in his tent and 'composing rhapsodies'. It came at a critical moment. For the morrow was Independence Day. He rode on the review between the ranks with the staff, as the cannon fired their salute. He dined with Wayne and his officers and drank the toasts; to the men of 1776, to the heroes who had fallen, to George Washington and to the French Republic. He delivered his Oration to the garrison, and on the 5th read an Address on *The Altar of Peace*. Both were published in 1798, the latter appropriately by the Missionary Society of Philadelphia.[6]

The Oration was largely ejaculatory:

O FRANCE: although I do not justify thy excesses, I venerate thy magnanimity ... INVINCIBLE FRENCHMEN! go on! ... The Popish beast has numbered his days ... Infatuated Britons! I feel for your insanity, although four thousand miles from your coast ... ANCIENT BRITONS! [footnote: The Welsh people] awake out of sleep! Open your eyes! Why are your tyrants great? Because you kneel down and cringe to them. Rise up. You are their equals! If you cannot rise, creep to the ocean and the friendly waves will waft you over the Atlantic to the hospitable shores of America ... Quit the little despotic island which gave you birth and leave the tyrants and the slaves of your country to live and die together ... Citizens and Soldiers of America! ... Banish from your land the remains of slavery!

and much more in the same vein.

In the Address, however, he got down to brass tacks. Significantly, it was the first time he had *read* a sermon. He blamed it on hoarseness and weariness, but perhaps the content had something to do with it. It was basically a plea for reconciliation with, and good treatment of, the Indian. Gideon, when going forth to war, had erected an altar to the God of Peace. This should be the model for the American army in the west.

> The philanthropist is every person's neighbour, the White, the Black, the Red, are alike to him; he recognises in each a brother . . . he knows how to make allowances for the prejudices of nations and individuals . . . In order to establish a durable peace, some sacrifices must be made on both sides. The love of conquest and enlargement of territory should be sacrificed — every nation or tribe having an indefeasible right of soil, as well as a right to govern themselves in what manner they think proper; for which reason the United States *purchase* the right of soil from the Indians . . . The desire of revenge should be immediately offered on the altar of forgiveness, even though thy brother transgress against thee seventy times seven in a day. Rational preachers ought to be employed to remove the ancient suspicions of the Indians, give them just notions of the great spirit, and teach them rules of moral rectitude. I am aware something more is wanted: unless husbandry and the mechanical arts be introduced with those missionaries, they will never be able to prevail on them to quit their ancient customs and manners. Government should therefore interfere and assist . . .
>
> Tis to be lamented that the Frontiers of America have been peopled in many places by men of bad morals . . . certain it is, that there are a great number of white as well as red savages. It will therefore be necessary to have such communications with the different tribes as to convince them of the good will of Americans in general . . . some Americans might have their residence in the Indian towns and the Indians, in like manner, reside in some of the principal towns on the frontiers . . . the Americans and Indians would become one people . . . Let us join the Indians in praying that the *Great Spirit* may enlighten their eyes and purify their hearts, give them a clear sky and smooth water, guard them against the bad birds, and remove the briars from their paths, protect them from the dogs of war, that they may never attend to their barking, but continue to keep the bloody hatchet in the ground and smoke the calumet of peace, until its odours perfume the air.

This, to a victorious American army determined to end the Indian menace in the north-west once and for all and to liberate the tide of settlement dammed up along the Ohio. 'Prudence is a rascally virtue,' said Rhees's friend Dr Benjamin Rush.

Whatever Indians might have thought of the discourse, many of the Americans present did not like it at all. David Jones was furious. This kind of talk from an ignorant newcomer was totally unfit for American ears. At dinner in the mess that evening there was an unholy row. Morgan John thought 'the poor chaplain . . . well roasted', but the mess dinners vanish from his journal. A man convicted of stealing a dozen bells was given a hundred lashes and then paraded around the camp with the bells tied about him. Rhees protested. 'What is Man?' He was present when they all smoked the pipe of peace at a conference of the chiefs which decided to postpone the treaty until all the sachems were in, but the Welshman had become *persona non grata* at headquarters.

And on 10 July, his diary carried the decisive entry:

> *The Retreat.* A British drummer, being taken prisoner by the French, was ordered to beat a retreat. 'A Retreat?', said he, 'there is no such march in the British army!' But the case is altered of late. The English at present have no occasion to learn any other march. It is with reluctance that I follow their example and it is owing to their rascality that I am obliged to retreat from Greenville to Cincinatti.

The occasion for his withdrawal is in fact obscure. He blamed the British at Detroit for continuing to stir up the tribes, despite the peace, thus making it impossible for a peaceable traveller to go on — 'Britannia blush! and endeavour to restore thy lost character by banishing thy courtiers where they sent the immortal patriots of 1793, Muir, Palmer, Skirving, Margarot and Gerrald!' But he linked with this — 'the jealousy of Jones'. It is quite clear that David Jones had a hand in it, no doubt Rhees's Address of 5 July also had its effect. For whatever combination of reasons, the route to the Illinois was closed. There was nothing for it but to return to the eastern states. After all, he had to be about his people's business.

He left on 10 July and he left in high spirits. He often enjoyed a good row and besides, friendly Cincinatti lay ahead. His three companions were very jumpy, startling at any sound, seeing Indians and rattlesnakes everywhere. Rhees, however, thought the rattlesnakes themselves were coming in for peace talks and his tone becomes whimsical. On watch one night, he was attacked by a host of enemies, who with their hostile weapons infuse poison into my flesh from head to foot. Although, Quixote-like, I destroy them by hundreds, the barbarians renew their attack and force me to lie down enwrap'd in my blanket, for fear of another invasion by a host of *royal* gnats and *aristocratical* mosquitoes.

At least his saddle and blanket made a better pillow than Jacob's.

It was in this light spirit that he cantered into genial Cincinatti just in time for Bastille Day. He had, after all, as he put it, 'stood on the ruins of the Bastille in Paris and felt the energy of those principles which shake Europe to the centre'. On this auspicious day, he announced (to himself) that he was formally 'taking possession' of the Miami lands on the Ohio as the Canaan of the Welsh People.

That day saw an equally propitious encounter. For, in Cincinatti, Rhees met James McKay. The Scotsman, having been appointed commander of its third expedition by the Missouri Company in St Louis, had been arranging for supplies and settling his affairs. He was passing through from New York to begin his three-year stint in Louisiana. This fortunate encounter warmed both men. 'It afforded me much pleasure', Rhees wrote home later, 'to meet with a man of his disposition and information engaged in the Indian trade.' McKay, in turn, found Rhees 'a worthy gentleman'. They talked long about John Evans and the Welsh Indians. McKay had doubts about the latter and could recognise none of the Welsh words Rhees mentioned. But he promised to keep his eyes open, to send regular reports, and to do all he could to help John Evans. He wrote later on:

> Though, during my former tour in the North West and upper part of the Missouri, I had heard nothing of a Welch tribe, I believed the Possibility of their existance and considering the light such a discovery might throw on the History of America was determined to use all the means in my Power to unveil the mystery. On my way from New York to Louisiana in 1794 [*sic*] I met a worthy Gentleman, Dr. John Rees, who, after informing him of my intended expedition, furnished me with a small vocabulary of the Welsh language written by himself, and informed me respecting a Mr. John Evans from Wales who was gone to the Illinois with the intention of travelling westward to see the supposed Welch tribe.[7]

On 15 July, Morgan John Rhees reluctantly crossed the Ohio into Kentucky and directed Primrose towards that distant Mecca, Rhode

Island, 'the sacred island of Roger Williams'. James McKay, armed with his Welsh vocabulary and the introduction to John Evans, set off down the Ohio to St Louis, to take charge of the last and most sustained Spanish effort to break through to the Pacific.

Notes

1. On this phase of John Evans's mission, see my *Madoc: the Making of a Myth* (Eyre Methuen, London, 1980), Chapter 9.

2. For Rhees's stay on the Ohio, I have used his Diary (now only in its rough, on-the-spot form) from 5 May to 16 July 1795, a section entirely omitted from J.T. Griffith's published version.

3. For David Jones, apart from the *Dictionary of American Biography* and the histories of the Baptists, I have relied on the rich historical records of the Great Valley Baptist Church, especially the copious genealogical and anecdotal transcripts of Isaac Cleaver and the Monthly Meeting Register 1790-1823. See also Louis H. Everts, *A History of Chester County* (1881). I am grateful to the pastor of Great Valley Baptist, Rev. Chester T. Winters, for his help with the church records and for his papers, lectures and collections on David Jones, whose lively biographer he is.

4. David Jones, *A Journal of Two Visits Made to Some Nations of Indians on the West Side of the River Ohio in the Years 1772 and 1773* (1774).

5. Great Valley Baptist Church, Monthly Meeting Register, February 1795-December 1798.

6. *An Oration Delivered at Greenville, Head-quarters of the Western Army, North-west of the Ohio on 4 July 1795* (Lang and Ustick, Philadelphia, 1798); *The Altar of Peace, Being the Substance of a Discourse Delivered in the Council House at Greenville, July 5th 1795, Before the Officers of the American Army and Major General Wayne*; prefixed by an address of the Missionary Society (Ephraim Conrad, Philadelphia, 1798).

7. For this encounter, see M.J. Rhees—William Owen, 24 November 1795, NLW 13222, fo. 461, printed in *Cambrian Register*, vol. i (1796), pp. 379-80 and in *National Library of Wales Journal*, vol. ii (1942), pp. 137-8, and James McKay, 'Indian Tribes', note 4, MS. in William Clark collection, Missouri Historical Society, St Louis; 1794 must be a slip, as Rhees was still in England in July 1794.

6 GROUNDING THE LAND OF LIBERTY

In August 1795, James McKay and John Evans nosed their four pirogues out from St Louis into the great river in one of the most memorable expeditions of western exploration.[1] Today, it is the memorials to Lewis and Clark which march along the Missouri; they have blotted out the memory of McKay's great enterprise and turned poor John Evans into the strangest ghost of that river of legend. In fact, the expedition was in every way comparable to that celebrated exploration and for as long as there were Spaniards in North America, they at least remembered it. 'The two most famous travellers of the northern countries of this continent,' a Governor of New Orleans called the pair in 1798 and, at the time, he was perfectly correct. As late as 1801, a man in the Governor's Office in New Orleans referred in pride and admiration to

> the struggle of *Sieur* Evans, agent of the company in 1796 to cause the British flag to be lowered among the Mandan tribe, when he caused that of His Catholic Majesty to be hoisted while on his expedition to find the Western Sea. In this, the English were repulsed, with the aid of the savage tribes, who from that hour, acknowledged the standard of His Majesty.

This man was also correct. In a minuscule struggle in the depth of a North Dakota winter, at the most western spearpoint of European enterprise in the Americas, John Evans won a victory of major imperial significance. He held the Mandans for Spain and they passed with Louisiana to the Americans. In the process he made himself an important pioneer of American geography; the great map of the Missouri which he prepared was of critical assistance to Lewis and Clark when they made their famous crossing to the Pacific nine years later.

He was deputy to a man who knew his business. Born in Scotland in 1759 to a family which claimed ancestors among the Irish nobility and at least one king, McKay had emigrated in 1776. A skilled western trader and wilderness man, widely experienced in the Canadian northwest, McKay had reached the Mandans from Canada in 1787, before he transferred his allegiance to Spain. A forceful, stubborn and imaginative man, his *Instructions* to John Evans were directly copied by President Jefferson for the Lewis and Clark expedition.

The thinking behind the expedition was sound. Two of the boats carried goods to buy their way through the Sioux and the lower tribes, a third was to sweeten the Mandans and the fourth was to sustain John Evans whom McKay personally chose to make the final leap to the Pacific. In 44 days they reached the Otos, found them in a state of rebellion and reduced them to order. As the winter gales set in, they reached the Omaha and were locked in endless wrangles with the wily and unscrupulous Black Bird. He milked them of their goods in sustained blackmail, but McKay established good relations with him, for he promised to bring all the lower tribes to obedience and to clear a way through the Sioux. By November the party was stuck among the Omaha, where they raised the first of the proposed chain of forts. They were faced with starvation and McKay organised a buffalo hunt. To lead it, he chose John Evans. The man from Waunfawr was away for 25 days, leading the hunt through the snowy prairies west of the Missouri. Characteristically he has left no record of this experience: did his eyes strain for footprints of the Madogwys? When he got back to the fort, the Missouri had frozen solid and McKay had come to the critical decision to hang on there for a promised assembly of the southern tribes and to send John Evans on ahead. The *Instructions* he drafted for John embodied a full imperial and scientific programme, but the Welshman's first sortie, in February 1796, was abortive. Some 300 miles from base, he ran into a war party of Sioux and was chased all the way back.

McKay summoned up Black Bird, got a parley with the Sioux and bought a clear passage. He scraped together all the trade goods that he could spare and committed them to John Evans. In June, the Welshman set out again. He made slow going, against the river and on his celebrated survey, was held up for weeks by the genial but stubborn Arikara, but (a demonstration of his skill, for he proved himself something of a genius with Indians) managed to talk them into letting him and some of his goods go. On 24 September 1796, John Evans finally reached the Mandan Indians, to be received as a hero. He deserved his day of triumph. He was the first white man effectively to reach them up the Missouri, the first to break the Sioux and Omaha blockade. He was the first to raise the standard of Spain which these Indians had not yet seen (doing so a week before Britain and Spain went to war back in Europe). At that moment, John Evans stood at the very rim of European empire in the Americas. Had the Spaniards been able to equip him properly, he might well have made that classic crossing by land to the Pacific a decade before Lewis and Clark. As it was, in a darkening autumn with the worst winter in the world closing in, John Evans at last came face to face with the reality of those White Padoucas who had stared up at him from all those maps back home.

At much the same time, hundreds of miles to the south-east, twenty Welshmen, axes in their hands, were confronting the hills, creeks and dense forests of Blacklick and the Connemaugh which were the reality of that *Gwladfa* which they had left a half-starved, angry and sometimes desperate Wales to build.

The launching of a *Gwladfa*, a national home for the Welsh, in western Pennsylvania, was as unexpected as it was abrupt. Its planting was the product of a conjuncture of forces stronger than the will of any individual, however dedicated. In July 1795, Morgan John Rhees had chosen the Ohio lands around the Miami mouth, within striking distance of the Missouri and the Padoucas, as the promised land. Within a year, however, the cross currents of an Atlantic world set in motion by the crisis of the French Revolution had driven him off course.

Until he reached the Atlantic states, Morgan John's return journey from Cincinatti in 1795 had been tedious.[2] Lexington he found as repulsive as when he had first seen it and he once more lost a night's sleep on the wilderness march, though this time because he was 'plagued by an old fiddler and a parcel of block-heads beating their stumps on the ground'. The party lost their boats in the Cumberland and Primrose had to swim, but otherwise, the trip was long, uneventful and dreary. He had time to muse on the extraordinary size of American raindrops, a good half as large again as the European variety. In this they paralleled American sermons: an hour and a half was counted a short stint. Preachers were peculiarly stretched by a sensational disaster at Alexandria, Virginia, where 27 people had been drowned crossing the river 'owing to drunkenness and contention'.[3]

Contention there was in plenty as soon as he reached the settled districts. In every township, John Jay's effigy was burning, for the terms of the Jay Treaty with Britain had been leaked and the country was in uproar. Morgan moved through the storms unperturbed until he reached Boston. New York had been devastated by fever and he had lost many friends, but much of September and October he spent in New England, revelling in its churches and colleges. Harvard's 14,000 books pleased him, but Yale lacked a good modern library. Rhode Island and its college were pure bliss, with the 'poor and despised Baptists' at last 'elevated above their neighbours'. The women were charming, too, and in Boston such veritable nymphs that it was small wonder that 'the inhabitants of this country are running a race as it were against time in the road to every manner of corruption.'[4]

It was in Boston, however, that he was deafened by the blasts of political controversy, the newspapers shrill and hoarse against each other 'with their trash of Jacobites, *Jacobins*, Aristocrats, Democrats, Federalists, anti-ditto and, worse than all, personal abuse'. He ran into the celebrated geographer Jedidiah Morse, who'd been clouted in the head while arguing with a crowd burning Jay's effigy: 'I wonder they did not knock your brains out . . . O, they could not do that, for if I had any brains, I would not have gone near them.'[5]

Morgan John was moving through a decisive moment in the revolutionary decade.[6] The new American republic, ringed and hemmed in by the British with their trading hegemony and their client Indians, by the Spaniards deploying their Indians to hold the south and deny Kentuckians access to the Mississipi, was trying to force its way in a world of mercantilist empires. As the new constitution went into effect, conflict broke out between Republicans and Federalists, as the former fought the Bank, the Debt, the 'Anglo-Saxon' policies of Alexander Hamilton. This fierce struggle assumed a whole new dimension under the impact of the French Revolution and when the flamboyant Citizen Genet, a Girondin, arrived as French representative, large crowds greeted him and Democratic societies of revolutionary temper mushroomed. It was Genet who enrolled George Rogers Clark and his *French* army in the west. He issued licences for privateers wholesale and unofficial sea war broke out between America and the Britain which was already being denounced for its commercial stranglehold and for its refusal to give up its posts within the north-west which had formally been ceded to the USA, but which the British retained as compensation for the American failure to make restitution to dispossessed Loyalists.

Faced with a threat of war with Britain alongside revolutionary France, fuelled by the passionate internal conflict, Washington and the Federalists took the desperate decision to come to terms with the British through their emissary John Jay. Jay's Treaty stopped the sea war, secured a British promise to abandon the posts (and the Ohio Indians) by June 1796, but dropped America's claims to freedom of the seas and seemed to accept the new republic's client status *vis-à-vis* the old country. To Republicans already deeply affronted by Hamilton's policies, it seemed a final betrayal, while Federalists, already in arms against a threat of *'sans-culotte'* revolution, were in turn revolted by Edmund Randolph's intrigues with the French Minister. The struggle to ratify the Jay Treaty rocked the republic. By April 1796, it had been done. By this time, the religious denominations had turned violently against the French Revolution and the election of John Adams as

President in 1796 opened several years of party conflict so severe that it seemed to threaten the cohesion of the state.

After Jay's Treaty, it was with France that unofficial sea war raged and the French attempt to bribe American envoys in the XYZ affair unleashed a gale of Federalist loyalism, whipped on by the vituperative expatriate William Cobbett, who pasted a huge portrait of George III in his Philadelphia window and created an American gutter press.[7] The crisis reached a paroxysm in the Alien and Sedition Acts of 1798, a campaign against *Jacobin* immigrants, British, Irish and French, a drive against Republican journalists and a thrust for war with France. Cobbett called for a spiritual renunciation of 1776 and got a surprising response; there was an attempt to replace the 4 July with the celebration of Washington's birthday. In riposte, the Virginia and Kentucky Resolutions against the Alien and Sedition Acts threatened secession. It was John Adams's break with his own party, his courageous despatch of a peace mission to France, which stopped the war clamour and threw open the bitter and hard-fought election of 1800, when Thomas Jefferson, supported by a massive inflow of the unpolitical into politics and, said aggrieved Federalists, by the massed votes of *Jacobin* immigrants, won through to the presidency in a 'second revolution', dismantled the Federalist party, though not the institutions it had created and managed to evoke a temporary consensus, nourished by western expansion and almost frenetic commercial growth in seas swept clear of rivals by the British fleet.

It was through these storms that the frail bark of the Welsh *Gwladfa* had to butt its way. His 'engagements to my own people and to Savannah' had spurred Morgan John on his way to the eastern states, but in Boston and New York, endless days of political argument distracted him. The men of the cloth were very hot for Jay and against democrats and Rhees teased them with quotations from Republican papers. What did these pestilential words 'Aristocrat' and 'Democrat' mean? In the Boston dining-room of Jedidiah Morse, Rhees flourished one set of definitions before gimlet clerical eyes:[8]

A mbitious	D ecent
R obber and	E nticing
I mpudent	M odest
S lovenly	O bliging
T urbulent	C areful
O utrageous	R eligious and
C rafty	A miable

R igorous	T radesman
A rtful	or other good citizen who wishes
T urk	a government founded on the
or one who wants an arbitrary	rights of the people, or one who
government and a share in the	endeavours to support such a one
administration thereof.	when established.

This modest and impartial characterisation had him arguing the toss all the way back to Philadelphia, which he reached by November. Argument did not stop there. Rhees threw himself into the lively Baptist and political world of the capital, made friends with Dr Benjamin Rush, shortly to be mercilessly pilloried by Cobbett in his *Porcupine's Gazette*, and resumed the fight for a purified and rational faith he had fought in Wales. He gladly paid thirty pence for Washington's epaulets but found too many men 'stretched the string of orthodoxy too tight'.[9] His temper was shorter than ever: 'Heavens! what narrow contracted minds some men have! It will take their snail creeping souls an eternity to crawl round a nutshell!' The marriage service had become something of an obsession with him. His yearning for a civil ceremony had surfaced several times in the western territories and at one service he exploded —

As for telling a parcel of trash after the clergyman, I take thee Mary — and I take thee John, for better or for worse etc., it must be ridiculous in the sight of sensible men ... Have a written contract and let the man and woman sign the same in the presence of witnesses, then the magistrate or minister pronounce them married without further ceremony.[10]

This latter assertion was soon to be put to its severest test. For in the First Baptist Church, Philadelphia, he had met Ann Loxley and, at her father's famous house in Spruce Street, by the Rev. Thomas Ustick, A.M., he was married to her in 1796, on the evening of 22 February — 'Being the anniversary of the Nativity of the Illustrious George Washington'.[11]

Morgan Rhees married a woman of character, charity and courage.[12] She was to become a mighty figure in Philadelphia religion and, in widowhood, raised a large family to a rich and respected adult achievement. It is difficult to penetrate to her through the formidable piety which encases her letters. After Morgan John's death, she wrote a rather unfortunate poem in two parts, *The Widow's Lament*, which is equally impenetrable. Rarely does the human being break through to visibility. 'I feel now', she wrote to her sister in 1806, 'that my heart was too much devoted to its darling idol and acknowledge the justice of God in removing him far from me.'

Marriage on Washington's birthday was perhaps an appropriate ritual, for in marrying Ann Loxley, Morgan John married into a tradition. If anyone could be said to embody in person an American revolutionary tradition, it was her father, Colonel Benjamin Loxley:[13]

> My father's name [wrote Ben Loxley in his journal], was Benjamin Loxley of Wakefield in Yorkshire in Old England, son of an ancient line of Loxleys in them parts . . . Industrious. Sober. Religious church-men and good warriors in defence of their Rights and Priviligous. My mother's name Elizabeth Loxley a daughter of Richard Pullan and Elisabeth his wife. A large and numerous family. Verry industrious. Farmers and Linnen weavers and Bleachers in Yorkshire near Nais-burra and Pately Brigs, Harrigate Spaws, Leeds and Bradford etc. Sober. Religious and Right Down Englishmen.[14]

In 1733, when Ben was 13, his uncle Francis Pullan came over from the Brandywine and offered his American farm to any of his nephews who went back with him. Only Ben would go. Lodged on his uncle's farm at Darby near Philadelphia, he was trained by Jenkin Jones the Baptist minister and apprenticed himself as a carpenter and joiner to Joseph Watkins of Abergavenny ('in Wales', as Colonel Loxley observes with commendable precision).[15] Free on 31 July 1742, young Ben started business on his own: 'I had a choice chest of tools and Books of Archatecture, an Bible and Psalm Book. NB the Tools were Saws, Augers, Bitts, Axes, Adzes etc such as I could not make myself – to the amount of £35-7-1½.' Though his uncle left him 'a great deal short' of what had been promised, 'I went on well and got plenty of work, good pay, many apprentices and servants.' He certainly did. Marriage to his master's niece, by whom he had three children, no doubt helped. She died in 1760 and he took as second wife Catherine, daughter of John Cox, a substantial farmer in Freehold, New Jersey, by whom he had twelve children. By the end of his life, Ben Loxley was still calling himself a 'house carpenter' (just as that wealthy Duplay with whom Robespierre lodged called himself a 'cabinet-maker': a trait common to such men as Thomas Hardy and Alexander Galloway the English *Jacobins*, like Ben Loxley type-figures of the new democracy of an old regime).[16] In fact he had become a renowned and successful building and engineering employer. When he drew up his will in 1784, he owned not only his celebrated house in Spruce Street (from whose balcony

George Whitefield preached and in which, when it was occupied by British officers during the War of Independence, the Quaker Lydia Darrach made herself a heroine) but a street of houses to its rear built of the red and black glazed brick he had brought from England; at least a dozen other houses in the heart of the city, tracts and plots elsewhere, a 200-foot wharf on the river, a small plantation in New Providence in the Bahamas, a farm nearby and some land on the Monongahela near Pittsburgh, managed by the Rev. John Corbly who was well informed about Welsh Indians.

That land had been pillaged by Indians during the war and Ben Loxley had suffered severe financial loss. For in the war he had made himself something of a hero. He recorded:

> In 1739 and 1740 I learnt Blakeney's Exercise of Gov. George Thomas and was chose an officer in the Melighia and at our Fort all through the Spanish war until 1747 . . . In 1755, after General Braddock's Defeat, I learnt Labratory Works and Gunery . . . I borrowed 4 cannon 4 lbers of Captain Andrew Hodge and mounted them on Traveling Carts and began the Artillery Company of Philadelphia.

As commander of the Philadelphia artillery, he served during the Seven Years' War (French and Indian War) and when the British came to confiscate the guns in 1765, he managed to hide everything except an 8-inch mortar, 'which they stole away privately and gave us plain hints that it would not be long before the British Army would visit America in a Different Manner than they had done to fight the French'. In 1775, 'when the Inhabitants of America found that the parlament of England was determined to Oppress and Chain down America to their Arbitrary wills', Ben Loxley was elected from Dock ward to Philadelphia's Committee of Safety: 'I was uneasy. I thought it was dangerous for me on acct of the Oaths I had taken to King George at the 3 times when I rec'd commissions under him (that I should be perjur'd).' He talked it over with some of his old comrades of the French war and 'we judg'd that King George had broke his Corronation Oath with us wherein He engag'd to protect all his subjects in free liberty of Conscience and lawful Rights and now he had broke that promise.'

Ben Loxley was very active during the war. He ran the Philadelphia artillery and arms works, took out his guns on 'shallops' to fight British ships. With his company at Amboy, he crept up to a British post, dropped a shell down the chimney 'and made the rascals scamper'. More: not only did he run a famous manufactory, he was appointed to manage the

Continental Army's arms laboratory, evacuating it when British troops came in sight of his house, performing further heroic deeds with his son (the Captain Loxley so affectionately remembered by a generation of Welsh Baptists) and suffering losses which he put at £6,000.

This personification of Poor Richard was, needless to say, a close friend of Benjamin Franklin's. He was in fact Franklin's technician. He made all Franklin's apparatus, often being awoken in the small hours to do so. In his own house, he kept a telescope, a camera obscura and 'an electrical machine'. Franklin's famous kite, with which he conducted his experiments in electricity, was a Loxley kite. It passed to his daughter Ann and was for years a feature of Morgan John Rhees's household.[17]

Morgan John married into a remarkably numerous family, a whole clan reared in one tradition which was fitting itself naturally into another, sending merchants and ship-captains into the Atlantic trade and stalwarts into the Jeffersonian Republicans. Benjamin Loxley junior commanded the *Pigou* and the *Penn*, vital instruments of the Baptist transatlantic international. One of the daughters married Lloyd Jones, captain and part-owner of the *Benjamin Franklin*, whose brother William was to serve as Jeffersonian Secretary to the Treasury. Ironically enough, it was Lloyd Jones's ship which was to carry the distinguished Frenchmen, including Volney, who were expelled under the Alien and Sedition Acts of 1798. He was given a signed testimonial by the Frenchmen in praise of his handling of the ship when it ran aground off Bordeaux.[18]

Morgan John followed Ann Loxley into Philadelphia's First Baptist Church which was a Loxley church, too, in the sense that Colonel Loxley had built it. And though the Welshman died in far-off Somerset county, his body was brought back to the Loxley family vault which Colonel Loxley had also built. Perhaps Morgan John may have felt at times that the universe was peopled by Loxleys, but they were clearly congenial, even if Colonel Loxley had 'a negro man Cuff' whom he bequeathed to his wife.[19] Morgan's first son was called John Loxley, taking precedence over the later Benjamin Rush and Thomas Jefferson Rhees; Ann Loxley he obviously cherished.

But by the spring of 1796, there was work for a Welshman, even a newly married one. It was on 5 October 1795 that the First Baptist Church of Philadelphia addressed an urgent letter to the local Association, demanding concerted action to deal with the unprecedented number of immigrants, particularly from Wales.[20] The celebrated Welsh Society of the city (which enrolled most of the elite of Philadelphia as 'honorary Welshmen') was revived — Morgan John was to write its new constitution in 1798 — precisely to deal with the newcomers.[21] For, after a lapse of forty years, the Welsh were once more coming into the eastern ports by the boatload. In an irresistible tide, which must have gladdened the shade of William Jones Llangadfan, the People were quitting their Egyptian task-masters and heading for Canaan. Their Moses had to be about his business.

Already, in the previous autumn, he had run into many of them. At Baltimore, on 23 August 1795, he had found enough Welsh newcomers to preach to in their own language. In New York, early in September, a crowd of Welshmen begged him for a sermon in the old tongue — 'Oh my countrymen, my poor countrymen. May God provide for you.' When he got back to the city in the middle of October, he ran into another bunch, just in from south Wales (at least 70 left Caernarvon in north Wales for New York that year). They were locked into 'a long conversation . . . What will become of us? O God! let the cloud move before us and lead us where the bounds of our habitation are fixed!'[22]

And even as Morgan John got back to Dr Samuel Jones's house at the end of October 1795, another and rather remarkable shipload of Cambro-Britons was coming up the Bay.[23] This was the *Maria* of Salem, no less than thirteen weeks out from Bristol, having run through a violent storm which dismasted her and before an Algerian corsair which pursued her. Now, as he sighted the Delaware, the captain turned in relief to his leading passenger and said, 'Well, Mr. Lloyd, there's no need to preach and pray any more. We come from the sea to the river.' Whereupon, as Mr Lloyd pointed out with some satisfaction, the *Maria* ran aground.

The mariner seems to have been under some strain. His ship was packed with Nonconformists from every corner of Wales. This was the company which was to prove decisive in the launching of the Welsh *Gwladfa*. The leader of the immigrants was Rees Lloyd, a Congregationalist minister from Pontypool in Monmouthshire. There were 'iron-men' from south Wales among the migrants; the Gwilym family of Cefn Amann were to be the first men to make iron west of the Alleghenies. Thomas Watkin Jones was taking people from Breconshire. There were a cluster of families from Llanbrynmair and the home district of William Jones Llangadfan. For it was on this ship that Ezekiel Hughes, who had first started on his project in 1793, at last reached the promised land.

After the conference with Morgan John Rhees at Llanbrynmair in the summer of 1794, Ezekiel Hughes had organised his vanguard party. This time, clearly, he meant to avoid Liverpool. He went to Bristol and arranged with the American owners of the *Maria* to pick up his party at

Carmarthen, in the spring of 1795. There was some delay and Hughes had to make a second trip. It was probably about this time that Rees Lloyd and the south Wales parties booked their passage in the same ship. Ezekiel Hughes's small group quit Llanbrynmair in July 1795, as the country was lurching into the desperate food shortage of that year. With Hughes went Edward Bebb and George Roberts and a dozen other young people, including four girls. They walked to Carmarthen but found the *Maria* was too big to get up the river. They piled into a small local craft piloted by William Hugh, but on a walk into the town, the men were suddenly threatened by the press gang. Thousands of people poured into the streets (Carmarthen was renowned for riot) and a merchant begged the migrants to hide, since 3,000 men were ready to fight the press gang if they laid hands on Hughes's party. The men loaded the women and baggage on to Hugh's ship and started to walk to Bristol. When they reached that city after four days, they heard that William Hugh's ship lay becalmed at Llanstephan. The women were stuck there for three weeks. Finally they started to walk themselves. No sooner had they left than the wind changed and Hugh's ship sailed. The women walked on but when they reached Bristol, found that the *Maria* itself had sailed with the new wind. The latter encountered William Hugh's ship in mid-channel, but he refused to hand over the luggage without proper warrant. The *Maria*, which had covered a hundred miles, turned back to within a dozen miles of Bristol. Hughes and George Roberts went aboard William Hugh's craft for Bristol, where they found the desperate women, who had hired a boat in a futile attempt to catch them. 'I think that day was the most unpleasant in my life,' said George Roberts fifty years later.

Rees Lloyd took command of the party, but their troubles had hardly begun. After a couple of weeks out, they were fired at by two British warships flying the French flag and boarded. For some hours, the migrants did not know whether they were to be taken prisoners by the French or pressed into the British navy, but after some hesitation, the officers allowed them to proceed. They were seasick all the way and in mid-passage, a sudden hurricane hit the ship so hard that it keeled over, its mast-head hitting the water, its mainmast splintering and its sails ripping. Rees Lloyd was hurled over the boats and nearly lost, saving himself by brute strength (and prayer). The mate, whose language turned the air blue around the Calvinist Welsh, called on God to damn his soul to Hell even more rapidly than usual, according to George Roberts, fell 'quite silent with his face blackish', according to Rees Lloyd. No sooner were they clear of this storm than the Algerian pirate hove into sight. Rees Lloyd climbed into a boat, turned his head to the gunwhales and prayed it off course. After this, Philadelphia on a late October night, with people from the Welsh and immigrant societies coming aboard with leaflets and the Welsh churches in the Great Valley waiting, was in truth a city of brotherly love: 'Although I had not been able to weep when leaving home, it was easy to let the tears fall now as I read these loving greetings in a foreign land.'

Party after party went through similar travail. 'The only news that this country affords', wrote Robert Williams of Llandudno to William Owen on 21 January 1796, 'is that a vessel sails from Carnarvon to America this month with about 300 Emigrants all Inhabitants of Carnarvonshire, Anglesey or Denbighshire.'[24] In the March of that year, William Richards Lynn was back in his beloved south-west Wales. He spent much of the month writing letters to Dr Samuel Jones in Philadelphia on behalf of emigrants who were leaving Cardiganshire and Carmarthenshire by the score. From St Dogmael's, near Cardigan, he wrote for Simon James, a weaver, elder at Blaen-y-waun Baptist and experienced itinerant preacher through north Wales: 'Where is this new country which you are going to secure to the Welsh and how are the poor moneyless emigrants to get thither?' A few days later, he was writing from St Clears in Carmarthenshire for Theophilus Rees, a man 'with a competent share of property' but with 'the disadvantage of knowing but little English'. He, with his family of eleven, were setting out with many other Baptists, 'together with a number of Presbyterians and other serious people to the number of six or seven score'. Baptists and other 'serious people' were multiplying hand over fist in a glorious revival, but so many of them were selling up and heading for America. There was much for Richards to do, but he was 'forced to return to hateful England' ... would that he could join them in 'your happy country' (in whose funds he had already invested £800). This party seems to have sailed from Milford Haven in Captain Williams's *Amphion* and to have reached New York in May. Like the people of the *Maria* they moved out into the Great Valley and around Philadelphia. They were delivering their letters to Samuel Jones during June and July and many of them made the long trek to launch Beula in the autumn.[25]

And from 1794 onwards through the decade, from chapel meeting and *gymanfa* and association, in every denomination, rises the same lament ... losses ... gaps ... departure of the brethren, from Ebenezer in Anglesey, from Dolbenmaen, from Rhydwilym, from Aberduar ...

Christmas Evans in Anglesey, master of the new pulpit style, raised his organ voice in protest: 'Ysbryd America yn trallodi yr Eglwys' —

'The Spirit of America afflicts the Church.' He denounced the Two Clever Talkers who were corrupting the Godly in Wales — 'Mr Gwladaethwr a Mr Mynd i America' — Mr Politician and Mr Go-to-America.[26] To read the Welsh-American correspondence of these years is an unnerving experience. Not only are family after family, sometimes whole communities, uprooting themselves. A whole people seems to be yearning to move. This, of course, is gross exaggeration. It was peculiarly a movement of Dissent, in the fullest sense of the word, and numbers, in any absolute terms, were not large. But in so small and self-conscious a people as the Welsh, the impact was shattering. 'Memorandum', runs one special entry in a parish register in the north-western peninsula of Llŷn, a remote and self-contained community of fishermen and small farmers faced with a threat of enclosure that was to bring them out into insurrection within a few years: 'Memorandum: that about twelvescore people emigrated from Llun to North America from the year 1795 to the year 1800 and that great many of them settled near Fort Skuyler.' In so miniature and so Welsh a community as Llŷn, the departure of 240 over five years was a cataclysm.[27] And more keenly even than the actual movement of people, an observer feels along his nerves the straining thousands behind them who could not move. During the terrible years of 1800-1, the scramble for the ships, the hellish crossings, with half the people dying in the foetid holds, seem desperate. Over in Beula, itself struggling to survive in the Pennsylvania wilderness, the news from Wales and the American ports made people ill.[28]

'What in God's name can I do?' — William Richards, back in Newcastle Emlyn in the tortured south-west in April 1801, was certainly desperate. He was writing letter after letter for the crowds thronging to his door ... 'The bearer of this, Daniel Davis, is about to emigrate to your country with his wife and seven children', ran a typical scrawl to Samuel Jones:

> He is by trade a mason and understands the farming business pretty well ... his wife has had some education and has sometimes kept school ... Two of her brothers are in the ministry in England among the Presbyterians ... I am ashamed to trouble you and Dr. Rogers so often with the concerns of these poor Emigrants but what can I do? It is hard to refuse these poor creatures ... I cannot describe to you the condition of our poor country, thousands of the poor move about the country begging bread ... Myriads would emigrate if they had money ... Your merchants and ship-captains are a most mercenary and unfeeling set of sharpers. They charge passengers near

double what they were wont to seven years ago. I wish a method was
contrived to take them over, and let them work at the money after
they got over.

The whole community in Newcastle Emlyn had asked William Richards
to devise such a scheme.[29]

With these penniless thousands at their back, it was in fact men like
Ezekiel Hughes, Theophilus Rees with his small competence, Thomas
Watkin Jones of the Old Hall, Glasbury, who went. This was probably
why it was so characteristically a movement of Dissent, why it was so
political in tone. In west and north Wales, to find Welsh *Jacobins*, you
have to look across the Atlantic. It was this movement, in all probability,
which initiated that emigrant tradition, the tradition of the 'exiles',
which was ultimately to be enshrined in ritual at the national eisteddfod,
with its special day, its poignant hymn, a moment more emotional than
even the Chairing of the Bard.[30]

There were two waves of migration in the revolutionary decade,
1794-7 and 1799-1801. Central to both was a grain shortage and famine
prices.[31] The crisis of 1795-6 was European; this was the crisis which
precipitated the last of the great *sans-culotte* revolts in France, at Ger-
minal and Prairial; in Britain, whole districts were convulsed by crowd
actions, and in some places the militia mutinied. Magistrates revived the
old paternalist economy, the war effort was paralysed, Pitt asked the
French for their peace terms. In Wales, every harvest from 1789 to
1802 was bad; in the often harshly poor upland areas as well as on the
coalfields, people were dangerously dependent on corn. Sufferings were
intense. Copper workers and colliers had rioted in Swansea during 1793;
during the first four months of 1795, price riots and corn actions broke
out all over Wales, Conway, Bangor, Aberystwyth, Narberth, Bridgend.
As the year unrolled, huge gangs of colliers scoured the north-eastern
coalfield in Flintshire; crowds seized Denbigh, marched on Abergele.
Fishguard, Bridgend and Carmarthen followed suit in the south; the
south-east was not far behind and at Haverfordwest in August, there
was virtually an insurrection. Troops went marching all over the Principality. It was through this turmoil that emigrants like the *Maria* party
threaded their way to the ports. In Carmarthen, 3,000 people were ready
to fight a way clear for them. This year was insurrectionary in temper.
At the end of it, the King's coach was mobbed in London, and in the
Two Acts, government suspended English liberties 'for the duration'.

Hardly had the country settled down when the French staged their
comic-opera landing at Fishguard early in 1797, to be swiftly bottled

up and captured and to create the legend of the 'ghost army' in red flannel petticoats. But the landing caused a panic, government cracked down hard on Dissenters, particularly Baptists, in the south-west, and there was a run on the Bank and a financial crisis, to accompany the naval mutinies; in 1798 came the Irish rebellion and its ghastly repression. No sooner had the country climbed out of this depression, broken off the peace talks with France and settled into that long haul of the Napoleonic War which entered into British national mythology, than the grain shortage of 1799-1800 hit it. Deep suspicions that this shortage was artificial made the risings, riots and crowd actions of 1800-1 more overtly political than those of 1795; shadowy *Jacobins* and revolutionary trade union lodges were sensed everywhere, under the hammer of the Combination Acts, the dragoons and the galleys. In Wales, there were massive insurrections at Merthyr Tydfil, in the north-west, in Pembrokeshire: there was another, and more desperate, wave of emigrants.

These climacteric moments, however, simply intensified an already painful malaise. 'There is a very great complaint in Wales against the English,' wrote Morgan Jones, Hammersmith to Pennsylvania, 'They go into the Principality and raise the rents of farms to so great a degree that the farmers there can't live upon them.'[32] This is a simplification; Wales, with its population suddenly increasing, was entering its travail of modernisation which the war enormously accelerated. Immigrant speculators, 'spirited proprietors', enclosures of arable, and more significantly, of commons, with their repeated, bruising impact on small farmers, labourers, the multiplying squatters moving up the hillsides to catch wartime prices, the displacement of traditional tenures by the annual lease, the wholesale commercialisation of agriculture, the inflation, the intrusion of machinery and the first factories into the world of the farm-based cloth industry, thrust rural Wales in particular into a prolonged social crisis, even as the iron industry mushroomed around Merthyr on the southern coalfield and there was a thickening of population on the coalfield of the north-east, around copper at Swansea and in Anglesey.

The rise of Nonconformity was evidently a factor in this crisis. In the last half of the eighteenth century, the Dissenting causes, for long stagnant, abruptly entered a phase of rapid growth; Methodism, which was itself to secede from the Anglican Church under persecution, in 1811, swept forward rapidly, particularly in the west and north. Within a couple of generations, the Welsh were to become a largely Nonconformist people, divorced from Establishment. The crisis of the Napoleonic Wars, in fact, registered the first tentative emergence of a 'nation' in

Wales, which (in marked similarity to the Czech people in central Europe) formed around a language and a religious line which was also a class line. The traditional leadership of the largely Anglicised gentry was beginning to be squeezed out as the new nation formed around its characteristic spokesmen, the preacher-journalists.

This process can be detected in gestation during the social crises of the French wars. It was in rural Wales that the shock was greatest. A generation later, in 1823, the anti-slavery crusader, Thomas Clarkson, went on mission to Wales.[33] As soon as he crossed from south-east Wales into Cardiganshire, the tone of his diaries changes abruptly. Nonconformists, now mainly Methodists, were timorous and uncertain; the gentry would not sit with them on committees. The social cleavage grew worse as he moved north and in Caernarvonshire he almost succumbed to despair. John Elias, the Methodist leader who towered over many Welsh minds like a Pope, did not dare meet Clarkson at home; they had to meet in secret in Chester. Not until Clarkson reached north-east Wales did he relax. He thought that, politically, one moved back fifty years going from England into eastern Wales, fifty years more going from eastern into western Wales. That spiritual frontier becomes visible in the 1790s, all the more so in that the Methodist conquest of north and west often moved out from bases established earlier by the Old Dissent (Llanbrynmair was precisely one).

The correlation becomes particularly striking when one maps the areas of 'disaffection' in Wales and compares that spiritual geography with the geography of emigration.[34] One region stands out with startling clarity, that great tract of country, embracing communities which were intensely Welsh in spirit, ranging from the Severn-Dovey belt of mid-Wales up into the northern heartland. It is precisely the cloth country, the webs of Merioneth and the flannels of Montgomery, an industry as scattered as the farms and hamlets which serviced it. This was the industry hit by the machines and the first factories in Newtown and Llanidloes and Welshpool; here was the monstrous growth in pauperism and the poor rates during the 1790s; here the virtual closure of Barmouth, the dislocations of inflation and wartime 'improvement' were felt most painfully.

And here, during the 1790s, was disaffection both rampant and peculiarly Welsh. During 1795 and 1796, there were large-scale riots against the militia, against the Navy acts. Bala, Barmouth, Machynlleth were storm-centres, whose shock waves ran out to mix with those created by the explosions on the north-eastern coalfield and Denbigh. At Llanbrynmair during the winter of 1796, large crowds gathered in defiance of the civil power. Their leaders were friends of Ezekiel Hughes and the men of the *Maria* — 'The Poor are oppressed by the Rich,' said one of them, John Ellis, in Welsh, 'and we are determined to have another government.'[35] Southern Merioneth was in virtually continuous turmoil during the mid-1790s. Troops were endlessly marching and counter-marching through Bala. And these were precisely the districts which generated the major thrust of emigration. 'There is not much call for women's labour in Cambria at present,' George Roberts of Llanbrynmair was to write from Beula, 'because only a little flax and wool is raised here yet.'[36] He took it for granted that 'women's work' meant carding and spinning. This was the country of William Jones Llangadfan, of Ezekiel Hughes, of the conferences on emigration at Bala and Llanbrynmair. This was the country of Edward Bebb who was to father the first native-born Governor of the state of Ohio. And in Bala in 1796, the taverns echoed to *Jacobin* and anti-*Jacobin* toasts.[37]

No less significant in the emigration registers was the south-west, that country which was to produce the Rebecca Riots of a later generation. The effects of the population explosion in Cardiganshire were peculiarly severe. In the post-war years, it was to be the most disturbed county in Wales. In the 1790s, that prolonged crisis was only beginning; it hit later than in the centre-north, but it becomes visible now. The rural area around the junction of Pembrokeshire, Cardiganshire and Carmarthenshire was a hub of discontent, with the colliers to the south-west and the town of Haverfordwest peculiarly 'Jacobinical' in spirit. And this region, too, was to supply its own distinctive quota of emigrants as was Llŷn in the north-west, for particular reasons of its own, probably related to the threat of enclosures, which provoked riots there and in the neighbouring quarry districts a few years later.

In the industrial regions, on the other hand, while there certainly were emigrants, society was more complex, open and developed and sufficiently wealthy to afford radicalism a purchase. The Merthyr district in particular nurtured a growing middle class and artisanry, in part staffed from the old Dissenting families of the area, 'sturdy Republicans' to a man, and in part from those easy villages of the Vale of Glamorgan where a species of liberalism had long flourished. In Glamorgan, there seems to be a virtually unbroken tradition running from the world of Dr Richard Price's father through the *Jacobins* into those Unitarian clans who could capture a working-class audience and make Merthyr the first radical town in Wales in the next generation.[38] In the 1790s, the two regional strongholds of radicalism in Wales were Merioneth-Montgomery and Merthyr. In the latter, radicalism could find a home *at* home; in the former, it took wing towards the Ohio. With good reason; in the middle 1790s, much of the population of Montgomeryshire and southern Merioneth was in spiritual secession from the British state, while Cardiganshire slithered into an occult and persistent malaise.

Not that public Jacobinism could get much of a purchase in those years.[39] Jac Glan-y-Gors brought out his *Seren tan Gwmmwl* (*The Clouded Star*) in 1795 and *Toriad y Dydd* (*Daybreak*) in 1797, Tom Paine in the British Tongue, but they were drowned in right-thinking and methodistical reaction. Two efforts to restart Morgan Rhees's *Cylchgrawn* failed. Even within the Baptist denomination, William Richards and his kin lost their fight for a 'natural and rational' religion against the newer spokesmen of a 'methodised', evangelical and 'vital' religion. The tone of public discourse for the generality was fixed by the Methodist Thomas Jones's *Gair yn ei amser* (*A Word in Season*), a quietist tract of 1798, for intellectuals by Walter Davies's cool scepticism and practical 'improvement', by the non-political, cultural and anti-quarian themes of William Owen's *Cambrian Register* of 1796.

The emigration movement and the troubled regions from which it emerged, however, were thoroughly disaffected in tone, intention and occasional overt declaration. These people were voting with their feet. In the USA, they were Jeffersonian Republicans. Like the British migration generally in these years, the Welsh movement was strongly artisan—small farmer—tradesman in character; most had their 'competences'. It was, further, a peculiarly *Welsh* movement. Rees Lloyd, for example, learned English largely in the Great Valley, where he moved after landing from the *Maria*. In March 1796, the minister of the Presbyterian church there wrote to him: 'I am much pleased that you have determined to learn the English language and I will with pleasure afford you every assistance in my power.' He sent him Morrison's *Grammar* and the first volume of Newton's works and promised to correct his letters. The English of Rees Lloyd's letters around 1800 is at best quaint, at worst bizarre. His wife Rachel signed by mark. Only at the end of his life, when he was a minister in Paddy's Run, Ohio, was Rees Lloyd writing good, if somewhat bookish English. His English 'family Bible', which passed to the Roberts family who cherished it, he picked up from a family called Hanson in the Great Valley.[40] Much the same was true of those of his congregation who followed him from 'Anglicised' Monmouthshire. The naturalisation records of Pennsylvania provide one striking illustration of the spirit of the migration. In those records, whose content was dictated to the clerk by the migrant, the Welsh rarely used the standard form for natives of Great Britain. Most indeed described their homeland as 'The Kingdom of Wales'.[41]

The thrust was towards a *Gwladfa*. In part, this was simply a natural desire to stick together in familiar company with a familiar language. 'I wish they may settle nearly together,' wrote William Richards of the group which moved out to Beula, 'as they may then have preaching in their mother tongue and be very comfortable.'[42] The people from Llŷn, for example, moved from New York upstate to the newly opened lands of Baron von Steuben beyond Fort Schuyler (Utica) and served as the nucleus of a flow which, after initial hardships, turned the Utica area and what became Oneida county into a dairy farming district of strongly Welsh character.[43] Others sought kinsfolk elsewhere, perhaps in the Carolinas. But the major thrust was far more consciously towards the creation of a new Wales in the west. It was channelled along the Baptist network; Samuel Jones and William Rogers were key figures; the old Welsh churches around Philadelphia a focus, unity an obsession. 'I hope of the Allmighty', said Rees Lloyd, 'by some means or other to direct us all to ficks upon some good spot of land where the poor Welsh people may have a comfortable Settlement.'[44]

And it was precisely here, in the realms of the imagination and the spirit, that the myth of the Welsh Indians worked its magic. Madoc had been the catalyst for the whole process. It was the revival of that myth, charged now with the regeneration drive of Morgan Rhees, the Druidic Jacobinism of Iolo Morganwg, which had initiated the America fever. Madoc had informed the first number of the *Cylchgrawn*, John Evans's journey, William Jones's line of settlements stretching to the Madogwys; Madoc and Jacobinism had been the message of the third number of the journal in August 1793, which inspired Ezekiel Hughes to his first essay in the remaking of a people. The Madoc myth massively reinforced a sense of identity. It called out the missionary impulse so strongly rooted in Welsh Dissent, visible even in Morgan Rhees's mission to the Parisian *sans-culottes*. Ministers and elders were obsessed with the back country, the Monongahela, Kentucky, the Ohio. Rees Lloyd had a son born to him four days after landing in America; he called the boy Ebenezer and dedicated him to missionary work among the Indians. William Tibbot left half his fortune to that Missionary Society of Philadelphia for which Morgan Rhees preached and which, after his Greenville experience, he helped to revivify.[45] Many of the leaders of the Welsh migration talked like sixteenth-century Spanish friars.

It went deeper than that. For the Madoc legend was an almost perfect mythic projection of both the hopes and the predicament of people who wished to be both Welsh and free, for Welshmen who were 'patriots' in the eighteenth-century, rather than the nineteenth-century, sense. English *Jacobins* in exile were to rally around Beula. The new Wales was to be an exemplar of *universal* liberty, much as Iolo's Druids were a Welsh and British exemplification of world truth. 'Dyma ni yn awr ar daith ein gobaith' — 'Here we are now on the Journey of our Hope,' Morgan John had Madoc declaim to the Welsh on the eve of their migration. Hope had to find its territorial anchorage. 'Here we are in the Land of Liberty,' one Welsh immigrant wrote (as if in response), 'Now, where do we ground it?'[46]

This was precisely the duty Morgan Rhees had assumed in 1794. The arrival of Ezekiel Hughes and the *Maria* party, with the others flooding in after them through the early months of 1796, carried the process begun then into its second phase. The newcomers organised *ad hoc* churches around Philadelphia. Simon James was to serve those in the Great Valley. Morgan Rhees organised Independents, Baptists and Methodists into a church in and around the city. Between November 1795 and November 1796, he celebrated many marriages at Pennepek and in Philadelphia. It is not clear whether he 'told a parcel of trash', but it was he who married David Francis the Ohio pioneer to Mary Rowland, William Griffith of Beula to Ann Evans. George Roberts recollected a communion for a mass congregation in July 1796, 'when we enjoyed a precious and reviving season'.[47]

The communion no doubt was to send off the Pennsylvania pioneers. The first act had been to organise that company which Iolo, William Owen and William Jones had called for. The Cambrian Company was formed early in 1796, with Morgan Rhees as president, William Griffith as secretary, based on Morgan's house in Second Street (a Loxley house, of course).[48] Its twelve articles took the standard form for such projects. Subscribers of 100 dollars were to elect commissioners on 1 November 1796, five of them, who were to make a block purchase of land, lay out a town plan, distribute 500 lots in the town to 'Mechanics and Professional Men' as a core and then sell the rest by auction. Outside the town, the land was to be divided into 640-acre sections, distributable by lot. Joint ownership of sections was contemplated but no one person was to be permitted more than four. The appeal was specifically transatlantic — 'Those who live in Europe cannot be too early in their application' and respectable — 'It is expected that the middle class of Citizens will view this opportunity as favourable to promote their interest and happiness . . . an association of virtuous Settlers.'

While the prospectus of the Company stated that 'it is not yet known whether the Company will purchase from the United States or

Individuals,' in fact, its language makes sense only in terms of federal land; 640 acres was the legal minimum for the sale of federal land. George Roberts reported that during 1796, Rhees made several applications and presented several petitions to Congress.[49] That it was the newly opened Ohio lands Rhees had in mind is clear from his appointment of Ezekiel Hughes as official searcher of the Company.

Hughes set out early in 1796 and he made straight for the site Rhees had selected in May 1795. He followed roughly in the footsteps of John Evans and Morgan himself. He took Edward Bebb of Llanbrynmair with him, walked to Pittsburgh, caught a boat to Marietta. General Putnam there tried to interest them in land, but they moved on to Limestone and thence to the mouth of the Big Miami on the Ohio. This was clearly the place to which Rhees had directed them. Hughes bought some 80 acres from Judge Symmes as a stake and a base from which to explore to the west. He had at that time only three neighbours and had to cut a path through forests to Cincinatti, but there was a regular boat service up river to the garrison which was still at Greenville. Bebb settled down with him and they were shortly joined by the Gwilym brothers who had been making iron on the Monongahela and at Redstone.[50] Morgan Rhees's Beula was clearly to rise on the Ohio.

There was no hope for it in 1796. Settlers had begun to move into the north-west and out from the Ohio bottom, but the tide could not freely flow until the passage of the land law of 1800. The riverine areas had been parcelled out among speculative companies and were the theatre for some of the more spectacular frauds, notably the miserable Scioto fiasco. The territory was riven by factional strife, with land legislation as a central issue. Not until 1800 did Congress pass a workable law.[51]

Hughes and Bebb chose to sweat it out on Blue Rock creek, but the Company could hardly lead the people into a Canaan whose title was insecure. In the long run, no doubt, it would have been better had they waited. But they did not know how long the wait would be and, in any case, how could they wait? The Welsh were milling about the heavily settled areas around Philadelphia and New York; more were coming in every month. Their letters were urgent. Under this pressure, Rhees turned to Dr Benjamin Rush.

It is not possible to say when Rhees and Rush became friends; their first surviving correspondence dates from 1797, when their relationship was already close. Morgan John named a son for the doctor. Rush was one of the inner circle of the American Philosophical Society, a friend of Thomas Jefferson.[52] A man after Rhees's heart, he was an Enlightenment thinker and dreamer to the very nerve-ends of his imagination.

Author of the first essay in psychiatry, he is said to have coined the
phrase 'mental illness'. He wanted New World medicine to be a new
world medicine. To break the dead generations of Gothic English, he
supported American spelling reform (shades of William Owen!) and
wanted the curriculum of a new federal university to be grounded in a
Course in the Art of Forgetting. And although Dr Rush diagnosed land
speculation, the American national sport, as quite literally a nervous
affliction, he had in fact laid out his money in vast undeveloped tracts
in Pennsylvania. The settlements he sponsored tended to be ideological
in character. It was he who found the land for Joseph Priestley, on
which a momentarily revolutionary Coleridge intended to plant *Pantisocracy*. His agent for his lands on the Susquehanna was William Cooper,
father of Fenimore Cooper the novelist, a judge who seems to have
been distinctly less literate than his son's buckskin heroes. Cooper and
Rush started a New Scotland on the latter's western lands through the
agency of John Craig Millar, son of the celebrated Scottish social philosopher.[53] It was perhaps natural that he and Rhees turned their minds
to a New Wales.

Rush had in 1794 patented a great tract of heavily forested hill
country south of the western branch of the Susquehanna, in the last
of the intramontane folds of the Appalachians. On 1 October 1796,
Morgan Rhees and his wife Ann bought the whole country, 43 named
400-acre tracts, totalling 17,400 acres on the waters of the Blacklick
and the Connemaugh, some 230 miles from Philadelphia and 80 from
Pittsburgh. It is difficult to penetrate to the reality behind the formal
deeds and bonds, but the 43 tracts were transferred to Rhees for £9,450
and were promptly mortgaged for that amount. In March 1798, Rush
conveyed six more tracts on Blacklick to Rhees for $3,748 under mort-
gage, while Rhees restored to Rush three of the original tracts on
Connemaugh for $1,781. Four hundred acres were reserved for a town
site, 200 for Rhees's cherished Christian Church and 600 for Rush,
though these were quitclaimed to Rhees as soon as the town plan had
been completed.[54] It is quite clear that, while Rhees was the active
agent and controller, the launching of Cambria, with Beula as its focus,
was in a real sense something of a partnership, in the tradition of Rush's
other liberty settlements of Pantisocracy and New Caledonia.

The first settlers moved on to the land in the autumn of 1796 and as
early as April 1797 Rees Lloyd had raised an Independent chapel there.
On 7 March of that year, Morgan John Rhees became an American
citizen and he led the second party up shortly afterwards.[55] In the
summer and autumn, he was back in Philadelphia following through,

with advertisements in the papers and a campaign for support among city notables. He was very active about the churches, assemblies and counting-houses of the capital and in October, presided over the first distribution of town lots. Beula was finally and legally launched when he and Ann patented the town plan on 2 November 1797.[56]

At that point, however, the holy ghost of the Welsh migration returned to brush his busy shoulder. In November, he was distracted by an urgent message from Dr Samuel Jones. After a silence of two years, a letter had come through from John Evans.

Notes

1. For John Evans's journey up the Missouri, see my *Madoc: the Making of a Myth* (Eyre Methuen, London, 1980), Chapter 9.

2. This account of his return journey is based on Morgan Rhees's diary; most of it (censored) has been printed in J.T. Griffith, *Morgan John Rhys* (USA, 1899 and Carmarthen, 1910), pp. 186-229.

3. Ibid., pp. 199, 195, 203, 210.

4. Ibid., pp. 210 ff.

5. Ibid., p.218.

6. This period in American history is well covered; for a quick assimilation, see J.C. Miller, *The Federalist Era 1789-1801* (New American Nation series, Hamish Hamilton, London, 1960).

7. For Cobbett, I have used his collected American works and, in particular, his journal *Porcupine's Gazette*; it makes hypnotic reading.

8. Reprinted in Griffith, *Morgan John Rhys*, p. 220.

9. Ibid., pp. 209, 212.

10. Rhees diary (original) *passim* and Griffith, *Morgan John Rhys*, p. 194.

11. Marriage Register, First Baptist Church, Philadelphia, p. 179. I am grateful to the officers of this church for allowing me to inspect their records; only through their records was I able to trace Morgan John Rhees's grave.

12. All the material on the Loxleys which follows is drawn from the Loxley papers within the Uselma Clark Smith Collection, Historical Society of Pennsylvania. Essential are a manuscript autobiography by Colonel Benjamin Loxley, supplemented by notes added by his kinsfolk, particularly his daughter Elizabeth, who married Lloyd Jones; a draft of Col. Loxley's will and scraps of correspondence. See here, A. Rees–E. Jones, 1 September 1806, Loxley papers.

13. What follows is drawn from Benjamin Loxley's draft autobiography and draft will, Loxley papers, Historical Society of Pennsylvania.

14. Presumably Knaresborough, Pateley Bridge and Harrogate Spa.

15. Abergavenny is in Monmouthshire (Gwent) to which, for some unaccountable reason, the English sometimes lay claim.

16. See my *Artisans and Sans-culottes: Popular Movements in Britain and France during the French Revolution* (E. Arnold, London, 1968; reprinted 1973).

17. For this intriguing detail see anonymous note attached to Benjamin Loxley's autobiography, Loxley papers; apparently Ann Loxley Rhees lent the kite to the editor of a New York paper and it disappeared.

18. The memorial is in the Loxley papers.

19. Draft of Benjamin Loxley's will, Loxley papers.

20. Minutes of the First Baptist Church, Philadelphia, 5 October 1795; see also A.D. Gillette (ed.), *Minutes of the Philadelphia Baptist Association 1707-1807* (Philadelphia, 1851).

21. Three volumes of the minutes of this society are in the Historical Society of Pennsylvania; on it, see George Vail, 'Backgrounds of Welsh music in colonial Pennsylvania', *Church Music and Musical Life in Colonial Pennsylvania* (Colonial Dames of America, Philadelphia, 1947), Vol. III, p. 365; and A.H. Dodd, *The Character of Early Welsh Emigration to the United States* (University of Wales, Cardiff, 1953).

22. Griffith, *Morgan John Rhys*, pp. 211, 213, 227.

23. On the *Maria* and its people, there are two essential letters: Rees Lloyd–Jonah Lloyd, 4 September 1837, Cambria Historical Society, Ebensburg, and George Roberts–Samuel Roberts, 1 March 1850; *Y Cronicl*, July 1850, printed in Alan Conway (ed.), *The Welsh in America: Letters from the Immigrants*, translated by Judith Lewis (University of Wales, Cardiff, 1961), pp. 17-20; there is, further, the memoir of Ezekiel Hughes from the Utica *Cambrian* with comments by Samuel Roberts, NLW 491, fo. 20; census returns, deeds and bonds from Cambria and Somerset courthouses may supplement here B.W. Chidlaw, *An Historical Sketch of Paddy's Run, Butler County, Ohio* (1876); see also E.G. Hartmann, *Americans from Wales* (Christopher, Boston, 1967), pp. 61-7, for this period.

24. R. Williams–W. Owen, 21 January 1796, NLW 13224, fo. 161-2.

25. W. Richards–S. Jones, 16 and 22 March 1796; for the £800, see 23 March and 4 August 1794: Pennepek.

26. This section is based on my reading of the Welsh correspondence of Samuel Jones, Philadelphia, and the letters of Iolo Morganwg, William Owen and others, the *Cylchgrawn* etc.; for some apposite examples, see J.J. Evans, *Morgan John Rhys a'i amserau* (University of Wales Press, Cardiff, 1935), especially pp. 37-40.

27. Transcripts of parish registers, Caernarvonshire, R. Ivor Parry MS., NLW 18334; and see D.J.V. Jones, *Before Rebecca: Popular Protest in Wales 1793-1835* (Allen Lane, London, 1973), Chapters 1 and 2.

28. See below, Chapter 7.

29. W. Richards–S. Jones, 3 April 1801 and 1800-1 *passim*: Pennepek.

30. This treatment of the social crisis and emigration in Wales during the 1790s is, of necessity at present, qualitative and impressionistic. It is basically grounded in my own experience of the primary material. For reference, the best sources are the works of David Williams: see the bibliography in the special 1967 number of the *Welsh History Review* devoted to him; his *Modern Wales* (John Murray, London, 1950; revised edn I.G. Jones, 1977) and *The Rebecca Riots* afford a first entry; I have found particularly useful Jones, *Before Rebecca*, D. Thomas, *Agriculture in Wales during the Napoleonic Wars* (University of Wales Press, Cardiff, 1963) and A.H. Dodd, *The Industrial Revolution in North Wales* (3rd edn, University of Wales Press, Cardiff, 1971). Hartmann, *Americans from Wales*, is a good general survey of emigration.

31. There is an outline sketch in my *Artisans and Sans-culottes*; I ground my comments in the work of my former student at the University of York, Roger A.E. Wells, whose PhD thesis, 'The Grain Crises in Late Eighteenth-century England', York, 1978, will become the definitive monograph; for Wales, see Jones, *Before Rebecca*, Chapters 1 and 2.

32. M. Jones–S. Jones, September 1796: Pennepek.

33. The Clarkson Diaries are in the National Library of Wales.

34. The really striking material here is that supplied by David J.V. Jones in his excellent *Before Rebecca*. If the material in the text and footnotes of Chapters 1 and 2 is reorganised along topographical lines and then brought into phase with

the emigration material provided here, a very clear and striking pattern emerges.

35. Ibid., p. 53.

36. G. Roberts–his parents, 13 October 1801, NLW 13189, reprinted in A.H. Dodd, 'Letters from Cambria County 1800-1823', *Pennsylvania History*, vol. xxii (1955), p. 139.

37. See my *Artisans and Sans-culottes* and Jones, *Before Rebecca*.

38. See my *The Merthyr Rising* (Croom Helm, London, 1978).

39. See, among other studies, Evans, *Morgan John Rhys a'i amserau* and *Dylanwad y Chwyldro Ffrengig ar lenyddiaeth Cymru* (Hugh Evans, Liverpool, 1928).

40. J. Gemmill–R. Lloyd, 18 March 1796; Lloyd Bible, in Cambria Historical Society; for Rachel, Deed Book 1, Cambria county.

41. Based on federal district courts and county courts, Pennsylvania, voluminous naturalisation records: Federal Record Centre, Veterans' Building, Philadelphia, City Hall, Philadelphia; 15 county courts.

42. W. Richards–S. Jones, 22 March 1796: Pennepek.

43. Hartmann, *Americans from Wales*, pp. 62, 65-7.

44. Rees Lloyd–S. Jones, 1800: Pennepek.

45. Rees Lloyd–Jonah Lloyd, 4 September 1837, Cambria Historical Society; will of William Tibbot, 16 February 1822, Will Book 1, Cambria county; preface to M.J. Rhees, *The Altar of Peace*, published by the Missionary Society in 1798.

46. D. Williams–R. Lloyd, November 1799, Cambria Historical Society.

47. Marriage Register, First Baptist Church, Philadelphia, list of marriages performed by M.J. Rhees 1795-6, handed over by Ann Rhees in 1808; G. Roberts, letter dated 20 July 1834, in *Y Cyfaill*, 1838, extracted in Griffith, *Morgan John Rhys*, p. 248; C.T. Roberts, 'Centennial History of First Congregational Church' (Cambria Historical Society, typescript, Ebensburg, n.d.).

48. The prospectus of this Company, several copies of which may be found in Cambria Historical Society, Historical Society of Pennsylvania and the William Owen letters in NLW, is printed in Griffith, *Morgan John Rhys*, pp. 244-7.

49. The best treatment of the land problem is Ray A. Billington's superb *Westward Expansion: a History of the American Frontier* (2nd edn, Macmillan, New York, 1960), see especially Chapter 12. See also G. Roberts in Griffith, *Morgan John Rhys*, p. 248.

50. See the full account on Samuel Roberts's memoir, based on the Utica *Cambrian*, in NLW 491, fo. 20.

51. Billington, *Westward Expansion*, Chapter 12.

52. To savour this remarkable man, try L.H. Butterfield (ed.), *The Letters of Benjamin Rush* (2 vols., American Philosophical Society, Philadelphia, 1951); and see Carl Binger, *Revolutionary Doctor* (W.W. Norton, New York, 1966: strong medical emphasis).

53. There is plenty of evidence in the Benjamin Rush papers, Historical Society of Pennsylvania; Judge Cooper's letters are frequently entertaining. See also Mary C. Park, *Joseph Priestley and the Problem of Pantisocracy* (Philadelphia, 1947) and Norman B. Wilkinson, 'Land Policy and Speculation in Pennsylvania 1779-1800' (unpublished PhD thesis, University of Pennsylvania, 1958).

54. All the deeds, conveyances etc. are in Deed Books 1-3, especially Book 2, Somerset county.

55. Prothonotary's Records, Philadelphia county, 7 March 1797, in City Hall, Philadelphia.

56. The original town plan was filed in Somerset county on 18 September 1798.

BEULAH LAND

From September 1796 to May 1797 John Evans was buried in the earth-lodges of the Mandans, living through a winter as severe as any on earth.[1] That winter shortened his life. It was a winter of growing frustration and anger. Within two weeks a small party of Norwesters from their northern base of La Souris came through. John Evans stopped them trading and packed them off. Their report caused consternation at La Souris and Riviere-Tremblante and at the Hudson's Bay post at Brandon House. Big John McDonnell of the Norwesters took the opportunity of sending a reconnaissance party back, carrying gifts and letters which for the moment were polite. The visit passed off peaceably in mid-December but Evans was firm in his replies, defending the Spanish monopoly and broadcasting McKay's prohibition of British traders.

By this time, his situation was desperate. His goods had run out and back down the Missouri, McKay was trapped among the Omaha and the Sioux. John had won the affection and trust of the Mandan chiefs, in a manner characteristic of him. They would, without doubt, have helped him, accepted Spain, given him a lift towards the Pacific, had the Spaniards been able to supply him. But in their empire, it was 'late afternoon getting on for evening'. The Norwesters, apprised of his weakness, decided to take over. The December expedition was ambushed by Pawnees, lost its horses and had an excuse for a further visit. The encounter was explosive. Numbers of the Mandans protested against John Evans's ban on trade with the British, carried the Norwesters' sleds in friendship even as the Welshman raised the Spanish flag in defiance and forced the Canadians to trade through himself. He sent strong protests to the Norwesters, but behind him, the Mandans were divided. Big John McDonnell replied with a declaration of war. He sent René Jusseaume, an illiterate but wily and vastly experienced *engagé* with plenty of goods against Fort McKay, as John Evans had renamed the blockhouse which Jusseaume himself had built. This was to be a decisive struggle for control of the upper Missouri and the route to the Pacific.

By that time, John Evans had been left isolated and starved 1,800 miles from his crumbling base. Behind him, the Missouri Company was in turmoil. Jacques Clamorgan had pressed on eagerly with his great plan and had won the support of the Spanish Council of State over the protests of Trudeau and the St Louis merchants, but a royal subsidy of

10,000 pesos towards the chain of forts was challenged and, faced with massive opposition, the governor Carondelet lost his nerve. The worst loss was the sudden death of young Andrew Todd in the yellow fever epidemic in New Orleans in December 1796. His colleagues pulled out of the enterprise and the vital Canadian support was removed. The whole ambitious enterprise ran out into sand and McKay was ordered home from the Omahas. At the same time, there was a sudden *sans-culotte* outbreak in St Louis. Carondelet sent every gunboat he could muster up the Mississippi under the Irish soldier Don Carlos Howard. Howard restored order easily enough in St Louis and Carondelet ordered him to sail up the Missouri and rescue John Evans. It was impossible; there simply were not enough supplies.

So John Evans, in March 1797, had to confront the strong and lavishly endowed Jusseaume expedition of the Norwesters with nothing but his own will and what loyalty he could command among the Mandans. In the circumstances, his achievement can only be called remarkable. He confronted Jusseaume head-on and won. The man from Waunfawr held the chiefs and many of their braves to their Spanish allegiance. Some of the tribe rebelled and Jusseaume got some of them into a plot to kill Evans. The chiefs moved into his hut to protect him. Jusseaume tried to shoot John Evans himself, but the interpreter frustrated him. The Indians would have killed Jusseaume had not the Welshman intervened. John Evans challenged Jusseaume to a duel and, in the end, the Norwester threw in his hand and left.

This miniature struggle in the wilderness had decisive imperial consequences, but John Evans realised that he could neither go any further nor stay. His sojourn had not been useless; he had gathered massive and accurate intelligence on the Missouri and the lands that lay beyond, as far as the Yellowstone and the Rockies. He had held the Mandans for Spain. But as an agent of a would-be great imperial company, he savoured the bitter taste of frustration. That frustration would be something more than the frustration of a loyal Company servant. After those cold and wretched months among the Mandans and their brother tribes, where now were the Welsh Indians of Madoc?

In May, promising to return with guns and goods, he and his little party set off down the river. It took them 68 days to reach St Louis. John Evans was greeted like a hero; he and McKay, after all, had done more for Spain than any others. Jacques Clamorgan, who took him into his household, immediately asked him to lead another expedition to the Pacific. There was a sad duty to perform first. Before moving to Arundel's friendly house in Cahokia, John Evans sat down on 15 July to write his long-awaited report to Dr Samuel Jones:

> Thus having explored and charted the Missurie for 1800 miles and
> by my Communications with the Indians this side of the Pacific
> Ocean from 35 to 49 Degrees of Latitude, I am able to inform you
> that there is no such People as the Welsh Indians.

A week before John Evans sat down to write his letter, the *Aurora*
of Philadelphia carried an urgent and exultant advertisement from the
Cambrian Company. It reminded professional men and mechanics that
if they moved into the new Cambria settlement before November 1797
and pledged themselves to build a house with a stone or brick chimney,
they would be entitled to four town lots within the limits of Beula.
Mills were now rising on the creek and upwards of a hundred people
had settled around Beula since the previous October.[2]

The promotion of Beula had begun in earnest in the spring of 1797,
when Morgan John Rhees had led the second pioneer party to the site,
to be followed by more settlers during the summer. Advertisements
summoned emigrants and others 'who have an enterprising spirit and
are willing, for a few years, to undergo and surmount difficulties in the
acquirement of independence'.[3] Beula was to be laid out, one mile
square, 395 acres were reserved for public buildings, schools, a library
and a seminary; 200 for a religious society, The Christian Church. Testi-
monials were quoted. The late John Craig Millar had thought the area
around the Connemaugh and Blacklick would become in time 'the
garden of Pennsylvania'; Colonel Elliott found it 'particularly adapted
to grass . . . fit for any kind of cultivation'. The surveyors John Harris
and Patrick Cassidy went into some detail. The former thought the site
sufficiently level, the tracts 'altogether tillable', the whole very proper
for pasture, abounding in meadow and well watered with streams ready
for mill-seats. He even mentioned wheat. The experienced Cassidy concentrated on the pastoral and sylvan potential, thought a quarter of the
land would make meadow and singled out its strategic siting, a mere
8-14 miles from the waterways.

The promoters admitted that the principal objection was 'the great
weight of timber', but pointed out that even the trees — walnut, hickory,
chestnut, linn, beech, poplar, hemlock, spruce — were of the best
quality, throwing in some speculative sugar trees and cherry for good
measure. But what they concentrated readers' attention on were the
commercial possibilities of the site. It stood, some 230 miles from Philadelphia and 80 miles from Pittsburgh, on the 'Juniata Road', between

the two, which, avoiding the worst of the mountain country, 'is likely to become the most public'; the portage from the Juniata to the Conne-maugh was similarly the shortest between eastern and western waters.

> This will, of course, cause it to be a natural deposit for stores, and it is not out of the scale of probability but Beula, being in the center of a new settlement, will in time be a manufacturing town, a seat of Justice and a considerable mart for inland trade.

There was nothing inherently unsound about this thinking. The aim of the founders of such settlements on the secondary frontier was to create a service centre of mixed production. In this hill country, agri-culture could be adequate but not much more. Hence Morgan Rhees's stress, in his writings and his later addresses to the Beula Seminary, on sylvan products, on potash, maple sugar, hence the special encourage-ment to mechanics and artisans. The ideal was a viable service centre which would, in effect, virtually create its own hinterland. As in all such communities, the emphasis was on craftsmen, roads and public buildings; the remarkable Cambrian Library planned for Beula was to be a vital growth factor. This was not a pipe-dream; this is precisely how many hill-country seats did grow – including that Ebensburg which was to rise a mere three miles from the Beula site and to flourish to this day.[4]

Admittedly, in this region of western Pennsylvania, the initial diffi-culties were appalling.[5] It was genuine wilderness, hardly scratched by white men before the Indian Treaty of Fort Stanwix in 1768. A handful of audacious pioneers, an Adams, a McGuire, had begun to carve out settlements, but beyond little Frankstown, there was very little except virgin forest. Its rolling hills were (and still are) beautiful; but for the timber, they strongly resemble the Black Mountains-Brecknock Beacons country of south Wales. But there was little chance here for that plateau farming and maple production which was to enrich Somerset county to the south. To the north of the Cambria district, timber was to be the mainstay, to the south around the town of Connemaugh, later called Johnstown, coal and iron. Ironically enough, just a couple of miles west of the Beula site, a populous coal town was later to take its name from Nant-y-Glo (Coalbrook).[6] Most crippling of all – the site *was* on the secondary frontier. With the major routes to the west close by, the opening up of easier lands in Ohio posed a deadly threat to the Cambria pioneers. The natural process of settlement here was slow.

The Welsh began it. An attempt had been launched in very similar style only the year before. The prime mover was John Craig Millar, son of the celebrated Scottish social philosopher John Millar. A hot-headed, brilliant but rather ill-balanced man, he had been one of the earliest 'Friends of the People' in Edinburgh and had migrated with his wife and some like-minded citizens to start a New Caledonia in the west. Old medical acquaintances from Scotland had contacted Benjamin Rush, who introduced him to key men in Philadelphia, notably to the Quaker Henry Drinker whose company (which George Roberts of Llanbrynmair was to join) held vast tracts in western Pennsylvania near to Rush's. Millar was going to take 12,000 acres from Drinker at the reasonable price of 10 shillings an acre and organise settlement. He was also keen to establish an agency for all proprietors west of the Allegheny Mountains. Drinker lent him £300 on a thousand acres to open up on his own in August 1796. But the young man died suddenly, a shock which nearly unhinged his father and drove his equally brilliant young wife Robina, youngest daughter of Dr Cullen, back to Scotland. Some elusive 'Jersey men' referred to in Rhees's correspondence seem to have been the only survivors of New Caledonia.[7]

More permanent were the German (Pennsylvania Dutch) settlers, including many of the Amish people, coming up from Somerset county to found Munster and cluster around Connemaugh under Joseph Yahns or Johns, a couple of years after the launching of Beula. To the north-ward, Catholics from Maryland began to group in 1799 under that remarkable pioneer, the Russian prince from Germany, Father Prince Gallitzin who called himself Augustus Demetrius Smith and founded Loretto. Irish and Scotch-Irish (Ulstermen) were soon filtering in here as everywhere along the mountain belt.[8]

The problem of such settlements as these could be expressed in an equation which took as its elements time, labour and morale. Timing was in fact the essence. Visible results had to be achieved in short order. Judge William Cooper, Rush's agent for the Susquehanna, was an old hand at this game. As he told Rush, the main problems were the moral ones presented by 'frightful appearance' and the 'length of the rout'. The only way to solve them was 'by spiritedly rushing upon them with a number of people . . . we must raise a party by way of breaking the ice.'[9] This was certainly the method Rhees and Rush tried to apply.

Quite obviously they seriously underestimated the difficulty of the land. No native American would tackle it. The weight of timber was crushing and much of the land turned out to be stony. Rhees thought one thousand-acre hill was so littered with rocks that it was worth scarcely a cent a hundred acres.[10] The settlers were precariously strung out at the end of a 30-mile supply line; they had to concentrate on communal necessities like mills. Brute realities drove many of the men to take work on roads and with waggoners. In these circumstances, a comparatively minor setback could cause cumulative delay which might prove morally disastrous. Moreover, all other land-holders in the area were similarly placed. There was sharp competition for population, particularly since Pennsylvania law required (in theory at least) that patented land be settled within two years. Little help and much hindrance could be expected from neighbours. Settlements like these were soon enmeshed in fierce local struggles over roads, township and county frontiers, court-houses, wagon trains. It was easy to succumb to the irrational.

Many such settlements failed or made false starts. There was a recognisable rhythm to the process. The first serious crisis came at once, after the first scanty harvest, when back-breaking labour in daunting isolation had yielded so little gain. Those who did not drop out at once tended to pull back from the proposed town into the little clearings on their farms, which made yet more difficult the energising of the settlement. The worst crisis of all often came with the opening of the settlement's first major road. This moment, which could mark the take-off for a community, could also signal its collapse. For Beula, the opening of the road would mean direct exposure to the endless train of Conestoga wagons creaking daily westwards towards easier land.

The venture was launched, however, in fine style. The town of Beula was patented by Morgan and Ann Rhees on 2 November 1797. It was ambitious. Beula was to be laid out on the side of a hill, straddling one of the creek systems which constituted the Blacklick. It was to be a mile square. There were two major roads, 100 feet wide, which quartered it — Sun and Joy. Two other good roads, Truth and Ray, ran north–south, while no fewer than fourteen, also 80 feet wide, ran east to west. The lanes and alleys running north–south were to be 20 feet wide, those running east–west, 15 feet. Roads and alleys took their names from beautiful and useful objects, creatures and qualities, rather in the manner of the French revolutionary calendar. Quince, Palm, Oak, Lamb and Kid coexisted with Zeal, Hope, Free and, perhaps less comfortably, with Oil, Wire and Quill. A town lot had a street frontage of 58 feet and stretched back 125 feet; four made an acre. Anyone who bought a 400-acre tract in Cambria was guaranteed four such lots; so were professional men and mechanics who moved into residence by November 1797 and built a good stone or brick chimney. 'Pompey', Robert Stewart the mulatto, who was counted a 'free white male' in the Census of 1800, had a stock of 40,000 bricks by that year, in the brickyard he had built on the edge of the well-stocked fishpool.[11] Apart from the 200 acres reserved for the Christian Church, 395 were set aside for court-house, school, seminary and library. Five hundred town lots were offered for straight sale at $10. Payment for lots, however, could be made 'in valuable books'.

This characteristic provision mirrored Morgan John's intense pre-occupation with the need to plant a major library in the wilderness. A small notebook, which passed to George Roberts, is the only surviving evidence of the library.[12] It lists books bought for or given to its stock. The list is far from complete. It omits the many books given by Benjamin Rush and simply makes blanket reference to other donations. Even so, the notebook lists 580 volumes. Rhees claimed that the library was approaching 1,500 volumes some years later. Most memoirs of Beula talk of 'a circulating library of 600 books'. Harvard at this date boasted 14,000. In this respect, at least, Beula must have been unique among frontier settlements.

The books themselves, as might be expected, were a very mixed bag. There was an apparently inexhaustible supply of Biblical commentaries and moral homilies — *Zimmerman on Solitude* and *Dodd on Death* seem to have been popular. But there were substantial shelves of serious scientific works, many practical treatises and encyclopaedias. Politics, poetry and the classics, both in translation and in Greek and Latin, were well represented. Most of the major thinkers then popular were available and there were multiple copies of Voltaire, Locke, Blackstone, Mably, Delolme, Brissot, Godwin, Paley, Grotius and Jefferson's *Virginia*. Citizen Richard Lee, who used to keep the *Tree of Liberty* in the Strand, sent Mary Wollstonecraft on the *French Revolution* and the *Rights of Women* besides three volumes of the radical journal *Pig's Meat* (one more of the British artisan's angry parodies of Burke's 'swinish multitude') and Griffith's *Morality of Shakespeare*.[13] Mathew Carey, the celebrated Philadelphia publisher, sent in a long and intensely practical list of medical and technical books, with a Welsh-English dictionary, while Dr William Rogers threw in a *Maxims of the Spanish Court*, presumably as a little light relief from the six copies of *The Various Readings of the Septuagint in the Alexandrian and Roman Copies*. There was little directly relevant to Wales and matters Welsh. *Llywarch Hen* was there and Warrington's *Wales*, together with sundry testaments and magazines (including, presumably, Rhees's own) but the only volume in Welsh given a specific title was the tome blazoned, perhaps appropriately, *Halleluia Drachefn* (*Halleluia Again*). Altogether, there were gifts from about a score of well-wishers in Philadelphia and New York, including the British *Jacobin* exiles Joseph Gales of Sheffield and William Young Birch of Manchester.

All of them were rewarded with Beula town lots. Joseph Priestley kept his indenture on display in his Northumberland house and Matthew Carey remembered his in his will.[14] Town lots were also thrown about in what seems a rather carefree manner, as payment to all manner of people for services rendered. 'Captain Robert Jones is entitled to six lots in Beula for the bay horse' ran one entry in Rhees's notebook.[15] Dry goods from Philadelphia, New York, Bordentown and Frankstown seem to have been paid for in the first year or so with town lots; Ralph Eddowes of Philadelphia got no fewer than twenty. Boudinot, Master of the US Mint, was given ten in return for books. Benjamin Rush was given three lots for window glass he supplied for the meeting house; Dr Arthur Blaney got four for his medical services to Welsh immigrants. Five lots were granted to the pioneer road-maker Patrick Galbraith for a clock, and, a comforting touch, as many as fifteen to John Hawkins, for a portable piano.

This makes it difficult to read much into the sales of town lots which duly went into effect from October 1797.[16] The first purchaser to be recorded in Somerset county deed book was, appropriately enough, Thomas Watkin Jones, the surveyor. An able and dedicated man, he owned the Old Neuadd (Hall) and an estate back home in Trenewydd, Glasbury, south Wales. He bought ten town lots at the earliest possible moment. Between 1 October and 24 November 1797, the sale of 134 town lots was formally recorded in Somerset court-house. Many known indentures were not so recorded. Of these 134, however, only 23 went to actual settlers in Cambria. Seven were taken up by pioneer settlers nearby like Thomas Durbin, a trouble-making Irishman, two Frankstown men and the speculator Zaccheus Collins, who held tracts in the district. The rest, over 100, went to sympathisers and book suppliers, Thomas Ustick, William Rogers, William Young Birch or to Philadelphia merchants. The Quaker Henry Andrew Haines figured as the largest investor with 30 lots.[17]

Of the 23 which went to actual settlers, eight were already 'improved' and carried a higher price. Rees Lloyd, who held four Beula lots, paid the standard $10 for only one of them; the others cost twice, thrice, seven times the normal. Apart from George Roberts, who held two, the other Cambria settlers named applied for single lots. The outlots and tracts around the town site, however, seemed to be filling up nicely. The high command of Beula, as it emerged around Morgan Rhees, was mixed. Thomas Watkin Jones was very active, seconded by John J. Evans, who opened a tavern, as did William Jenkins. Simon James began to make a name for himself as a surveyor and land agent and Thomas Ustick, a kinsman of the minister of the First Baptist Church in Philadelphia, seems to have been in charge of building. Thomas Phillips and, above all, William Tibbot were the makers of mills. Two of the settlers counted as 'gentlemen', Joseph J. Moore, who was to pen a famous *Beula Lament* on the death of Washington, and Ebenezer Hickling. George Roberts, writing to Benjamin Rush several years later, complained that the only doctor anywhere near the settlement was a man in Indiana town, thirty miles away. He added, 'I am inclined to think that the doctors that have been inclined to settle in these thinly settled, healthy and poor parts of the country are not the most skilful in the world.'[18] Hickling served in lieu. He was a young apothecary from London, whose father, also an apothecary, was a preacher of the Universalist doctrine of Elhanan Winchester. Winchester recommended the young man to Rush when he migrated to America, to lodge with the Universalist's mother-in-law. He was among the first to move out to Cambria, where he was invariably known as The Doctor.[19] To the hopeful eyes of these leaders, a hundred people moving in to attack the Blacklick forests in the summer of 1797 must have seemed an encouraging sight.

The first shocks, then, were in many ways the worst. Rhees, who had been busy around Philadelphia through the winter, went back up to Beula in the spring of 1798. He was shattered. 'What shall I say?' he wrote to Rush on 26 July, 'I could scarcely believe my eyes nor my ears, such a change I could not have conceived.' Rush had been asking for a report to insert in the press. All Rhees could reply was 'I must beg of you not to print anything respecting our settlement except our transactions of the 4th of July.' The whole project was threatened with immediate collapse.[20]

The very foundations had given way. A year of unremitting labour had been succeeded by a winter of unrelieved disaster. Clearing the ground had proved much harder than expected. There were stones everywhere. Particularly serious was the failure of the mills. 'My sawmill and seat are completely gone,' said Rhees, 'after spending the best part of last summer in erecting and sinking at least on them 1,000 dollars.' The loss of the mill was deadly serious. It threw the settlers into depression and set back essential improvements by more than a year. The people had been too hard pressed in trying to get the sawmill working, in starting on a new one further down the creek and in helping Thomas Phillips set up a gristmill on the Connemaugh, to spare time from the harvest and sowing turnips to do any serious work on major buildings. More had been directed to the road, which had been stopped, as everything else had been, by a long and desperately hard winter. The settlers had been forced to work out to get money and neighbouring settlements had proved hostile and extortionate.

Worst of all had been the collapse in morale. Rhees's own brother had taken to drink and his breakdown had cost Morgan John nearly a thousand pounds. Dr Hickling had also suffered something like a nervous breakdown. 'I almost despaired last week of his recovery.' Poverty and accidents and the sheer grind of the settlement had made many of the pioneers disaffected: 'others who were very sober, industrious people when I left them last summer are entirely devoted to the Stinking God, whisky.'

It is clear that many never recovered from this first, shattering experience. Some seem to have quit at once. Others were scarred by an insecurity and a susceptibility to panic which were to prove permanent, particularly since all the winters were hard. Rhees had no hope of any newcomers during 1798 and was afraid that deserters would malign the enterprise. But he had by no means given up. Many were still firm in the cause and he had hopes of some of the backsliders. 'In the midst of these calamities, Providence smiles on the industry of many of the settlers. They will have a tolerable crop of grain and an abundance of vegetables.' He had taken full command himself. The new sawmill should cost only a half of what digging the race for the first one had taken. There were two men burning lime within two miles of town. The major problems were the debts which had built up on Rhees's shoulders and the endless demands for an easing of the terms of mortgage and lease which were pouring in on him. But he was determined to recover swiftly, to press on. His health had suffered, but his spirits were reviving and little John Loxley Rhees was as plump as a pumpkin and beginning to prattle.

The failure of the mills and other communal services was doubly grave in that it plunged the settlers into deeper dependence on the wages of others and 'working out'. There can be no doubt that Cambria land was very difficult and, in places, impossible. Rees Rees, one of the first men up, wrote to Rush in 1805:

I have gone through a great deal of Hardship for some years, but it is something better now. I went the first year to the next settlement past of us called Frankstown and carried 30 bushels of grain that year on my back, which is the distance of 20 miles, sometimes I was oblidged to go 4 or 5 miles further. I carried all the grain I used so far the first year. I feel the effects to that in my limbs to this day.

He had lost too much time from his plot, working out to get money for grain, victuals and iron.[21]

The essential need was to preserve faith that it would be 'something better' in a reasonable time. There was certainly some potential in the land. By 1801, George Roberts, who had cleared some 8 to 10 of his 50 acres a couple of miles east of the town site, in which he held two lots, had a dozen cattle and four pigs and could write to Llanbrynmair, 'I have hardly a trace of the fear of poverty that dogged me for some years in Wales to a sinful extent.'[22] Others were successful. In a tax return for what was then Cambria county which survives from 1810, most of the Welsh were solidly placed among the mass of substantial taxpayers, and while few of them could equal a handful of their German and Irish fellow-settlers, the man most highly assessed in the roll, at nearly $800, was in fact Rees Lloyd, who by then had cleared 34 acres of his 350 and owned a horse and four head of cattle. In that tax list, the 53 Welsh heads of families, rather over a third of the total number, accounted for nearly 60 per cent of the total assessment and were credited with 24 horses and 81 head of cattle.[23]

William Tibbot, whose successful erection of mills probably saved the settlement in the last resort, at that point had cleared 4 of his 57 acres, raised a grist mill, ran a horse and four head of cattle. By the time he came to make his will in 1822, William Tibbot was having some trouble with his second wife. He wanted himself buried with his first one and left the second only some clothes and one dollar (she challenged the testament). But to his son Richard, he left the eastern end of one tract, 112 acres together with the house he lived in. To his son Jabez, he left the western end of the tract together with his sawmill and the house he had bought from William Jones. A 107-acre tract with his grist mill, dam and race, he left to his son Festus. He was able to leave $250 together with obligations totalling another $250 to his two daughters who married sons of Rees Lloyd, with an extra $50 each for their husbands. The profits of stock he held in the Pennsylvania Turnpike were to go to the Board of American Indian Missionaries, together with the $20 at least he expected from a settlement in Wales. His books and his clothes could be divided three ways.[24]

Luck or skill could certainly enable men to break through after the desperate early days. Rees Rees, who had carried all that grain in the first year, had been preceded on the site by William Griffith, a Methodist from Cardiganshire who had crossed with the Simon James party and had been one of the very first men up in the winter of 1796. In 1804, he wrote in a wretched spirit (in part of course functional!) to beg a favour of Benjamin Rush:

By my own ignorance, it happened that the land that I have settled upon is far worse than but few places that have been settled by any of the Welch people excepting such of them that have long ago left us and their improvements. I have through great difficulty partly cleared and improved about 12 acres of land and although the weight of timber is inexpressible yet the stones that is in every part of it (excepting a very few acres of wet meadow ground) disheartens me more than the weight of timber and withal the land is so poor that it is in vain to attempt to raise either wheat or corn in any part of it. On that account I have put in no winter grain this fall only one bushel of rye and by being put too so hard by providing the necessaries of life for myself and family (although our victuals as to their quality and cloathing have been I believe more scanty than but few in the state) my fences are so far out of order that I am realy ashamed to see them so that I have not attempted to keep a hog this upwards of two years. I have through great labour raised a good stock of cattle but the labour that I have had by cutting Lynn for them in the winters togeather with living too much on vegetable food and several other hardships that I have suffered since I have settled here has hurted my health very much so that I cannot sustain hard labour as I could formerly and indeed cannot look at the cattle that I have raised as my own by thinking of what is to be paid for the land before I am entitled to it.

He recognised the generosity of Rush's 'behaviours' towards the settlers in forgiving them much interest and one-eighth of the principal; this would be a large sum on 100 acres, never mind the whole settlement he had sold. But he could not meet the present terms even if he sold all his stock. He couldn't pay the interest without annually decreasing that stock. He had been 'making my moan' to Thomas W. Jones. He asked Rush to postpone interest payments for four years and to forgive him a quarter of the principal.[25] The response to his petition is not known, but in the tax return of a few years later, with a wife, a teenage son and three young daughters, he was said to have cleared ten of his 200 acres and to own a horse and three head of cattle.[26]

His old comrade Rees Rees wrote his begging letter to Rush two

months later than Griffith. After agreeing that it was something better
now, he asked for 50 acres of donation land (a practice started in 1801).
His land was producing grain but to produce more, he would have to
cut down the 20 acres of good sugar camp he'd cleared, and sugar was
his most profitable crop. If the 50 acres were granted, he would buy 50
more and add them to the 100 he already owned. In the tax return, Rees
Rees, with a wife, four young girls and one teenage daughter, was said
to have cleared 15 acres of his hundred, and was credited with a horse
and five head of cattle. His assessment was $210 to William Griffith's
$252.[27]

Both died within a year of each other in 1831-2. Rees Rees's will
contained merely a curt injunction to his sons-in-law, who included
Jabez Tibbot, to sell his property and distribute the money after the
death of his widow. William Griffith left his wife (who had a mahogany
bureau) a carding machine, with its dam, race and machinery, all his
bees, half his grain, potatoes and household goods, two cows and a
horse, the house adjacent to the western end or *pen* (head) of his barn,
all his bottom land and pasture field and the partly cleared area north
of the garden. His daughter Gwen got the part-tract of 90 acres, 42
perches and her husband, Richard Tibbot, was given $5 and a heifer.
Other daughters and their husbands were given a total of $100 and 'the
rest' went to his son Griffith, together with those 'books I cherish'
(even though he signed by mark) – a Welsh Bible and Baxter's *Saints*.[28]
Of course, William Griffith *did* come from Cardiganshire!

Despite the dreadful collapse of hope and morale in 1798, then,
there was clearly something to build on. Thomas Watkin Jones, eagerly
supported by John J. Evans, who took out no fewer than 11 town lots
in Beula and started a shop to supplement his tavern, threw himself
into remedial action.[29] Characteristically, Morgan Rhees and his men
at once turned to political action. They sent in a petition to Somerset
county to have Cambria made a recognised township, with the voting
station at Beula. They voted two to one in favour of the Republicans
against the Federalists in Miles Phillips's house, when the petition was
granted in June 1798. Equally characteristically, however, this action
by Somerset county (which had itself been formed only in 1795) en-
raged the Germans of the south. Under Joseph Johns and John Horner,
they protested against this 'high-handed Welsh outrage', pointing out
that they had to walk 18 miles through almost unbroken forest and
over often impassable streams to take part in town meetings and to vote
(which they did roughly fifty-fifty between Republicans and Federalists).
Their request was granted in the December and the German area was

included within another township.[30] The squabble is symptomatic. In reporting the creation of the new Cambrian township, Rhees had said to Rush:

> there is not a doubt but we shall soon have a new county and it is not improbable but that the seat of justice will be at Beula, at any rate it will be the most centrical situation and on account of its Library will have superior privileges to any town west of the Allegheny.

This prospect was central to their thinking and the reasoning behind it proved correct.[31]

The Library got its charter from Pennsylvania in May 1798 and in September, Rhees allotted no fewer than 350 town lots to it. For several years he delivered the annual keynote oration at the school. In the same year he brought out a short-lived newspaper, *The Western Sky*, edited at Beula, largely written by Rhees, and printed at Philadelphia by Conrad, printer to the Missionary Society. His addresses at Greenville were published, too.[32] This sustained publicity was followed up in 1799 by what became an annual visit to the state assembly, where he lobbied endlessly for Cambria, trying to get it made a county with Beula as the capital, trying to interest other land-holders in an alliance.[33] Back in the west, new roads to Huntingdon in the north and Somerset in the south were authorised and Thomas W. Jones began to supervise the physical work of cutting them through the forests. There seems to have been a spurt in building during 1798 and 1799, reinforced by the first recruits from another wave of emigration from Wales building up over the terrible years from 1799 to 1801. Log cabins, often with stone or brick foundations and brick chimneys, were now rising and Thomas Phillips started on the stone foundations of a massive building designed for public purposes.[34]

It was all in vain. The winter of 1798-9 was even worse than the previous one. When Rhees got back to Beula from the assembly, he found there had been another disaster to the mills. The sawmill was useless and it would cost more to repair it than it would have done to build something effective in the first place. There was still trouble over gristmills, too. No money had come in towards the road either, but they were going on with it 'by anticipation'.[35] Thomas Ustick, the building supervisor, also wrote gloomily. Rush's window-glass had come, but Ustick had not got on with the doctor's house, 'as the Situation of your lots does not Suit for building a house of Lush Magnitude though the Cituation is very pleasant, but will not do for business I think'. It would be better to build on Joy Street. He had engaged a carpenter from Greensburg to build two rooms and the man meant to build a house himself during the summer. Ustick added, 'in all provability we shall make considerable improvement here in the coarse of the summer but in order for that to take place it will be necessary for all who are consirned to doe what they can for us.'[36]

In fact, the settlement was beginning to break up. Rhees found that two families had already left and that more were leaving. Moreover, more and more were beginning to protest and complain: 'There are some bad characters among ourselves which I am anxious to see on their journey, they have done much mischief by poisoning the public mind with jealousies and false alarms.' The answer was a further attempt to build up an alliance to populate the western counties. The *Western Sky* set itself to attract settlers and to win the approval of speculators like Henry Drinker and Zaccheus Collins. Rhees and Thomas W. Jones were soon claiming that Beula would shortly be ringed by 500 busy and prosperous farmers. Another slate of town lots was showered on Philadelphia merchants and landowners and Rhees began to argue the case for a cartel of land-holders, financed by a levy, which would employ Thomas Watkin Jones as an agent and field manager and develop the whole area with Beula as a focus, rather in the style of the Holland Company of New York.[37]

It was at this time, in fact, that Henry Drinker and Zaccheus Collins began to employ both Jones and Simon James as agents. Drinker, as early as February 1799, sent Thomas W. Jones the plans and outlines (which were, characteristically, still very vague and inaccurate) of some 25 tracts totalling over 10,000 acres which he held near the Beula lands. The agency he transferred to Jones from Patrick Cassidy with an order to get the lands settled.[38] Zaccheus Collins, who was also vague about his tracts, followed suit and in the following year signed a contract with Simon James for the peopling of his land. Simon James leased from Collins a tract originally patented to a John Hall of about 400 acres, on which he had already begun to make improvements. He was, within ten years, to clear and enclose 100 acres, 12 of them meadow, and to plant and maintain at least 200 apple trees. He was to build a good log house at least 16 feet square and a log barn, each end of which was to be 24 feet square. He was to live on the site. At the end of the ten-year span, he was to be free to purchase the tract for $1,082 on easy terms. This was a standard form of contract, in that from this base James was to attract settlers to this and other tracts, on sub-leases with similar stipulations.

A brief fragment of a report which Simon James prepared for Collins three years later bears its own witness to the struggle to populate Cambria:

house F.	Edward Evans on Tract Courtney.	GOING
house Q.	David Reese (tract John Hall) cleared about 12 acres on 100 at 10/–	DEAD
house V.	Simon James (John Hall) cleared 18 acres, 100 donation. Exclusive of his own labour.	
house	William Thomas (John Hall) blacksmith. 100 acres at 20/–	GOING
house	Samuel Jones (John Hall) cleared 9 acres. Cost 100 besides his own labour (50 acres at 20/–	GOING
	N.B. Simon James has 166 acres left.	
house	Thomas Powell, Baptist minister. Cleared considerably on John Ives Tract.	GOING

John Reese made some clearance on George Steed Tract but left it, finding it too hard to clear.

Mr. T.W. Jones procured two settlers by virtue of my power to him, viz.

William Davies on T.M. Cope Tract on south end.

William Price on C. Jervis Tract, on south end.	DEAD

Mr. Thomas Reese has settled on J. Parrish Tract.[39]

This deadly struggle produced in 1800 what was virtually a rebellion within Beula. By this time, shiploads of the Welsh were once again coming into the ports and Beula-Cambria was the natural destination of many of them. At Beula, the critical achievement was the final opening of the road, after much labour and the shouldering of much debt. Its immediate effect was disastrous. By June 1800, Rhees, after another fruitless session at the state assembly, was gloomily reporting to Rush, 'Settlers, chagrined with disappointments, are quitting our settlement in different directions.'

Once again, the mills had failed: 'The second sawmill has been taken all to pieces.' Moreover the gristmill could not be finished. In the event, it had been little needed, for during the summer there had been a mass exodus. This 'Clearfield expedition' remains obscure, but evidently a substantial number of settlers, some out of spleen, many, said Rhees, 'duped from a sense of their duty', had quit the settlement to look for better land elsewhere. They returned in defeat. Many then left but many others, in a spirit which ranged from the surly to the resigned, were remaining. The prime mover in the affair had been Ebenezer Hickling. Its failure turned him into a remorseless enemy. He quit the settlement and, according to Rhees, henceforth did all he could to undermine it. Joseph Moore had also been involved but now repented of it and had agreed to act as deputy surveyor under Thomas W. Jones.

And the atmosphere had turned poisonous. Rhees talks of 'the torrent of opposition and slanderous reproach which has been poured on my head . . . It has been the study and glory of some mischief makers among us to drive every newcomer away . . . I have threatened to take legal measures.' The expedition and the mass defections threw the settlement's financial affairs into chaos, Rhees was now being throttled in a dense and complex web of debt. The third sawmill was raised in July and cost another £1,000.[40]

Frustration bred malice and recrimination. The community was becoming claustrophobic. 'Mrs. Phillips has followed her husband down the country,' Rhees exploded at one point, 'and we all hope she never will return to live here.' It is impossible now to get at the cause or occasion of these quarrels, but they could be deadly. A story was current years later, for example, about a Mrs. Phillips who had disrupted the funeral service for her young son Thomas, when she interpreted the minister's address as implying that the dead boy was the only one in the family who had been any good. The body had been carried off in dudgeon from the graveyard and buried in a lonely fenced-off grave in the woods. Some Beula people, irritated by this performance, at once bought the freedom of the indentured labourer the Phillipses had brought with them; the lad apparently died on the spot from shock and was promptly buried in the now-vacant grave which he himself had dug![41]

Small wonder that Rhees's annual address to the Beula Seminary that September was distinctly defensive in tone:

We have laid the foundation of a seminary of learning, and considerable property, with an extensive library, have been given towards its support. The value of these have not yet been realised agreeable to our wishes. We have met with obstacles, have yet to encounter difficulties and probably to stem a torrent of disappointments. Are we prepared to meet them? Have we resources equal to the undertaking? Some of you reply in the affirmative and others reluctantly say No! In this divided state, what is to be done? Shall we proceed or leave the fabric unfinished? Is there amongst us no Zechariah to stimulate the people to action?

There was little doubt about Morgan John's reply. He summoned them to battle yet again, ending with the call — 'On with Jefferson! Jefferson and liberty! Jefferson and peace!'[42]

To Benjamin Rush, he spoke in more desperate terms — 'One effort more! and then, if I do not overcome the Philistines, they must conquer me.'[43] But, indeed, in the autumn of 1800, he seems temporarily to have rallied the Cambria settlers. Many of those who had gone on the Clearfield expedition were afflicted with a certain shame. Despite the psychological bruising the community had suffered, there was an inflow of newcomers during 1800, and to an outsider, Cambria and Beula were beginning to present a respectable appearance. At the Census of 1800, the township was credited with a population of 445 souls and 88 heads of families. Some were German and more Irish, but over 50 families were Welsh and it was they who gave the settlement its character. There were now 60 to 70 cabins in and around Beula, many with stone foundations. More impressive buildings were in the course of construction. There were two chapels, a school, an embryo seminary and Freemason's lodge. William Tibbot and Thomas Phillips had their mills going at last. Many of the men had taken work on the roads as teamsters and some of the Phillipses had themselves started a wagon service to Philadelphia. By this time, Rhees, Thomas W. Jones and Hickling were all JPs and associate judges of Somerset county. John J. Evans was employed by the county and a Somerset court was once held at his tavern.[44]

It was at this time that Rhees finally yielded to the promptings of Pennsylvania's Jeffersonian Governor McKean. In his great purge of the Federalists, McKean had twice offered the key administrative post in Somerset county to Rhees, but had been refused. By this time, however, Morgan John was worn down, anxious about his financial prospects and the security of his growing family. He finally accepted the post of Prothonotary and Clerk of Courts of Somerset. George Washington Loxley, his brother-in-law, moved into Beula at this time, perhaps to act as his representative and, though the Welshman at this stage continued to maintain close contact with Cambria, he took up official residence in Somerset town towards the end of 1800. 'Debt! Debt!' he cried to Rush:

> Cure me once of this malady, doctor, and I promise never to be afflicted with it again. Money! Money! if the love of it is the root of all evil, the want of it to a man of business is the *great devil* . . . were it not for the office, which I refused twice, I should soon run ashore without bread for my family. The ways of God which are equally

mysterious in the wilderness as in the ocean are not known till often travelled and even then, like the Hebrew alphabet, must always be read backwards.[45]

He soon had need of a cipher. After yet another dreary wrangle at the Pennsylvania assembly in the spring of 1801, he returned to a Beula in which the temporary equilibrium of the autumn of 1800 had broken down. In May 1801, he addressed a truly desperate letter to Rush:

Something must be done or our settlements are undone. My health is impaired and every feeling of soul harassed by a perverse and crooked generation . . . Several of our settlers returned towards Philadelphia, others are going to the westward. A Mr. Lloyd, one of our ministers, is now travelling in quest of a better country. He is likely to do us considerable injury. I had given him 50 acres of land in fee and all the encouragement in my power, but since our road has been opened and the travellers become numerous, himself and others have been seised with a kind of mania for migrating to some paradise where they may live without work.[46]

This was the first mention of Rees Lloyd as a dissident and it was even more serious than Rhees had indicated. For the defection of Lloyd signalled an organised Welsh secession from Cambria and the breakdown of the Beula project as Morgan John Rhees had conceived it.

Notes

1. For Evans's experiences on the Missouri, see my *Madoc: the Making of a Myth* (Eyre Methuen, London, 1980), Chapter 10.
2. *Aurora* (Pennsylvania), 7 July 1797; this and other cuttings are in Cambria Historical Society.
3. Examples of these in Cambria Historical Society and see reprint in J.T. Griffith, *Morgan John Rhys* (USA, 1899 and Carmarthen, 1910), pp. 249-52.
4. My comments are based on Ray A. Billington's *Westward Expansion: a History of the American Frontier* (2nd edn, New York, 1960), on my reading of the correspondence between Benjamin Rush and William Cooper, and on my observation of the area.
5. For the general history of the district, see H. Wilson Storey, *History of Cambria County*, 3 vols. (New York, 1907); W.H. Koontz (ed.), *History of Bedford and Somerset Counties* (New York, 1906); and W.H. Egle, *History of the Commonwealth of Pennsylvania* (Philadelphia, 1883).
6. Launched later in the century. The streets have Welsh names, the inhabitants Slav, though there are still Welsh families in the area. One Pennsylvania-Dutch (German) farmer told me he steered clear of Ebensburg-Nant-y-Glo because it was

a Welsh town. This comment, which appears to me lunatic, should perhaps be recorded.

7. For this brief encounter, see the correspondence between Rush, John and John Craig Millar, Edward Fisher and John Black of Edinburgh and Henry Drinker in Benjamin Rush papers, vols. 4, 5 and 24, Historical Society of Pennsylvania.

8. See Wilson Storey, *History of Cambria County*, and the material in Cambria Historical Society.

9. William Cooper—B. Rush, 23 March 1790, Benjamin Rush papers, vol. 26.

10. M.J. Rhees—B. Rush, 26 July 1798, Benjamin Rush papers, vol. 14 (all the Rhees—Rush correspondence which survives in this collection is in vol. 14).

11. Federal Census 1800, Somerset county, Cambria township, in Somerset court-house; *Cambria Freeman*, 20 January 1872.

12. Notebook in Cambria Historical Society.

13. On Citizen Richard Lee, see my *Artisans and Sans-culottes: Popular Movements in Britain and France during the French Revolution* (E. Arnold, London, 1968; reprinted 1973) and the occasional hostile references in William Cobbett's American journal *Porcupine's Gazette*.

14. Edward Carey Gardiner collection, Mathew Carey section, box 84a, Historical Society of Pennsylvania; Priestley's indenture is still on display in his Northumberland (Pennsylvania) house.

15. The material in this paragraph is derived from Morgan Rhees's library notebook in Cambria Historical Society.

16. Recorded in Somerset county and Cambria county, Deed Book 1 in each case, court-houses of Somerset and Ebensburg.

17. Haines had been a benefactor to Joseph Priestley; see Mary C. Park, *Joseph Priestley and the Problem of Pantisocracy* (Philadelphia, 1947).

18. George Roberts—B. Rush, 9 January 1812, Benjamin Rush papers, vol. 14.

19. E. Winchester—B. Rush, 18 February 1792, 13 March 1793, Benjamin Rush papers, vol. 20.

20. For the material in this and the following three paragraphs, see M.J. Rhees—B. Rush, 26 July 1798, Benjamin Rush papers, vol. 14.

21. R. Rees—B. Rush, 23 January 1805, Benjamin Rush papers, vol. 14.

22. George Roberts—his parents, 13 October 1801, NLW 14094, reprinted in A.H. Dodd, 'Letters from Cambria County 1800-1823', *Pennsylvania History*, vol. xxii (1955).

23. Cambria county tax assessment 1810, Ebensburg court-house. This material has also been used to some extent by Kate Alletha Standish, 'The Racial Origins of the Early Settlers of Cambria County', (unpublished AM thesis, University of Pittsburgh, 1934), but my calculations differ from hers; she adopts criteria for 'Welsh-speaking people' which I do not seem to understand. I have based my identifications on the copious material available in the deed books, will books, minutes, rolls, dockets of the quarter sessions of Somerset and Cambria counties, and in Cambria Historical Society.

24. On Tibbot, see Cambria county tax assessment 1810; Census return, Somerset county, Cambria township, 1800; his will dated 16 February 1822 and registered 26 December 1827, is in Will Book 1, Cambria county. There is copious material on him, particularly in connection with the First Congregational Church, Ebensburg, in Cambria Historical Society.

25. W. Griffith—B. Rush, 2 December 1804, Benjamin Rush papers, vol. 6.

26. Cambria county tax assessment 1810, Ebensburg court-house.

27. See R. Rees—B. Rush, 23 January 1805, Benjamin Rush papers, vol. 14; Cambria county tax assessment 1810, Ebensburg court-house.

28. Cambria county, Will Book 1, Ebensburg court-house.

29. Somerset county, Deed Books 1-4 and Cambria county, Deed Book 1, in

Somerset and Ebensburg court-houses.

30. Somerset county, Quarter Sessions, petitions, June and December 1798.

31. M.J. Rhees—B. Rush, 26 July 1798, Benjamin Rush papers, vol. 14.

32. The seminary and library are mentioned frequently in Somerset county Deed Books; the *Western Sky* is known now only by report.

33. M.J. Rhees—B. Rush, 11 December 1802, Benjamin Rush papers, vol. 14, where he says he attended the legislature for three successive years, and frequent references in the correspondence.

34. Somerset county, road dockets, *passim*; M.J. Rhees—B. Rush, 28 September 1799, Benjamin Rush papers, vol. 14; *Cambria Freeman*, 10 June 1871, 20 January 1872; *Cambria Herald*, 2 September 1873, 12 August 1894.

35. M.J. Rhees—B. Rush, 28 September 1799, Benjamin Rush papers, vol. 14.

36. T. Ustick—B. Rush, 10 February 1799, Benjamin Rush papers, vol. 10.

37. See Somerset county, Deed Books; newspaper advertisements in cuttings at Cambria Historical Society; M.J. Rhees—B. Rush, September 1800—December 1802, Benjamin Rush papers, vol. 14; Zaccheus Collins: papers and letter-book 1801-4; Henry Drinker: letter-books 1796-1800, 1800-2, all in Historical Society of Pennsylvania.

38. H. Drinker—T.W. Jones, 28 February 1799—11 October 1800, Henry Drinker letter-books 1796-1802, Historical Society of Pennsylvania.

39. This contract and report are among the Zaccheus Collins papers, Historical Society of Pennsylvania.

40. On the crisis of this year, the Clearfield expedition, Hickling and the feuds within Cambria, see M.J. Rhees—B. Rush, 4 June, 21 July 1800, 10 May 1801, Benjamin Rush papers, vol. 14.

41. This story by an old Beula resident was remembered in the *Cambria Herald*, 12 August 1894, and thought good enough to reprint in the *Mountaineer*, 27 June 1938. However unlikely it seems and however it has grown in the meantime, few Welsh people, I think, would find it hard to believe at least the original incident! It is impossible to say whether this fiery Mrs Phillips who did not shrink from the ultimate deterrent was the same as the woman Morgan John was glad to see the back of; there were several Phillips families.

42. Rhees's address of 22 September 1800 is in the Gratz collection, Historical Society of Pennsylvania.

43. M.J. Rhees—B. Rush, 10 May 1801, Benjamin Rush papers, vol. 14.

44. My calculations from the Census return, Cambria township, Somerset county for 1800; appointments and offices in Somerset county, Quarter Sessions records; impressions of Beula from memoirs, local histories, etc. in Cambria Historical Society.

45. M.J. Rhees—B. Rush, 17 September 1801, Benjamin Rush papers, vol. 14; Rhees's name is very prominent in the records of Somerset county 1800-4; one of his charges to the Somerset Grand Jury, in characteristic style, is in the Gratz collection of the Historical Society of Pennsylvania.

46. M.J. Rhees—B. Rush, 10 May 1801, Benjamin Rush papers, vol. 14.

8 EXODUS

The fate of Beula was decided in the critical conjuncture of 1801. The new land law at last passed Congress. It was the first workable land law for the new territories. Lowering the minimum purchase to 320 acres, it extended credit to 75 per cent of the price. It was from this moment that the tide of settlement really swept out across the Ohio, generating in its rear an Ohio fever as contagious as Kentucky mania.[1] At that very moment, emigration from Britain and Wales suddenly accelerated. Under these twin pressures, Beula cracked.

It was the migration which first registered on settlers' minds. The grain crisis of 1800-1 in Britain was in many ways even worse than that of 1795-6.[2] It was made all the more intolerable by a widespread suspicion that the shortage was artificial and by a totally negative response by government and Parliament to a massive campaign of petitioning, in which *Jacobins* surfaced once more. Whole districts seethed with sedition and a serious, insurrectionary underground took shape.

Once again, great waves of revolt, riot and protest swept across many regions. This time, the Volunteers mutinied. In the aftermath of the Irish rebellion and its ghastly suppression, repressive measures pressed hard on *Jacobin* and working-class movements growling back into action, even as trade unionists organised massively to defeat the Combination Acts. Widespread war-weariness sharpened subversion. By late 1801 there was wholesale disaffection in many areas which, after the peace of Amiens, spilled over into symptomatic spurts of rebellion and the Despard conspiracy.

Wales could not escape. From early in 1800, disturbances spread across mid-Wales from Towyn and Machynlleth and the dragoons were sent in. In the spring, a spectacular popular action convulsed the new industrial areas around Dowlais and Beaufort and in the autumn the Merthyr district erupted into massive insurrection. By early 1801, the whole of north Wales was said to be disaffected and arming and in the dreadful spring there were explosions in Pembrokeshire and the southwest. Troops scoured Wales; men were hanged, shadowy but ubiquitous *Jacobins* reported. Pikes were being made in both north and south and a revolt in the north was genuinely feared. In these circumstances, many of the Welsh once again voted with their feet.

Even in struggling Cambria, people were appalled at the news from home. There was worse to come. For some reason, possibly the very abruptness of the emigration movement, the sea-crossings of 1800-1 were marred by heart-breaking tragedy. In one letter home on 13 October 1801, George Roberts reported two terrible disasters. In one vessel recently arrived in Baltimore, eight children and forty adults had died, some of them in the harbour itself. In the ship used by his own sisters earlier, 53 out of 102 passengers had died at sea. Four young widows had come with his sisters to Cambria and they were only now recovering. Two people died on the way inland to Beula, leaving four children as stranded orphans. The death-list was harrowing: 'Abraham Tibbot, William Davies the mason, Ann o'r Allt, David Price and David Harry's children, Evans's wife from Llanidloes, John Evans and his children, Morgan Owen, Idris Thomas and his children, James Mills and his daughter. Twm bach had been brought into Cambria, having lost his parents ... For God's sake make sure your water is good, keep it out of the heat ...' The news from Wales and the Atlantic crossings was so bad that George Roberts had taken to his bed for ten weeks.[3]

With Welsh people dying on the crossing like blacks on the slave ships, the letters from the survivors in Philadelphia and New York had a shattering effect in Cambria, all the more poignant for their restraint and the high vision of America they expressed: 'Through the mercy of the Lord', wrote David Williams, shoemaker of *Coomddwynant*, spokesman for a decimated group just into New York from south Wales, addressing himself to Rees Lloyd whom they all remembered:

> we have the priviledge to take the pen in hand to acquint you from the Land you called Land of Fridom ... We are now like ship must founder. Do not know where to go. Some say hear and others there. Now I desire of you to send me a true intelligence of your settlement by the return of post. I will try to come to your settlement.[4]

Rees Lloyd could take no more of it. It was probably a hard decision for him. He was one of the most successful settlers in Cambria and Morgan Rhees had just given him 50 acres. But he had also just lost his little girl Rachel to the wilderness. On 23 March 1801, he wrote an anguished letter to Samuel Jones Pennepek.[5] Did he know of any comfortable spot of land to direct his fellow-countrymen to? Lately many letters had come pouring in from Wales and from people who had already crossed and Rees Lloyd was at his wits' end:

> I do not blame this settlment. I am rather thinking it will go on, and

that shall be a flourishing country here in time. Great improvements made on the roads and in Beula this year. But it is too hard for poor people make a living upon this land on the account of its heavy clearing and slow producings. It require good deal of money and a strong team and to buy their provitions the twice or thrice first years. I cannot with a clear conscience to encourage my poor countrymen and friends to depend much on this place and 'tis a heavy trouble to my mind to see honest and industrious people working hard and after all could not aquire an Independent Situation.

He thought such a land as Cambria ought to be granted at a low price or at ten or twelve years without interest: 'There is many new settlements in the western territories and near the Lakes and flattering encouragements to settle in them.' He was in a quandary because of his ignorance. He did not want to lead people into a 'discomfortable situation', but something had to be done. 'May the Lord direct us.' His inclination was towards the 'military land' (the Ohio) and he begged Samuel Jones for information. His own sons and their friends were anxious to form a Welsh settlement in a better country. In fact a group had approached Rees Lloyd himself to act as a searcher, but he asked the Philadelphia minister to keep the news to himself: 'I would rather to keep it secret for some laid out much of their property in this place.'

A little later he sent Samuel Jones the terms (in Welsh) of a New Society which many of the Welsh had formed. All were to have equal rights. Every denomination was to live together, if its members so wished. All pledged themselves to two days' labour a month on behalf of those who went to look for land. 'There is some report lately', added Lloyd hopefully, 'that there shall be a vast deal of land this summer for the settling of it.' The organisation of this Welsh society was the death of Morgan John's Beula.

The root cause was evidently the brute reality of a difficult settlement, but there were clearly other sources of friction.[6] The stress on the integrity of the denomination in this new society is one indication. Rees Lloyd was a man of high and dedicated sectarian temper. Born in 1759 at Llanboidy in Carmarthenshire, he entered the ministry at the age of 21 and was called to Ebenezer Independent chapel in Pontypool to assist old Edmund Jones. He had been ordained on 29 April 1795 in Pontypool by five ministers, with prayer and the laying-on-of-hands. David Jones of the Great Valley would have approved.

When Rees Lloyd finally quit Cambria in 1817, to serve in Paddy's Run, Ohio, he gave its land to the First Congregational Church of

Ebensburg. The terms of the covenant were striking. The Independents
of Ebensburg were bound to the strictest orthodoxy: the divinity of
Christ, the Atonement and the absolute necessity of the effectual work
of the Holy Ghost in the conversion of sinners. If a majority deserted
this creed, the church was to pass to the minority. If the whole community deserted it, the church was forfeit and was to pass to the nearest
congregation of English Presbyterians.[7]

In 1811, Lloyd wrote a book, *The Richmond Alarm*. A playhouse in
Richmond had been destroyed by fire. Lloyd interpreted this as the
judgement of God and wrote in approval of divine censorship.[8] George
Roberts and William Tibbot, who were to serve as co-pastors of the
Congregational church, seem to have been men of similar temper.
Roberts, made a judge in 1807, took great pains to enforce moral
legislation, however obsolete, inflicting fines on those (generally Irish
drovers) who worked on a Sunday and who swore on any day, and
carefully noting the facts in Morgan Rhees's little library notebook.
Their cause (and the Baptists') were in fact to lose many of the next
generation wholesale, John Lloyd and Festus Tibbot among them, to
the Campbellites whose church, in final irony, stands to this day, in
permanent rebuke to Baptists and Independents alike, as the First
Christian Church of Ebensburg.

Ironically, this, of course, was the title of Morgan John's original
religious society. There is no need to point out that there was little of
the sectarian about him. Moreover, just as Roberts and Tibbot tended
to rally to Lloyd, Thomas W. Jones, John J. Evans (who, as a tavern-
keeper, was called 'professing to be Christian', by Roberts) and Thomas
Phillips were close to Rhees. None of these men would take an oath in
court; they affirmed. In 1799, Thomas Watkin Jones, together with
Ebenezer Hickling and Joseph Moore, formed a Freemasons' Lodge in
Beula. Morgan John, out of 'the good opinion and respect' which he
held for the Masons and 'for the furtherance of their views', gave the
Lodge two lots in Lamb Street.[9] It comes as no surprise to learn that
when a son was born to Thomas Watkin Jones, the young man called
him Voltaire — Voltaire Goldsmith Jones, no less.[10]

Perhaps too much should not be made of this, since George Roberts
was himself surprised at the good relations between Baptists and Independents in Cambria. It remains a fact that Morgan John's *Christian
Church* was stillborn. The seven articles of this church make striking
reading. They vividly recall Beth-Shalom black church in Savannah and
indeed Roger Williams's original covenant for Rhode Island.

The first five ran:

This Union shall be called the Christian Church. It must never be called by any other name, nor controlled by any particular opinions of any man or party of men. Jesus Christ is the only head, believers the only members and the New Testament the only rule of brotherhood. In intellectual things, every member shall enjoy his own opinions and converse freely upon any subject; but in discipline, minute conformity with the commands of Christ is required. Every separate society that shall unite with this Association, shall have power to receive their members, elect their officers and in case of misconduct, to discipline them.[11]

This strikingly liberal and New Testament creed must have grated on the sensibilities of many reared on that close, devoted, but often crabbed dedication to Biblical text and the minutiae of doctrine which were beginning to colonise the minds of the Welsh. The Christian Church never got off the ground. As early as April 1797, Rees Lloyd led a group of 12 Independents, 11 Methodists and a new member to form Ebenezer Independent chapel a little north of the Beula site. They raised a twenty-foot square log chapel, with a roof of clapboard and not a single nail. Though numbers fell off in the early years as people quit, they held communion once a month.[12] The remainder raised a chapel in the north-east corner of Beula. Since their minister was Morgan Rhees, it was more ambitious in scale, but in practice, it rapidly evolved into an orthodox Baptist cause (in so far as any chapel with Morgan John as minister could be called orthodox!) As is customary in such matters, at least in Wales, passionate loyalties soon crystallised around them. Many people were to keep on going to the Baptist chapel in Beula into the 1870s, even after Beula itself had disappeared and the Baptists themselves had moved into Ebensburg. Many more had themselves buried in the grave-yard of what was, to them, a transplanted version of the *hen dŷ cwrdd* (the Old Meeting House).

No matter how humane Rees Lloyd's motives, those who remained loyal to Beula could see it only as desertion and there was a struggle. Rhees summoned up his energies for one last fight. He rushed first to the state assembly of Pennsylvania. The creation of new counties was in train and the boundary lines proposed were harmful to Cambria. He denounced 'enemies' who were trying to prevent the population of western Pennsylvania. It is impossible to identify these people now. Rhees singled out a senator Johnston who was a Federalist, but so were Gurney and Jones whom he hoped to rally and the motives were probably more brutally self-interested. Rhees and Rush managed to get the Bill postponed.

Rhees urged Rush to offer donation land to hold the settlers and in fact began to give out lots of 50 acres in the summer. Rush finally agreed by the October of 1801. He promised to give 50 acres out of every 400-acre holding to anyone who cleared two acres in a year and in six years built a log house and barn and planted a hundred apple trees. This seems to have held a sufficient number of the old settlers and attracted enough of the new to keep Cambria alive through the exodus of 1801-2.[13]

For in 1801 the lands west of the Ohio, divided into sections, were offered for sale. Ezekiel Hughes and Edward Bebb of Llanbrynmair and their friends the Gwilyms from Cefn Amman, who had sweated it out so long, moved into action. Hughes bought sections 15 and 16 along the Whitewater, the first man to buy land beyond the Miami. Bebb bought a half-section on a fork of the Whitewater. These purchases became the nucleus of what grew into a celebrated Welsh settlement, Paddy's Run. And how ironic it was that the rise of this settlement, on the site which Morgan John Rhees himself had selected way back in May 1795, should now menace his Beula! For while Ezekiel Hughes went back to Llanbrynmair to fetch people, to marry a Bebb and to cause a sensation in his American hat, Edward Bebb went to Cambria to marry a Roberts and tell them about the Ohio settlement. David Francis, who had been married by Morgan John back in Philadelphia, joined him.[14]

And at this critical stage, the final decisive factor came into play — the beaky nose of David Jones of the Great Valley. The 'fighting pastor', who had still not kicked the bucket, was on another of his periodical sorties into the west. He came into Cambria at a critical moment. In that divided community, there was little doubt about his choice. Rhees met his second defeat at the old man's hands. Simon James and John Rees joined David Jones and all three went deep into Ohio. There, on behalf of Theophilus Rees, another of the first-comers to Beula, and many others, they bought the whole of the north-east corner of what became Granville township and the settlement of Welsh Hills. Oddly enough, Rees Lloyd did not join them. 'I had gone away, too,' he wrote many years later, 'except the over-ruling Providence had ordained me to stay in some extraordinary manner which I cannot relate now.' But this expedition was decisive. In 1802, led by the Indian scout Jimmie Johnson and moving through Wheeling and the newly opened Zane's Trace, a party moved to Granville to begin settlement. About the same time, James Nicholas took another party from Cambria to the Miami area. Edward Bebb's son William, destined to be Governor, was the first white child born in the settlement.[15]

Morgan Rhees recognised his personal defeat. In 1802, in a complicated series of transfers and exchanges, he restored to Benjamin Rush all the lands of the original grant which lay outside Beula proper, and established himself finally in Somerset. There he began at last to flourish and to find some peace of mind. He made an efficient Clerk, found a friend in Otto Shrader of the Pennsylvania-Dutch community and proved popular. In default of a Baptist community, he used to preach to his clerk who bore the rather un-Baptist name of John Sullivan. A chapel was later launched by people who remembered Rhees with affection. A Benjamin Rush Rhees and a Thomas Jefferson Rhees (who died in infancy) were born. His letters grow calmer.[16]

Peace, however, he was not to find this side of the grave. Benjamin Rush granted several of the restored tracts to the Philadelphia Anti-Slavery Society and in 1805 handed over the remainder to his son Richard who was anxious to get rid of them.[17] Beula at this point still existed, though there were only nine families in residence, most of them, interestingly enough, craftsmen. But Thomas Watkin Jones and John J. Evans acquired many properties from Rhees, who still maintained a house in the skeleton town. And while decimated Beula was serving at this time largely as a staging-post on the route to the Ohio settlements, there was still a substantial Welsh population in Cambria. The whole troubled issue was re-opened when, in March 1804, Pennsylvania created Cambria County. The Welsh were occupying the centre of the new juris-diction. Within a year, a county seat was to be chosen, no more than seven miles from that geographical centre.

All over the new county, men girded themselves for action, for to be chosen as the seat of justice and administration might make a township's future.[18] Over in Loretto, Prince Gallitzin stayed aloof; he did not want lawyers mixing with his innocent people. But Munster put in a claim. Rhees, roused to his last battle, went into action for Beula. He travelled to Washington and got the mail extended through the town. The faithful John J. Evans became postmaster and made his first report in January 1805.[19] However shrunken, Beula after all, was still in existence, with a post office, a road and what had been a remarkable library. Morgan John was spent out, but he felt that the seminary with its library would carry the day, since the authorities were primarily concerned with the provision of land for public buildings in the new centre. He, with Rush's help, tried to get Philadelphians to pledge books and a 'trifling donation' if Beula were chosen.[20]

The events which followed were quite remarkable.[21] For in August 1804, Rees Lloyd bought from Benjamin Rush one of the original tracts — Mere — which had been part of Rhees's purchase in 1796 and which he had restored in 1802. On this tract, Lloyd announced the plotting of a new town which he called Ebensburg, some say in memory of his son who died in the Great Valley, others in memory of Ebenezer chapel Pontypool. The first town plan was an unfinished draft which ended in a dotted line. Late in 1805, Lloyd, in a complicated transaction with the executors of William Jenkins, bought 100 acres of another tract (again one of Morgan John's originals) and added a chunk of it to the town. The town plan itself was not patented and filed in court until July 1807, two years after the battle was over. The *Small and Elegant Atlas* by the celebrated Aaron Arrowsmith and Samuel Lewis, which was published in 1804, was still showing Beula as part of Somerset county, without a trace of Ebensburg.

The launching of Ebensburg was unmistakably a direct attack on Rhees and his Beula.[22] During 1804 there was an inflow into Cambria and Lloyd reported a religious revival. No fewer than 29 families were admitted into the Independent chapel in the course of the year. A new and larger chapel was built. There was evidently a rally around Lloyd and against the Beula intransigents. The battle was fierce. Ebensburg won. According to the historian Walkinshaw, it defeated Beula by only two votes.[23]

Lloyd won by generously pledging a whole slate of town lots to the support of public buildings, the court-house and the jail.[24] It is to be noted, further, that he also pledged town lots totalling a third of the town's area, to Nathaniel W. Sample, a minister from Lancaster county who was an assemblyman and apparently an influential one. Lloyd established a close liaison with Sample. One of his sons went to live with Sample but after a few months left him, addressing his father in trenchant terms — 'Finding the pursuit of wealth incompatible with learning and the Christian character, I have relinquished it.'[25] Sample himself seems to have been less rigid. Entering into his inheritance in Ebensburg, by skilfully driven alleys, he doubled it. 'A fine performance by a Christian minister!' wrote one former Beula resident, still irate in 1873.[26] Rees Lloyd's town was a much smaller and simpler affair than Beula. His street names differed, too. The street directly facing Beula was named Triumph. Lloyd named one street after Sample. Another was named after one of the three new county commissioners, to whom Lloyd had also conveyed town properties. This was Alexander Ogle, known as Spoony Ogle because he once denounced President van Buren for living in Oriental luxury when he discovered there were silver spoons in the White House.[27] Alexander Horner of the German community, another commissioner, was also honoured, but not John J. Evans of

Beula, third of the commissioners. Lloyd named one street after himself, another after his daughter Fanny, whose name, fortunately for the dignity of the county seat, he spelt Phany (it has gently mutated into Phaney). To achieve his end, Rees Lloyd mortgaged himself to the hilt and was unable to pay off the mortgage until 1818. Civic memorials pay tribute to his generosity and with reason. It should also be noted, however, that the county leased or sold back to him a large proportion of the property he had given it. When all is said, one cannot help feeling that Beula died, not with a bang but a whimper.

For die it now did. The siting of the seat of justice at Ebensburg proved decisive. It was said that some houses were literally moved up the hill from Beula into the new town. Many of 'Pompey''s chimneys certainly were. Beula church itself finally moved into Ebensburg, though Morgan Rhees's school was run as a pay school by Henry George for some time and there were burials in the old churchyard as late as the 1870s. The little site was soon celebrated for its ruins and its lonely graveyard. As the very stones crumbled, it became the 'ghost village'. No house was built there after 1804. Perhaps it can be said finally to have died when Thomas Watkin Jones died in 1808, at the age of 36; at the very latest when John J. Evans went in 1829. Much of the land ultimately passed to one man, Griffith Lloyd, who, in 1844, was the first to report the Beula ghost.[28]

Notes

1. Ray Billington, *Westward Expansion: a History of the American Frontier* (2nd edn, New York, 1960), especially Chapter 12; Rhees's diary has a little material on the problem, as seen from Cincinatti in 1795.

2. For a brief and vivid picture of the situation as it affected Wales, see D.J.V. Jones, *Before Rebecca: Popular Protest in Wales 1793-1835* (Allen Lane, London, 1973), Chapters 1 and 2; my thinking is derived from the York PhD thesis of my friend Roger A.E. Wells, on the grain troubles and popular disaffection of 1795-1801: 'The Grain Crises in Late Eighteenth-century England', York, 1978.

3. These appalling stories are in a letter from George Roberts to his parents, reprinted in A.H. Dodd's collection, 'Letters from Cambria County 1800-1823', *Pennsylvania History*, vol. xxii (1955), cited above.

4. David Williams—Rees Lloyd, probably November 1799, Cambria Historical Society.

5. For this letter and the one that follows, R. Lloyd—S. Jones, 23 March 1801 and n.d. (but clearly a little later): Pennepek.

6. This sketch of Rees Lloyd is based on a memoir by George Roberts, published in *Cyfaill*, vol. i (1838) and translated in *Biographical Cyclopedia of Cambria County* (Philadelphia, 1896), on C.T. Roberts's typescript 'Centennial History of the First Congregational Church' (Cambria Historical Society, Ebensburg n.d.), on

the material collected for the anonymous *Home Coming Celebration of the First Congregational Church, Ebensburg* (1934) and on the heterogeneous material in Cambria Historical Society.

7. Deed, 21 November 1817, Cambria county, Deed Book 1.

8. From George Roberts's memoir, cited above.

9. Deed, 18 December 1799 in Somerset county, Deed Book 1 and Quarter Sessions records, *passim*.

10. Testament of Thomas Watkin Jones, 30 May 1807, Cambria county, Will Book 1. This only son seems to have suppressed his name and taken his father's — at least on a sentimental pilgrimage to the Beula ruins in 1871, he was called T.W. Jones junior (*Cambria Freeman*, 10 June 1871).

11. J.T. Griffith, *Morgan John Rhys* (USA, 1899 and Carmarthen, 1910), pp. 264-6, reprints it from the Welsh journal *Seren Gomer*.

12. Many details in Cambria Historical Society; see in particular the centennial history by C.T. Roberts. David Benedict, *A General History of the Baptist Denomination in America* (Boston, 1813), pp. 600 ff, gets the facts right but misinterprets the split.

13. M.J. Rhees–B. Rush, 10 May 1801–11 December 1802, Benjamin Rush papers, vol. 14; there is considerable correspondence about the donation land in the Rush papers.

14. See B.W. Chidlaw, *An Historical Sketch of Paddy's Run, Butler County, Ohio* (1876); William Harvey Jones, centennial oration at Granville, reprinted from the Utica *Cambrian*, in *Weekly Tribune* (Johnstown, Cambria county), 5 January 1906; memoir of Ezekiel Hughes, reprinted from the American *Cambrian* by S.R. (Samuel Roberts, Llanbrynmair) with comments, NLW 491; all which material should be set against the history of Beula-Cambria which has now been reconstructed.

15. Rees Lloyd's comment is quoted from a letter he wrote to his brother Jonah in Wales on 4 September 1837 in C.T. Roberts's centennial history of Ebensburg; David Jones's presence is indicated by William Harvey Jones (see footnote 14) and the records of the Great Valley Baptist church.

16. M.J. Rhees–B. Rush, 1801-4, Benjamin Rush papers, vol. 14; Somerset county, Deed Book 3; Cambria county, Deed Book 1; *Cambria Freeman*, 20 January 1872.

17. Cambria county, Deed Book 1 and Benjamin Rush papers, *passim*.

18. The story of this struggle is told, with some circumstantial detail (often incorrect, however, on particulars concerning Beula) in L.C. Walkinshaw, *Annals of South-Western Pennsylvania* (New York, 1939), Vol. II, pp. 315-30; see also H. Wilson Storey, *History of Cambria County*, 3 vols. (New York, 1907) and W.H. Koontz (ed.), *History of Bedford and Somerset Counties* (New York, 1906).

19. M.J. Rhees–B. Rush, 21 March 1804, Benjamin Rush papers, vol. 14; an official statement from the US Postmaster-General of 1936 about the Beula post office (it shut down in 1807) is available in Cambria Historical Society.

20. M.J. Rhees–B. Rush, 21 March 1804, Benjamin Rush papers, vol. 14.

21. All the deeds, bonds, conveyances, mentioned in this paragraph are recorded in Somerset county, Deed Book 3 and Cambria county, Deed Book 1. The *Atlas* was presumably prepared in 1803.

22. There is an entertaining, but cock-eyed, account of the struggle in Julius Chambers, *Lovers Four and Maidens Five* (Philadelphia, 1886), the section entitled 'The Cymric Agonistes'. Chambers claims (in total falsehood) that Morgan Rhees could not speak English and once reduced a polite Philadelphia circle to hysterical laughter by reading 'Behold the Lamb of God' as 'Look at God's little sheep'. He calls him vainglorious, measuring all distances from Beula town pump. He says the most vicious boycotting was practised against each other by the two towns, which

is conceivable, but adds that local opinion thought Ebensburg won because it built a church first, before a market house, whereas Beula reversed the procedure! The book is interesting, however, as an extreme example of the common practice of mistakenly reading the Beula-Ebensburg rivalry right back to the original settlement of 1796.

23. On the growth of Ebenezer Independent Chapel, the C.T. Roberts's centennial history which used early, and now lost, records.

24. For all the deeds, bonds and conveyances mentioned in this and the succeeding paragraphs, Cambria county, Deed Book 1 and County Commissioners' Minute Book.

25. David Lloyd–Rees Lloyd, 6 March 1809, Cambria Historical Society.

26. *Cambria Freeman*, 5 September 1873.

27. A gem I found first in Julius Chambers's *Cymric Agonistes*, which turned out to be a standard historical anecdote.

28. The literature on the 'ghost village' is quite substantial; there are even novels based on it. On this first ghost, which was a poltergeist afflicting Lloyd's twelve-year-old daughter, see N.B. Wolfe, *Startling Facts in Modern Spiritualism* (Chicago, 1875). The modern ghost is a weeping female in white who tends to linger on Nant-y-Glo railway bridge. She was reported again by three different persons the night after I visited the Beula graveyard. As a Welshman, I found this both proper and reassuring.

9 WORLD'S END

Morgan John Rhees saw nothing of this; perhaps he was lucky not to. After his last journey to Washington and the launching of rival Ebensburg, he could do little but wait. On 22 November 1804, he was buying land from his friend Otto Shrader of the Pennsylvania-Dutch community of Somerset county, but at the end of the month, he was suddenly taken ill. On 3 December, he made his will.[1]

His most valuable possession was an eight-day clock, assessed at $40. Two round looking-glasses were also thought expensive and a tea-urn inscribed MJR sufficiently distinctive to fetch $14. His five pictures, however (one wonders what they were), were not worth much. He had eight Windsor chairs, an armchair, one master bed with curtains, two other beds (one broken) and two children's beds. There was a portmanteau and a small mahogany writing-desk. He owned one cow and one share in Somerset library; his clothes were put at $22. There were $160 cash in the house.

His books were valued at $334. There were 120 of them, with a parcel of drawings (his own?) and some maps. He had a plan of Wilmington, where that Baptist brother had kept such a smart young lass in the house and a French grammar, souvenir perhaps of an earlier excitement. He owned a Homer's *Iliad*, a Pope's poems, Buffon, Locke, *The Gleaner*, Thomson's *Seasons*, Priestley, the Voyages of Sir John Hawkins, an abridged Gibbon and, perhaps appropriately, 'one *Great Evil of Prodigality*'. His real property in Somerset was valued at $729, in Beula at $169. His executor was Thomas Watkin Jones. The Voltairean ratified Morgan John's will in Somerset county court on Christmas Day. He managed to sell the Somerset lands for $700, but was left in the red.

For on 7 December 1804 Morgan John Rhees finally gave up. His body was taken back to Philadelphia to lie among all the Loxleys.[2] After 44 years that brief, bright flame went out. It was not relit until the twentieth century.

The name of Morgan John Rhees was made illustrious by children and descendants.[3] His widow Ann did not die until 1849, having founded the Baptist Sunday Schools of Philadelphia. His son John Loxley Rhees, born in the room in the Loxley house in Second Street where Lydia Darrach had overheard British officers plotting the attack she reported to George Washington, lived a long, worthy, but rather obscure life as principal of Philadelphia's Model School, though he served as Grand Worthy Patriarch of the Order of Sons of Temperance. Morgan John Rhees junior, too, laboured in a decent, local and bachelor honour as a Baptist minister, getting his DD from Rochester and serving at Wilmington, where he also had his housekeeper. Benjamin Rush Rhees, however, born in Beula, lived up to his name and became a famous doctor. Short with black, curly hair and dark blue eyes, he was a lively and attractive man, a poet and classical scholar as well as an expert on eastern diseases. Trained in Philadelphia's medical school, first in the country, he made two journeys to the East Indies, fought the yellow fever and the small-pox in his city, turned the Loxley House into a medical centre and school and, his father's son, launched Jefferson Medical College in the teeth of resistance from the old guard. He died young, but his son William Jones Rhees, named after a Jeffersonian Secretary to the Treasury, went on to become first secretary and archivist of the Smith-sonian Institution; from the same family stemmed Dr Rush Rhees, President of Rochester University. Another university president, of Columbia, New York was the product of the marriage of Morgan John's daughter Elizabeth to Nicholas Murray, Irish immigrant and convert from Catholicism, author of the *Kirwan Letters* against Papism, whose grandson was Nicholas Murray Butler; into his family passed Morgan John's stained and tattered journal of his epic journey of 1794-5.

The man himself, however, was soon forgotten. Even within his own Baptist denomination, the kind of world outlook he and William Richards and J.R. Jones Ramoth had fought for was defeated. The victory Rees Lloyd won in Pennsylvania was repeated all over Wales.[4] That eighteenth-century democracy, the first British (and American and French) democracy, certainly persisted, into a new world of in-dustry and a working class, reform Bills and Welsh self-consciousness; it informed at least the first phases of the British and Welsh Chartist movement. But these new preoccupations, new imperatives were neces-sarily different. It had to fight a losing battle against the overpowering hegemony of the new political economy and its evangelicalism. Within the Welsh-speaking world, it rapidly became a minority sensibility. And in those regions of the spirit where Methodism and its 'methodised' dependencies ruled supreme, it was eclipsed. In the second generation of Nonconformist advance and the first of hegemony, Mr Politician had gone to America and good riddance; Methodist John Elias presided as a Pope with his Bulls of Bala; Baptist Christmas Evans established a style which was crassly imitated by too many *crach-pregethwyr* (quack-preachers), a farandole of charlatans, with a religious *revival* 'every seven years'. A whole generation was branded with a crabbed, narrow, pedantic, self-taught and self-obsessed image which later generations of Welshmen were to recoil from, in an act of spiritual parricide; for these men were also shapers and moulders of Jesuit power.[5] But even after that third generation, when horizons broadened, when Nonconformity became a creative force, the first democrats of Dissenter Enlightenment found no place. It was the new men who created the first history of the new Wales, to which Morgan John and his kin, if they were remembered at all, were merely prologue. In mid-century a man of unusually liberal and genial temper, Dr Lewis Edwards, in the journal *Traethodydd*, one of the rare genuinely intellectual enterprises of those first years of a nation created by preacher-journalists, remembered Morgan John's *Cylchgrawn* and wrote well of it. But it was necessary for the reconstructed Welsh to emerge from their narrow tunnel before they could, by an act of imaginative will, recall their founding fathers. Even then, the recapture was slow, partial, uninformed. A Pennsylvania Welshman wrote a decent and pious memoir of Morgan John in the early years of the twentieth century. It was an act of filial homage, but even he omitted from the diary all mention of that journey to the frontier through the Kentucky wilderness and censored the remainder.[6] When Morgan John finally found his way into the *Dictionary of National Biography*, his life was written by Ramsay MacDonald, the man who led and broke the Labour Party; it is, appropriately, a shoddy job.[7] In this, of course, Wales was simply an exaggerated symptom of a British affliction. These 'first men' look the 'last men' of another time. The first generation of Welsh and British democrats figure as precursors, a false dawn; they enter tradition by an indirection.

But if Morgan John Rhees had to wait long to become visible once more, John Evans, of course, had to wait even longer; indeed, in some senses, he is waiting yet.[8] After those dramatic months on the far Missouri, perhaps the rest of his life was bound to be anti-climax. In any event, it was brief; John Evans was dead five years before Morgan Rhees.

He took a job as a surveyor in Lorimier's district of Cap Girardeau, hoping to settle there, but soon ran into an avalanche of troubles: he had difficulty getting his money out of incoming American settlers, some business ventures failed, he lost much property in one of the Mississippi floods and he was robbed. Land promised him did not materialise and he slumped into one of the fits of depression which had begun to assail him. He began to drink heavily and, his health already undermined, to collapse into alcoholism. Clamorgan wanted him to lead another expedition towards the Pacific but could get no support. The new Governor,

Gayoso de Lemos, wanted to use him as a frontier commissioner on the Missouri under the treaty with the USA but in the end, as an act of charity, took the Welshman into his own household. When Dr Samuel Jones wrote to him in March 1799, the reply he received from the US Consul in New Orleans, written on 3 August 1799, was a shock:

> The inclosed letter from you to Mr. John T. Evans fell lately into my hands and I was induced to open it that ... I might advise his friends of the fate of that unfortunate man who died not long since in this City after being for some time deprived of his reason. Chagrin and disappointment in his Views contributed, I fear, to hasten his end.

'Is there one thing in the possession of Ieuan ab Ivan that he would not sacrifice to the cause of the Madogion? No, not one; even my precious life would I lay down for their sake.' Poor John Evans, at 29, had been true to his word. He had lived more in seven years than most men in a lifetime. Now the boy from Waunfawr was tipped into a lonely grave in a southern city in a Catholic land. He was forgotten more quickly than Morgan John Rhees, slipping out of history as unobtrusively as he had out of London in 1792. Yet this man, strangest ghost of the Missouri, left immediate legacies more positive than Morgan's, for in his resolute pursuit of error, he had stumbled across truth.

A few months after his death Napoleon Bonaparte took back the continent and sold it to the USA, sweeping all those imaginative, worried, prickly and quarrelling men in New Orleans and St Louis into the margins of history after John Evans and Morgan John Rhees. President Thomas Jefferson, with the aid of the American Philosophical Society, Dr Benjamin Rush and Dr Samuel Mitchill of the *Medical Repository*, had long been collecting material on the far west, and in May 1804, sent Merriwether Lewis and William Clark off up the Missouri from St Louis on the expedition which was to take them to the Pacific. Essential to the first phase of the enterprise was John Evans's material. Jefferson's instructions to Lewis and Clark were modelled on those which James McKay had issued to John Evans. The President sent to the explorers first a summary and then the whole of the journal of McKay which incorporated Evans's. Above all, the explorers had John's great map of the Missouri, which proved of critical assistance to them. The quest for Welsh Indians had no more remarkable consequence than this. Madoc made John Evans into an explorer of America and into as much of a 'precursor' as Morgan John Rhees.

Not that the failure of his mission did anything to stop the remorseless advance of Welsh Indians into the west! His report home of 1797, duly summarised and 'improved' by Morgan John was an anti-climax. It makes curious reading and may have been censored by the Spaniards (in his cups, one man claimed, John boasted that he knew more than he would ever tell but had been paid to keep his mouth shut!) He spent most time on his first madcap venture and devoted much of the rest of his space to a description of the Missouri; Mandans were scarcely mentioned and Padoucas not at all. From a man commissioned to find Welsh Indians, the report reads very oddly indeed and, after an initial depression, was rapidly discounted by the Welsh at home. John clearly had not gone far enough. And even while Lewis and Clark were at the Mandans, a Welsh Indian story came bubbling in full strength out of Kentucky, to be supported by many others, to circulate around the newspaper network and to lodge in the history of Louisiana published by Colonel Amos Stoddard, the American officer who took over St Louis, in a volume of 1812 which established a new orthodoxy for Madoc and his Indians.

By that time, however, the Madoc myth was rapidly losing its symbolic power, even if migration had mounted to a desperate peak. Wales's little clerisy of radical intellectuals, in any case, had other problems on their minds. William Richards Lynn had to report to Dr Samuel Jones in 1798 that he was in deep trouble. After the French landing at Fishguard, he had rushed to the defence of the Baptists and others who had been scapegoats in a witch-hunt. His Welsh pamphlet on the subject had provoked fury and had brought threats from the Establishment. He had planned an English version: 'It was hinted to my friends by one of the most moderate of the Clergy that if I wrote and published in English they would not answer for the consequences.' He was also threatened with prosecution over his recent English-Welsh Dictionary: 'Something under the words *Buccaniers*, *Fast Day* and *Pope* gave great umbrage to the Clergy and others'![9] Iolo Morganwg's comment on the Fishguard landing would certainly have landed him in a Bastille:

Breeches, petticoats, shirts, shifts, blankets, sheets (for some received the news in bed) have been most wofully defiled in South Wales lately on hearing that a thimblefull of Frenchmen landed on our coast. I hope that you will have the goodness to compassionate our unfortunate washwomen. Our *Dragooners* sent us some companies of Dragoons after the old women of Pembrokeshire had secured the *damned Republicans* as it seems we are requested to call them. Are there no lamp-irons in Downing Street? I fear that the hemp crop of the last season failed. We must allow that the French are beforehand with us in the most useful arts and sciences, witness their invention and use of the *guillotine*.

In the same letter to William Owen, he reported that he had received an 'affecting' letter from the transported martyr Palmer in Botany Bay. He was sending copies to the *Jacobins* in London.[10]

William Owen's brother, John the publisher, had also got into trouble. He had published a libel on our *happy constitution*, Owen reported to Iolo. The House of Commons tried to force him to give up the anonymous author. The Ministry prevailed on him to refuse, and as a reward Wyndham, the Secretary for War, got Edmund Burke to make him a present of the famous *Letter to the Duke of Bedford*, which had an extensive sale, but 'regardless of the above-mentioned gift, Mr. Burke came upon him for the profits. This produced a quarrel and ended as all quarrels usually do, to the favor of the strongest side and Sionyn is now a bankrupt.' He was shortly to emigrate to 'General' Bowles's country. Iolo, however, was not only translating Bishop Watson's *Apology for the Bible* into Welsh, in the hope of provoking a parallel translation of Paine's *Age of Reason*; he was battling with the newly formed Board of Agriculture under Arthur Young. Both Walter Davies (who ultimately wrote the Welsh reports) and Iolo had been approached by the Board. Walter had begged Iolo's help. Iolo's survey of Glamorgan, however, had 'gone beyond the queries of the Board in many curious matters' (one can well believe it!). The publisher Chalmers, though he thought Iolo 'wild' (his word for a Democrat, said William Owen), wanted it as a separate publication, along with Gray's *Bard* in Welsh. Iolo denounced the Board as 'a nickname; it has views, to answer which I am not quite pliant enough to tell a few smooth lies'.[11]

This kind of Jacobinism, however, had become largely a matter of private correspondence. In his letter of June 1797, introducing his new and non-political *Cambrian Register* (Walter Davies had warned him off democratic notions) and Yorke's study of the royal tribes of Wales, William Owen was apologetic. This was no *Cylchgrawn* — 'the book is to be a mere aristocratic *tegan* [trinket] to be given away only amongst a dozen or two intimate friends' and the journal 'answers the purpose of the publishers very well by their *own* account.'[12] Public defeat and an enforced shift of emphasis were recognised. Jac Glan-y-Gors's pamphlets battled on. In 1798, Thomas Roberts Llwynrhudol, who was so passionate a Madoc man that he earned the title Father of the Madogwys, brought out *Cwyn yn erbyn Gorthrymder*, *Protest against Oppression*, but it was a hard fight. Thomas Evans, Tomas Glyn Cothi, a Unitarian who was jailed in 1801 and was accused of singing Welsh versions of French revolutionary songs, had published a journal intended to be a successor to the *Cylchgrawn* which was passionately pro-American and preached emigration. David Davies of Holywell followed suit in a periodical which became almost totally obsessed with Glan y Gors's pamphlets. They did not last into 1797 − 'the hearers are becoming thinner.' For a while, even Dr Samuel Jones broke with William Richards because of his alleged Deism.[13] In the insurrections, riots, emigrations, explosions of 1800-1, certainly there was plenty of 'subversion', but there was little connection with the Gwyneddigion and the *Jacobin* intelligentsia − except over American migration. The exception was Merthyr Tydfil and its hinterland, rapidly growing with the iron industry into the major urban centre of Wales in whose vicinity Tomos Glyn Cothi was to serve as Unitarian minister for twenty years. Here much of the Jacobinism of the Vale and the hills tended to come to a focus. It was perhaps the one area of Wales where a continuous tradition of radicalism stretched from the pre-industrial into the industrial era.[14] But already here, the terms of discourse were shifting. In any event, after the resumption of war, it was not a heroic French republic Britain was fighting but the empire of Napoleon. Iolo and Jac Glan-y-Gors sang the praises of Nelson and the Volunteers. The public image of the Gwyneddigion and their kin became the Board of Agriculture's reports, the *Cambrian Register*, and, of course, their great achievement the *Myvyrian Archaiology*.

What they did not lose was their American commitment. Through all the pulses of emigration fever, it registers time and time again. In 1796, William Owen was getting ready to go; his brother did go. When he heard that the ironmaster Richard Crawshay was planning to establish a settlement in the USA, Iolo Morganwg formally applied for a post there, and got a dusty answer. William Richards announced that he was leaving his library to be divided equally between Rhode Island College and the Beula seminary. His books did in fact go to Brown University.[15]

In these circumstances, the new reports of Welsh Indians from 1804 set off another flurry of speculation, strongly reinforced by Amos Stoddard's history of Louisiana and George Catlin's celebrated study of the Mandans.[16] For a while the Padouca Hunt was on again. William Richards was correct, however, when he wrote to William Owen in 1800, 'I conceived great hopes, one time, of John Evans's adventure being attended with success, but now the scene is closed. And we shall probably never see such another adventurer rise up.'

In the late eighteenth century, as in the sixteenth, the Madoc myth served a recognisable and, in some senses, a valid purpose. Not only did it meet some psychological need, it was itself an integral element of a particular historical conjuncture. With the death of John Evans and of Beula, this is no longer true. In the new Wales of the nineteenth century, Madoc survived, but largely as a minor descant, a matter of after-dinner rhetoric, eisteddfod patriotism and children's verse. Madoc became a particular preserve of Welsh-speaking Wales and as Welsh remorselessly shrank, so did he. If the myth served any purpose at all in the nineteenth century, it was in America, where it grew to monstrous proportions and even lodged in the margins of scholarly discourse for a while. Characteristically, a stir of interest which may be detected in our own day tends to focus more closely on the Mandans, on peoples who have disappeared, on enterprises forgotten by history. The myth concentrates fears of a loss of historical identity. The peculiar bite which the legend acquired in the age of revolution never returned.

For Madoc himself, Nemesis struck in 1858. In response to the offer of a prize for an essay on Madoc at the Llangollen eisteddfod of that year, Thomas Stephens, a chemist of Merthyr and one of the finest critical intelligences Wales has produced, wrote a devastating study, subjecting the whole legend to a remorseless critique which left hardly anything of substance. The eisteddfod committee, on the grounds that the essay was on the *non*-discovery of America by Madoc, disqualified it. Stephens mounted the platform to protest, the chairman ordered the band to strike up. There was uproar and outrage. It was, in short, an unholy eisteddfod scandal, almost as characteristic a feature of nine-teenth-century Welsh culture as a chapel split. The essay was finally published posthumously in 1893.

Since that date, belief in Madoc has to rest on faith rather than works. The faithful, however, survive in some number, particularly in the USA. In 1947, the Welsh Indians were identified as the Kutenai of British Columbia; in 1951 a book argued the case all over again, citing new evidence. In 1953 the Daughters of the American Revolution raised a plaque to Madoc at Mobile and in 1966 a rather sophisticated apology for him was published. Whatever sceptics or scholars might say, the Madogwys have gone on thundering across the prairies.

So, of course, have more plebeian Welsh in actuality. The migrations of the 1790s opened another cycle, a movement which did not stop and has not stopped.[17] Statisticians are convinced that, in terms of the total Welsh population, grounded on a strong industrial base, emigration has been relatively unimportant. Wales stands at the opposite pole to Ireland.

Nevertheless in a small, tightly knit community, its effects have been much more severe than merely quantitative evidence would lead one to expect. There is scarcely a family in Wales, certainly no extended family, which does not have its American or Canadian dimension.

From the 1800s onwards, the settlements in Ohio, Pennsylvania, New York acted as foci for movements which soon transcended them. After the farmers and the artisans went the miners, steelworkers, tinplaters. Wilkes-Barre, Scranton, Youngstown, Pittsburgh, Edmonton, Calgary became household names in Wales. The 'exiles' found their day at the national eisteddfod. But never again did this migration carry that powerful, millenarian, national charge of the 1790s. Later movements were less ambitious, more careful, more practical. They grew as Oneida county and Utica in New York grew, by gradual, piecemeal assimilation; friends moved to friends, in a miniature and molecular process like a coral growth. This turned Utica for a time into the strongest centre of Welshness in the country, but many communities followed the same pattern. The Welsh displayed their customary contradictions as emigrants. What modern Welsh nationalists would recognise as Welshness faded very quickly, particularly in the industrial conurbations. Even in Beula, English-language services had to be introduced as early as 1813. A diffuse yet persistent current of Welsh feeling, however, remained strong. On only two occasions can one detect some echo of the spirit of the 1790s. The Welsh sector of the great Mormon migration had its own passion, though a sectional one. And from the 1860s, there was a serious attempt to create a *Gwladfa* in Patagonia in the Argentine. This, though now beginning to fade, was without doubt the most successful. So successful was it that the very word *Gwladfa* acquired a precise geographical location.[18] With the contradictory development of *Gwladfa* and metropolis, it created that tragi-comic situation in modern times, in which people speaking only Welsh and Spanish returned to the homeland to find they could not make themselves understood. The spirit of the 1860s, however, strong, deep and sometimes bitter, was different from that of the 1790s; it was more inward-looking, more exclusive, more effective in its own terms, but also more narrow; its very siting demonstrates also its desperation.

Never again after the 1790s was the Welsh diaspora to America to carry that sense that Welsh was the vehicle of universal liberty, universal values, that the *Gwladfa* was the geographical anchorage of a universalism which made the Welsh into a chosen race of a particular, peculiar, but non-exclusive kind. Never again was it to be suffused with Iolo's Druidic and *Jacobin* vision, was it to turn defeat at home into a transatlantic

assertion which was *not* defensive, never again was it to create a Kingdom of Wales which found Madoc — here we are now on the journey of
our hope — a sufficient symbolic myth.

Looked at in the long perspectives of a history which many fear may
now be drawing to its close, the curve of Welsh development takes a
sudden upward kick in the 1790s; there is a sharp, spasmodic and jagged
jerk in the graph; a kind of rupture. It was one of those sudden spasms
that indicate the movement of deep, structural change below the surface.
The migrations, the Jacobinism, the Madoc fever of the 1790s, minority
phenomena though they all were, were symptoms of the painful emergence of a new social order, a new set of values, a new nation. The
development of this new society made its first exemplars 'out of date'
very rapidly. Before Napoleon had been defeated, even before the
Methodists had officially become Nonconformist, the *Jacobins* and
Madocians were beginning to look like creatures from another time.

And, curiously, the world into which these Welsh frontiersmen moved
acquired something of the same quality. This was certainly true of the
men who tried to make Spanish Louisiana work. Today, it takes an
effort of will to remember that St Louis was once Spanish. All that
labour and frustration, blown away as if they had never been. To a
degree, it is true even of the Americans. The USA begins, in reality,
with the constitution which went into effect from 1789; the USA as a
continental power begins with the Louisiana Purchase. In a manner
which parallels the history of British democracy, many of those 'first
men', the men who lived before the first American consensus, the Jeffersonian, can look like the 'last men' of something else.

Yet what a potent generation this was, on both sides of the Atlantic!
The Welsh among them, on their peculiar mission, moved into and
through a tense and complex field of force, as empires collided and dis-
solved. Their frontier proved a frontier of illusion, but no less than their
disillusion, their dreams and their labour were on a heroic scale. And
when that revolutionary decade ends, one is left less with a sense of
bathos than with a realisation that so much of human history has been
like this. What the experience leaves in the mind is a wry sadness touched
with a wholly appropriate irony and indeed comedy; sometimes, too,
an obscure resentment against reality for being so unjust. For what
remains to mark the passage of these people but some rubble scattered
on a hillside in western Pennsylvania?

The tragi-comic ending of Beula can stand as their epitaph, meagre
recompense for all the labour and the hope invested in that sad square
mile. In Ebensburg, a Tibbot and a Griffiths and an Edwards still stand

sentinel over the hill-top cross-roads, but down in Beula, above the lonely marker, there is just a handful of gravestones, Watkin Jones's staring stonily at the minister's recumbent among leaning heads, facing down to the creek and the west where so many of the others went. So much backbreak and heartbreak, so much hope and delusion, so much malice and anger and despair, to make a comfortable settlement for the poor Welsh people, and most of them carried far away in the end, as if by some giant shrug of a westering ocean.

Notes

1. Somerset County Will Book 1.

2. His grave proved difficult to find. In 1860 the First Baptist dead were transferred to Mount Moriah cemetary in what is today west Philadelphia. The cemetery's records are in a bad state; the grave was found by quartering the cemetery and searching it; it lies in plot 112 across Cobb's Creek.

3. Summary accounts in J.T. Griffith, *Morgan John Rhys* (USA, 1899 and Carmarthen, 1910); supplementary information from Mrs Mary Murray Brown of Mount Kisco, New York, who owns the 1794-5 journal and is a niece of Nicholas Murray Butler.

4. R.T. Jenkins, 'William Richards o Lynn', *Trafodion Cymdeithas Hanes Bedyddwyr Cymru* (Welsh Baptist Historical Society, 1930).

5. I am in accord with the views genially and charitably expressed by R.T. Jenkins, one of Wales's most admirable historians, who seems rather neglected and who has left little in English.

6. Griffith, *Morgan John Rhys*.

7. The life by W.H. Allison in the *Dictionary of American Biography* (supplement 1) is even worse.

8. On John Evans's last years and the consequences of his mission, see my *Madoc: the Making of a Myth* (Eyre Methuen, London, 1980), Chapter 11.

9. W. Richards–S. Jones, 19 March 1798: Pennepek.

10. E. Williams–W. Owen, 7 March 1797, NLW 13222, fo. 131-4.

11. Information derived from W. Owen–E. Williams, 1 January, 15 June 1797, 1 April 1798, NLW Iolo 322, 323, 325; W. Davies–W. Owen, 20 June, n.y., NLW 13224, fo. 173-5; see also W. Owen–E. Williams, Alban Eilir, 1796, NLW Iolo 32 321.

12. W. Owen–E. Williams, 15 June 1797, NLW Iolo 323.

13. W. Richards–S. Jones, 13 March 1803: Pennepek; and see R.T. Jenkins, *Hanes Cymru yn y Ddeunawfed Ganrif* (University of Wales paperback reprint, Cardiff, 1972); J.J. Evans, *Dylanwad y Chwyldro Ffrengig ar Lenyddiaeth Cymru* (Hugh Evans, Liverpool, 1928).

14. See my *The Merthyr Rising* (Croom Helm, London, 1978).

15. W. Owen–E. Williams, 1796, NLW Iolo 321; W. Richards–S. Jones, 6 June 1797: Pennepek; E. Williams –W. Owen, 17 June 1800, NLW 13222, fo. 145-7; E. Williams–R. Crawshay, 20 June 1800 and reply, June, NLW Iolo 865; Crawshay replied, 'My son and self are no emigration men or promoters of it. But as you wish to go there I wish you as speedy a passage as you run away with from my table on the sight of Mr. John Wood'; an enigmatic but clearly ominous comment!

16. On the later history of the myth, see my *Madoc: the Making of a Myth*, Chapters 11 and 12.

17. From a vast bibliography, one may select as a useful general survey, E.G. Hartmann, *Americans from Wales* (Christopher, Boston, 1967).

18. On the Patagonia colony, see R. Bryn Williams, *Y Wladfa* (University of Wales Press, Cardiff, 1962) and Glyn Williams, *The Desert and the Dream* (University of Wales Press, Cardiff, 1975).

INDEX